GREAT WATER
GREAT FISH

GREAT WATER

GREAT FISH

The worldwide guide to fly fishing

JOHN ROSS

CHARTWELL
BOOKS, INC.

Author's Acknowledgments

Special thanks go to on-line friends of the International Fly Fishing Association (IFFA), many of whom provided information and photographs for this book. An organization of dedicated and knowledgeable fly fishers worldwide, membership information can be obtained from Bob Kloskowski at (bjkk@gomontana.com) or from the IFFA website: *http://members.xoom.com/IFFA/ffl.htm*. In similar vein, check out: *http://www.where-to-fish.com*, another excellent source of international fishing information.

I also want to thank my editors at Quintet – Keith Ryan and Diana Steedman – and creative director Richard Dewing. Working with them has been a pleasure and without their unstinting efforts, this book would not be what it is.

And under the category of best for last, I'm indebted to my wife Katie Anders, herself an angling travel writer. Her love, patience, understanding and keen insight empowers me.

Picture Credits

The Publishers would like to acknowledge the following contributors of photographs:

Hans Abplanalp LRPS, CH 3800 Interlaken, Switzerland. email: abpl@tcnet.ch pages 49, 50, 51; Allsport page 56; Angling Times, Emap Pursuit Publishing Ltd., Peterborough PE3 8DZ, England page 63; Barry and Cathy Beck, Benton, Pennsylvania, email: thebecks@epix.net pages 2, 28, 29 left, 30 right, 40, 41 right, 42, 43, 45, 98, 99, 100, 101, 102, 103, 113, 114, 116, 117, 122, 125 right, 126, 131, 137, 142; Denver Bryan www.denverbryan.com pages 6, 34, 37, 38, 41 left, 44, 94, 95, 96, 97, 124, 128, 132, 138, 139 right, 140, 141, 144, 145; Frontiers http://www.frontierstrvl.com pages 12, 18, 19, 21, 85, 120 right; Alistair Gowans http://ds.dial.pipex.com/ally.gowans pages 30 left, 46, 66 left, 68, 77 right, 78, 81, 104, 105, 106, 107, 108 left, 109, 110 right, 111; Images of Africa Photobank, Lichfield WS13 7EX, England: pages 14, 16 Carla-Signorini Jones; 15 left, 15 right David Keith Jones; 17 Friedrich von Horsten; Life File Photographic Library, London SW17 8QY, England: pages 22 Gina Green; 23 John Dakers; 24 Aubrey J. Slaughter; 25, 27 Emma Lee; 26 Joseph Green; 47 Su Davies; 48 Ron Gregory; 55, 119 Nigel Sitwell 69 Jan Suttle; 79, 82, 110 left Cliff Threadgold; 83 Caroline Field; 108 right Graham Burns; 112 Jeremy Hoare; 146 Wayne Shakell; 147 Louise Oldroyd; 148 Life File; New Zealand Tourist Office page 9; Barry Ord Clarke www.flyshop.no/barry pages 10, 11, 57, 58, 59, 60, 61, 62, 70, 71, 72, 73, 74, 75, 86, 87, 88, 89, 90, 91, 92, 93, 120 left; John Ross email: jross@crosslink.net pages 29 right, 31, 32, 35, 36, 39, 123, 125 left, 127, 129, 130, 133,134, 135, 139, 143, 150; Harry Salmgren, email: salmgren@flyfish.pp.se pages 52, 53, 64, 65, 66 right, 67, 76, 77 left, 80, 118, 121; Sri Lankan Tourist Board page 20

A QUINTET BOOK

Published by Chartwell Books
A Division of Book Sales, Inc.
114, Northfield Avenue
Edison, New Jersey 08837

This edition produced for sale in the U.S.A., its territories and dependencies only.

ISBN 0-7858-1060-9

This book was designed and produced by
Quintet Publishing Limited
6 Blundell Street
London N7 9BH

Creative Director: Richard Dewing
Art Director: Simon Daley
Designer: Paul Wright
Project Editors: Keith Ryan, Diana Steedman
Editor: Andrew Armitage

Typeset in Great Britain by
Central Southern Typesetters, Eastbourne
Manufactured in China by Regent Publishing Services Ltd.
Printed in China by Leefung-Asco Printers Ltd.

Contents

Introduction

We had finished dinner at the inn on the Miramichi and were lounging around the table drinking the last of the wine. Bob, a fellow guest, turned to me and asked, "What's the best place to fish?" I was nonplussed. Was he serious? Maybe this was the opening line for a joke. My normal response to this question is, "The place you plan to fish tomorrow," or words to that effect. Bob was genuine, however, and really wanted an answer. I tried to ask him what kind of fishing he liked, what climates he enjoyed, whether this species or that attracted his interest more than another. The answer grew long and Bob, I'm afraid, became somewhat bored. He wanted a list.

Well, in a way this book is for Bob. He'll find information on more than 1,000 different locations around the world where the fishing is very good. At any given time, each could be the best place to fish. Some of the waters – Norway's Alta, England's Itchen and Test, Henry's Fork in the US – are recognized worldwide as superlative sport fisheries. The others are highly regarded by fly fishers of the country where they are found. All offer good sport.

Defining the "best" river is tough. Some judge a river based on the size and number of the fish it yields. Others base their assessments on the fame of a river as reported in magazines. For a few, the quality of a river is related to cost. And there are others for whom the zenith of the sport comes with the greatest technical challenge or exploring waters that have seldom if ever been fished before. For me, a "best" river is like a "best" double gun. It fits me and my style (or lack thereof). I know my limitations (they are many) and preferences (few but firmly, some would say stubbornly, held). Just what makes a "best" stream is a matter of personal preference. Which is more important: big fish or numbers of fish? Do you prefer relative solitude or are you willing to share a pool with two or three other anglers? Is casting to rising fish your cup of tea or are you more at home dredging nymphs and streamers through deep silent runs? Do you prefer to fish with a guide or would you rather "freelance?"

For me, the context of the river is almost as important as the quality of the fish and the fishing. Has the river played an important role in angling history like the Test, the Beaverkill, and the Letort? Is it found in a region of stunning natural beauty? Are human comforts close at hand? Or is it utterly isolated in pristine wilderness?

And then there's what Katie, my wife, calls the "Ahh" factor. Does the water sing to you like the Fire Hole does to me with its boiling mudpots, or the Test at the old mill. Is its sweep, like that of Tierra del Fuego, so grand and glorious that it leaves me without breath? At times I want a little stream high in the mountains where the bellies of brook trout are as bright as the flame Azalea that blooms along the bank. At other times, I want to lean against the current of a cold and heavy river, casting endlessly to rise a salmon or steelhead of respectable if not record weight. Fishing always nourishes my soul, but my palate, as do those of other anglers, varies with the season of my mind.

Passionate anglers who travel the globe in pursuit of stellar fly fishing experience will find a lifetime of waters in this guide. So too will those anglers whose business or vacations carry them across international borders. For the latter, recent improvements in tackle, namely the development of multi-section, medium to heavy weight rods, means that a basic fly fishing kit can be packed inside one's usual luggage. A few extra days tacked on to a trip, and a bit of prior planning, can add an interesting angling interlude to what would be an otherwise routine trip to London, Tokyo, Moscow, or Buenos Aires or any of a hundred major cities around the world.

So, rather than in-depth profiles of a few magnificent fly-fishing destinations, this book is a global guide to good fly fishing. It is the first step down the trail of discovering places throughout the world where angling may suit your tastes. Each chapter refers to agencies to whom the traveling fisherman may apply for permits to fish, for accommodation at lodges and hotels, and for information on traveling to and around the respective countries. The Resources section beginning on page 152 collects together detailed contacts, phone and web addresses country by country. The process is like exploring a new stream. Unlike other fishing books, this guide is not meant to be read. It is meant to be used.

Travel tips

Right **Lakes of New Zealand provide solitude, and huge browns and rainbows.**

Flying half way around the world in search of salmon to make your reel sing is a lot like planning a jaunt to fish in the next state or province of your own country. The steps are essentially the same – you'll decide where you want to go, when you want to go, and how much you want to spend. International travel is, of course, more complicated.

The key factor is time. With the exception of those fortunate few globe-trotting anglers who can zip off to Pago Pago at the drop of a hat (filled to the brim with cold cash), most of us need lots of time to put together an international fishing adventure. The more exotic the destination, the more time you'll need. And the more popular the locale, the further in advance you must book. The best beats on Norwegian and Icelandic salmon rivers are often reserved a year or two in advance. Start planning a year to 18 months ahead.

Choosing the Destination

What will it be? Bonefish on Christmas Island? Salmon on the Panoi? Sea-run browns of Tierra del Fuego? Big rainbows on Henry's Fork? Conjure up the perfect trip in your mind. What will make you happiest? But in conceiving the ideal international angling foray, it's also important to ask yourself some questions:

What are your angling preferences? Punching long casts with heavy streamers into howling winds may not be your idea of fun. Rather, you may fancy those short, precise casts of exquisitely

tied dries, to wary browns rising in the cresses. Some anglers of the "been there, done that" school of fishing visit angling locations as if they were collecting merit badges in Scouting. Others seek new venues because they're intrigued, say, with the notion of fishing for yamame in the picture-book mountain streams of Japan, or sea-run browns at midnight in the shadow of an Irish country inn. On the other hand, if your fishing trip calls for new skills – use of a two-handed or Spey rod – practice, practice, practice before you go.

How much time can you commit? If there's one rule that holds true in international travel, it's this: Everything takes longer than expected. And if you're traveling to places where tourism infrastructure is just developing – republics in the former Soviet Union, for instance – you'll learn that patience is not just a mere virtue, it's a way of life. Vagaries of travel and weather play hob with the best laid plans. Allowing a couple days extra at either end of the trip may permit you to spend one more day on a river that is just falling to fishable levels.

How much money can you spend? Only you care how much you spend on a trip. It's a shame to louse up a trip worrying that expenses are out of control. Make a budget, add 20 percent contingency, and then try to stay within it.

How important are the comforts of home? At the end of a day's fishing is a hot shower, cold toddy, and freshly made bed high on your list of priorities? Or do you mind a borrowed sleeping bag

and the most rustic of baths – a mid-day dip in the stream? Even the best fishing, after a few days, may not compensate for accommodation and board that are lower than your usual standards.

And finally, are you comfortable in other cultures? The famous line from *The Wizard of Oz*: There's no place like home, applies to fishing as well. Anglers in every country have their own traditions. While Americans may practice catch and release, it may be considered unethical in some countries and illegal in others. Guides who work for blue-ribbon operations may speak your language, but those who work for smaller outfits most likely will not. You will do yourself a huge favor by taking time to learn some basic phrases in the native language before you depart. Knowing something of the local history, religion, geography, flora and fauna will enrich your trip as well. There is more to fishing than fishing.

International Communications

While English may be the primary language of fly fishing and most governmental tourism offices have English-speaking staff, it's important to remember that queries submitted in the language of the country to which you plan to travel get the best and fastest results. Norman Crisp, a biologist who fishes widely throughout the world uses this trick to improve responses: his first letter to a tourism office is written in the country's language. In it he requests the information he needs in

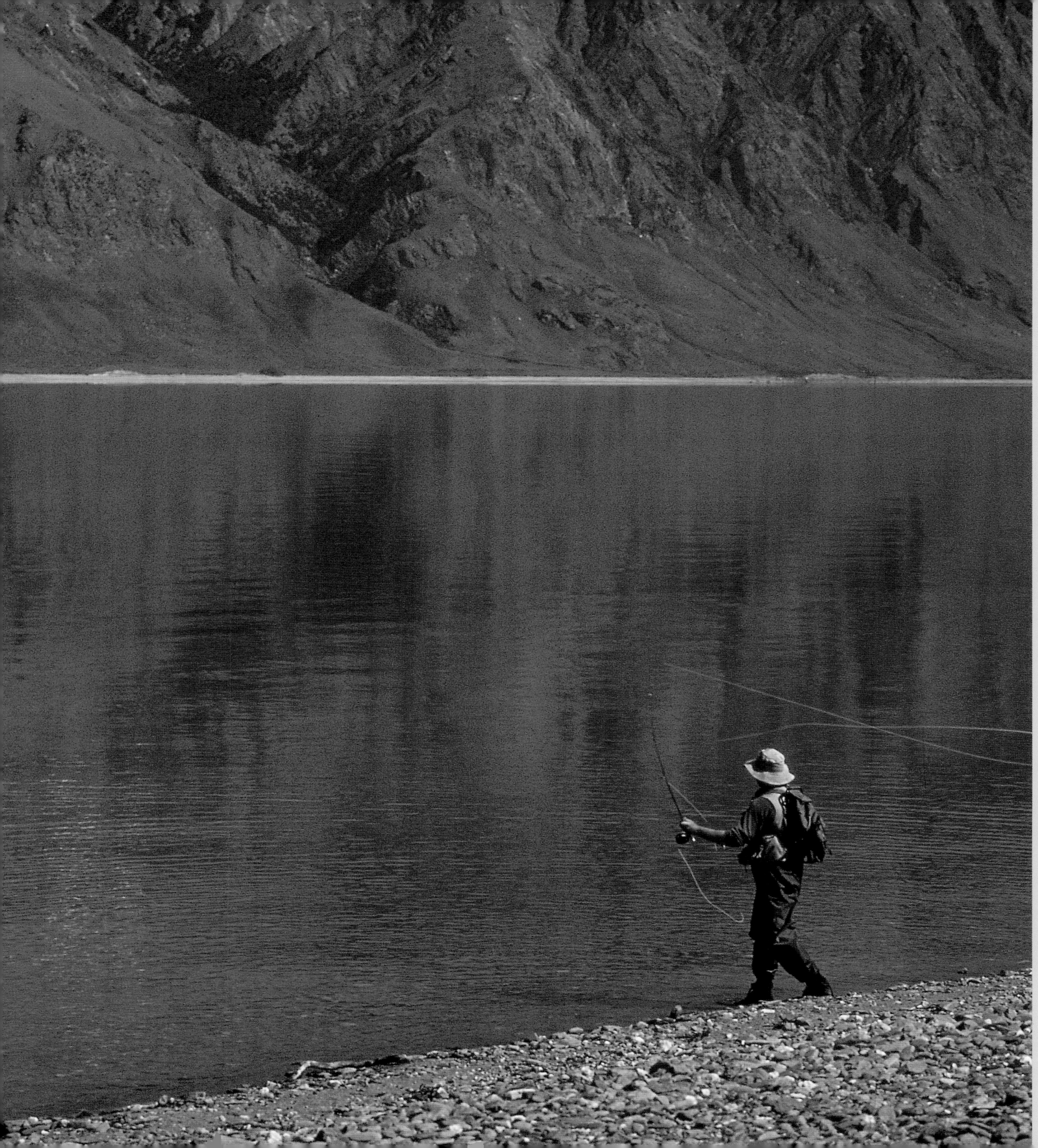

English, if possible, and he notes that his command of the country's language is very poor. Norm takes advantage of the language skills of staff and students at a nearby university and pays them to translate documents for him. The price is quite reasonable, the quality of the information he receives in return is very high, and the goodwill he engenders is of inestimable value.

More and more, fax and e-mail are the preferred modes of communication between angler and potential guide or lodge in another country. Unlike mailed letters, faxes and e-mail know no time zones, and are almost instantaneous. And the World Wide Web is an amazing library chock full of information about fly fishing. Hours spent fishing the net for articles on international angling are well spent indeed.

Anglers are anglers the worldwide. Local guides know where the fish are, what they feed on, and when they feed. Local guides who are fly fishers generally will be pleased to recommend a pattern or two for their clients to try. The wise traveling angler bends these on his tippet and fishes as the guide instructs. Try it the guide's way first. If it fails to produce or you want to try your own ideas later, there will be plenty of time to do so. When separated by language, as you may be when fishing with a guide overseas, it's not so much what you say that's important, but what you do. Take your lead from your guide. Common sense, courtesy, and respect can become the foundations of more than just a week's good fishing. The relationship between a guide and client is human and sometimes personalities just don't mix. Air your concerns quietly with the English-speaking owner or manager of the lodge. He may be able to shuffle assignments a bit.

What to pack

Airlines, these days, are increasingly fussy about weight limits on baggage. And, while a major carrier may permit two bags, the last leg of your trip on that former military helicopter may not have room for even a quarter of that. Ask your booking agent for the lowest maximum weight on any flight segment, and let that be your top limit.

Break baggage into two categories: the essentials and the basics.

The Essentials The essentials are those things which you cannot be without: medications (carry copies of prescriptions as well) and prescription eyeglasses (at least two pairs in addition to polarized glasses for fishing), money (enough cash in local currency to cover transportation to the closest city with a bank that accepts credit or ATM card withdrawals), and identification (passport and a copy thereof carried in a different place on your person). A fanny pack, belted around your waist, is a great place to carry the essentials, as well as a small flashlight and a Swiss army knife with scissors, screwdriver, corkscrew, and file. You may have room for a paperback or two for those interminable airport waits. Make copies of your airline tickets and itinerary as well. And carry a basic health history (current list of immunizations, allergies, and medical problems) compiled with your family doctor. Carry also extra copies of your medical insurance card, but keep in mind that your medical insurance may not be honored in another country. Check with the authorities of the countries you will visit, in advance, for the best information. If you book your trip through an agent – a highly recommended

practice, by the way – she or he will be able to give you good guidance here.

The Basics If you've taken care of the essentials you'll survive your trip and most likely won't go broke. But what about luggage, clothing and traveling tackle? Add it up: waders, wading boots, rain jacket, sweaters, etc., etc., etc. None of it's light and most is bulky. Tackle satchels – those waterproof over-the-shoulder bags with a bevy of outside pockets – are perfect carry-on bags for traveling anglers. Even if you keep the weight down to 22 lbs, you can still pack medications, extra glasses, Gore-Tex hat (wear the jacket), mini shaving kit, camera, waders, ultra-light wading shoes, fingerless gloves, flashlight, extra batteries

for camera and light, two reels with floating and sinking lines, and a ziplock bag with a two pairs of heavy socks, and light-weight polypro long underwear, a polar fleece sweater, two short (five to seven piece) traveling rods and whatever tackle (nippers, forceps, flies, leader, etc.) you want crammed into the side pockets. Rain and good fishing go together. Wear a Gore-Tex parka shell and a pair of sturdy walking shoes or boots.

Pockets in the jacket can carry clean underwear and dry socks in ziplock bags. A bag containing these essentials fits under the seat or in the overhead bin. And, if need be, you can live out of it for a week.

Electric power varies from country to country with most using the European standard of 220 volts at 50 cycles. In North America 110 volts is standard. Many modern appliances are dual range and will

work, using the correct plug adapter, with either. But some function only with one or the other. If you have questions, check with the manufacturer. Batteries are another story. They're fairly universal, but in other than major cities, can be in short supply. Before you leave, replace or charge batteries in everything that you intend to bring along (watch, flashlight, tape player, camcorder, and camera.) Where feasible, bring spares.

Web leaves you with a pretty rosy view of fishing. Everyone always catches big fish, cloudy water magically clears, the sun shines and all's right on the stream. Well, sometimes. There are days, of course, when slow is too kind a word to describe the fishing. Changing weather patterns or fluctuating water levels can turn a normally superb fishery into a mediocre one overnight.

And the further in advance one must plan a trip, the greater the likelihood that river conditions will change before you get there. It's the nature of the beast. What to do? Base your selection of a fishing locale on reliable information … work through a booking agent, talk with other anglers who have extensive experience fishing the waters where you're headed, and remain in close contact with the lodge or guide you plan to use. Your booking agent is a key player in all of this. He or she thrives on repeat business as do lodges, but more so. If you've booked a trip and the fishing where you're headed has taken a terrible turn for the worse, a good agent will let you know and do his dead level best to book you elsewhere.

It's hard not to get carried away by the sweet pictures presented by books and articles, but you've got to remember that fishing is fishing. Sometimes it's just not up to par.

About booking agents

There are two schools of thought about whether to book a trip through an agent. On the plus side: agents know many more lodges than most of us. They have inspected the lodges and understand the clientele that the lodge serves. And they know about the fishing. In most cases, you'll pay the same price for a week at a lodge whether you book through an agent or do it yourself. (If you book through an

Tackle When it comes to international travel, long rod tubes are cumbersome at best. Some air carriers will permit you to carry them aboard, but most prefer that they be checked, and left to the tender mercies of baggage handlers. You can tape three long rod tubes together for added structural rigidity, but still your rods face substantial risk from damage or theft. Thanks to improved composite materials and breakthroughs in ferrule design, there is now a carry-on solution.

The most exciting development in fly rod design is the proliferation of multi-section travel rods produced by US manufacturers. The R. L. Winston Rod Co., (PO Box 411, 500 South Main Street, Twin Bridges, MO 59754 USA, 406-684-5674; fax 406-684-5533; http://www.winstonrods.com) offers a series of five-piece 9-foot boron-graphite rods in six, seven, eight, nine, ten, and 12 weights. These rods pack down to about 2 feet and are easily carried inside one's duffel. Winston's are top

of the line rods, no doubt about it. A fine custom rod maker, Dave Lewis of Performance Fly Rods (Rt. 4, Box 440, Harrisonburg, VA 22901 USA; 540-867-0856; email: Hyrods@aol.com), builds a stout six-piece, eight to nine weight 9-foot rod that slips into a carry-on bag. Both Winston and Lewis also make five-piece travel rods in two to five weights for trout. Among the most practical of the new breed of traveling rods is the seven-piece, 8-foot, five-weight Vagabond by Thomas & Thomas with sections about 15 inches long. And the oldest and finest of these multi-piece traveling trout rods is the tiny Smuggler series from The House of Hardy, (Alnwick, Northumberland, NE66 2PF, UK; 1665 602771; fax. 1665-602389.)

Great expectations

Skimming through fishing books such as this one, piles of magazines, and articles on the World Wide

agent, the lodge pays the agent a fee of about 15 percent, but it costs you the same either way.)

On the down side, some agents have exclusive relationships with one or more lodges. There's a quid pro quo in this. In exchange for being the sole representative of a lodge in, say the US, the agent pledges to provide the lodge with so many guests per year. If an agent is the sole representative for a lodge, you can bet your bottom line that his priority is filling that lodge with guests. Sure, he wants guests to be satisfied. That keeps him and the lodge in repeat business. But rest assured that he's going to try and sell you on that lodge.

Agents who represent many lodges have a different perspective. Their bread and butter comes from establishing relationships with clients who may not want to go to the same lodge year after year. In the main, their job is to help you find the fishing vacation of your dreams – and then book it through them. If things go awry on your trip as they sometimes do, and you booked it through an agent, you'll have greater opportunity for redress than you will if you've booked it directly. Agents are generally current on international travel and airline regulations, and they provide a wealth of practical information that will facilitate your fishing vacation.

If you're working with an agent, should you talk directly with prospective lodges as well? Yes! And beware of the agent who tries to keep you from it. Remember, it's your trip of a lifetime, and you must satisfy yourself that this trip is going to meet your expectations. At the same time, if you're working with an agent who has recommended a lodge, it's frankly unethical to book the lodge directly without going through the agent.

The task of selecting an agent is much the same as picking a lodge. Below is a list of some of the best. Call them, ask about their services, talk with them about their relationships with the lodges they represent, and obtain a list of

references, particularly of people who live in your area. Find out if they will be attending any of the fishing shows in your area, and if so, arrange to meet them in person.

Below are booking agents with extensive international expertise. In addition, in the Resources section at back (page 152), is a list of agents who specialize in one country.

Angling Travel Holidays Orchard House, Gunton Park, Hanworth, Norwich NR11 7HJ, UK. Ph and Fax: 1263 761602

John Eustice & Associates 1445 SW 84th Ave, Portland, OR 97225, USA; Ph: 503 297 2468; http://www.johneustice.com

Fishabout PO Box 1679, Los Gaitos, CA 95031, USA; Ph: 408 354 4396; Fax: 408 395 4676; http://www.fishabout.com

The Fly Shop 4140 Churn Creek Rd, Redding, CA 96002, USA; Ph: 800 669 3474; Fax: 916 222 3572; http://www.theflyshop.com

Frontiers 305 Logan Rd, PO Box 959, Wexford, PA 15090-0959, USA; Ph: 412 835 1577; Fax: 412 935 5388; http://www.frontierstrvl.com.
UK Office 18 Albermarle St, London W1X 3HA; Ph: 171 493 0798; Fax: 171 629 5569

Gage Outdoor Expeditions Northstar East Building, 608 Second Ave S., Suite 166, Minneapolis, MN 55402, USA. Ph: 800 888 1601

Get-Lost Tours 78-14 153 Ave, Howard Beach, NY 11411, USA. Ph: 718 738 9069.

Kaufmann's Streamborn Fly Fishing Expeditions, Inc. 8861 S.W. Commercial, PO Box 23032, Tigard, OR 97281, USA. Ph: 800 442 4359; Fax: 503 684 7025; email: kaufmanns@kman.com; http://www.kman.com

King's Angling Holidays 27 Minster Way, Hornchurch, Essex RM11 3TH, UK; Ph: 1708 453043; Fax 1708 446413

Jim McCarthy Adventures 4906 Creek Drive, Harrisburg, PA 17112, USA; Ph 717 652 4374; Fax: 717 652 5888

Off the Beaten Path 27 E. Main St, Bozeman, MT 59715, USA. Ph: 800 445 2995

Orchape 6, Rue d' Amaillé, 75017 Paris, France; Ph: 43 80 30 67; http://www.spav.com-progc-orchape.com

Orvis Historic Rt. 7A, Manchester, VT 05254-0798, **USA** 802 362 3750; http:// www.orvis.com (NB: ask for Orvis Endorsed Lodges and Outfitters. This is not a booking agency per se, but Orvis approves a number of lodges and guides worldwide.)
UK Office Unit 30, Vermont House, Northway, Andover SP10 5RW; Ph: 1264 349500

Pan Angling Travel Services 5348 West Vermont, suite 300A, Indianapolis, IN 46224, USA; Ph: 317 240 3474; Fax: 317 227 6803; http://www.com-panangling

Quest! Global Angling Adventures 700 3595 Canton Highway, Suite C-11, Marietta, GA 30066, USA; Ph: 770 971 8586

Roxton Bailey Robinson 25 High Street, Hungerford RG17 0NF, UK; Ph: 1488 683222; Fax: 1488 689730

Tightline Destinations 248 Spring Street, Hope Valley, RI 02832, USA. Ph: 800 933 4742

Transmarine PO Box 601732, N. Miami Beach, FL 33160, USA; Ph: 305 412 3818; Fax: 305 412 3637

World Class Adventures 275 Corporate Ave., Ste. 800 Kalispell, MT 59901, USA. Ph: 800 515-7988

Africa

Think of the Pyramids and ruins of Carthage, testimony to the temporal nature of civilization; of vast deserts and rivers unchanged from the beginning of time; of exotic cultures in perpetual collision; of flora and fauna utterly foreign to all but those who live in harmony with it. This is Africa, the second largest continent and probably the most diverse – more than 1,000 languages are spoken here by just 12 percent of the world's population who live in a constantly evolving melange of 50 countries. From Ra's al Abyad (Cape Blanc) in Tunisia, to its southernmost tip at Cape Agulhas in South Africa, the continent spans 5,000 miles. It is very nearly as wide and contains about 22 percent of the world's landmass. The continent's geography is dominated by the Sahara, the world's largest desert. To the north are the populous and more developed nations of Egypt, Algeria, Libya, Tunisia, and Morocco. South of the desert are the countries of East, Central, and West Africa, lands of high plateau and rainforest jungle.

The most extensive fissure in the earth's crust – the Great Rift – runs about 3,700 miles from the Mediterranean at Port Said to the mouth of the Zambezi on the Indian Ocean across from Madagascar. Emerging from the Red Sea on the coast of Eritrea, the Great Rift spawns volcanoes which give Africa its highest mountain, Kilimanjaro (19,340 feet). As the rift sinks beneath the Indian Ocean, a new string of highlands – the Drakensbergs – forms the escarpment between the temperate interior plateau of southern Africa and its sweltering low coastal

Far left **Swamps of the Okavango Delta hold tiger fish.**
Center **Sun cracks the dawn south of Mombasa, hot-spot for fly-fished sails.**
Left **No Falls are grander than Victoria and angling from nearby lodges is excellent.**

a member of the barbel family indigenous to Africa, provide consistently good sport on fly rods. And in the last 40 years or so, a number of lakes have been stocked with both largemouth and smallmouth bass from the United States. The coast has its share of saltwater species – ladyfish, queenfish, garick, and grunters – which all fall prey to a well-presented fly.

South Africa, with the exception of some of the intensely managed trout streams and tiger fishing, of course, is probably not a fly-fishing destination of the caliber of Alaska, Argentina, New Zealand, or Russia. On the other hand, where else can you fish for trout while watching the exotic game of the veldt? Tourists planning a safari in southern or eastern Africa will miss a real bet if they fail to bring along a couple of rods and a box or two of flies.

Kenya

The coast off Mombasa offers fly fishing for blue-water species, particularly sailfish. From mid-November to mid-January is the peak season, and fish tend to run in the 70 to 80 lb range. Anglers normally fish from 20 to 23-foot skiffs, though larger sportfishermen are available. Hemingway's at Watamu near Malindi, about 62 miles north of Mombasa, is headquarters for fly fishers after sails.

Some of the mountain streams have limited stocks of rainbows, which the government is attempting to enhance. And largemouth bass are quite plentiful in Lake Naivasha, about 62 miles northwest of Nairobi.

regions. Though brook trout can be found in the upper reaches of streams on the shoulders of the Atlas range in Morocco and Algeria, and headwaters rising on the flanks of Kilimanjaro carry rainbows, the best trout fishing in Africa is found along the inland side of the escarpment that embraces southern Africa.

As they were in South America, trout – browns and rainbows – were stocked in Africa by early settlers. Generally speaking, headwaters that gather in the uplands are favorable for trout. They breed in many streams, and many streams carry self-sustaining populations. But summers are quite dry with less than 10 inches average monthly precipitation. Winters are not much better. About 40 inches falls, on average, in July. Thus streams

are thin and shallow and while adequate to sustain trout, they run quite low in winter. The best rivers are privately held by syndicates or clubs which manage their waters intensely through stream improvement (weirs and small impoundments) and by selective culling of fingerlings and feeding. As a result, a number of streams produce quite respectable rainbows, some up to 11 lbs, with most fish averaging 1 to 2 lbs. Trout have also been stocked in a number of large impoundments, and fly fishing here can be quite good.

Trout, however, are not the only players on this field. Tiger fish, reputedly the most aggressive freshwater sport species, are found in many rivers, and they readily take almost any pattern that's presented. Largemouth and smallmouth yellowfish,

these ruffians tend toward the bright, big, and gaudy, though there's a bit of a movement toward top-water flies such as mouse patterns. On average, these fish run between 4 and 8 lbs; anglers can expect a dozen strikes in a morning's outing. The best time to fish the upper Zambezi is when waters are low – typically from September to December. Most fishing is done from fiberglass boats, but mokoro, native dugouts, are also used. Marking the end of the Caprivi Strip near Kasane, some 30 miles west of Victoria Falls, Impalila Island Lodge sits on an island where the Zambezi and Chobe rivers meet. Not only is this a gathering spot for anglers, but it's a jumping-off spot for visiting Chobe National Park for viewing of elephants, hippo, lions, and buffaloes.

Tanzania

Just across the border from Kenya is Kilimanjaro, Africa's highest peak. Its western summit is called Ngêje Ngêi – the House of God according to the Masai. Rainbows are found in several streams that rise on the mountain, stocked by settlers. The fishing is an interesting adjunct to game viewing in the region. More significant is fishing from October to March for sailfish off Dar es Salaam at the southern end of the Zanzibar Channel and further south near Mafia Island. Tiger fish are found in Lake Tanganyika.

Mozambique

With the exception of some tiger fishing in the lower Zambezi River, angling in this subtropical land below the escarpment is limited to saltwater species. But what saltwater fishing it is! The best waters are located in the Bazaruto Archipelago about 30 miles south of the mouth of Rio Save. Flats here hold springers (ladyfish) to 22 lbs, kingfish (trevally) to 26 lbs, and queenfish (jacks) to 33 lbs. These are not sandy flats, the bottom is more marly and wading is difficult. Fishing is best on incoming tides from October through May. Bonefish, *big* bonefish, are caught in these waters as well, but not on the flats. Anglers use heavier spinning or casting gear with bait and weights in the surf. Among lodges offering saltwater fly fishing is Benguela Lodge on Benguerra Island just south of Bazaruto.

Zambia/Namibia

Tiger fish are the premier game fish for fly-rodders in South Africa. They strike with unparalleled viciousness, leaping like salmon until utterly exhausted. Typically, anglers have used a bit of metal leader to prevent break-offs, but increasingly heavy monofilament is doing the job. Flies for

Zimbabwe

The Zambezi splits the border between Zimbabwe and Zambia. Tiger fish abound in the river, as well as species of freshwater bream that are similar to but larger than crappie in the US. Numerous lodges are found along the river, particularly in the area of Victoria Falls near Livingstone. Down stream, the 155-mile-long Lake Kariba is also an excellent venue for tiger fish, most in the 2 to 6½ lb range. Charles Norman, author of *Fish the Southern Seas*, having fished most of this water, maintains a current list. In addition to warm-water species, rainbows and browns have been stocked in the rivers and lakes of the mountains near Nyanga along the country's border with Mozambique. Largemouth bass are now quite common in Zimbabwean waters.

Botswana

The Okavango Delta is a magical place. It is a vast wetland of swamp, rivers (the Okavango and the Thaoge), and scores of lagoons surrounded by Africa's second largest desert, the Kalahari. The water draws thousands of big-game animals and provides some of the best tiger fishing in southern Africa. You will fish from native canoes and other shallow draft boats that are more stable than they appear. This area is very primitive and hard to reach, but the fly fishing makes up for its inconvenience. Tiger fish run in the river and lagoons hold threespot and redbreast tilapia in summer. Beautiful olive and thinface largemouth bream are available in winter. Guma Lagoon Camp with its comfortable tents sits on Okavango's front door.

South Africa

There are two schools of thought about just what constitutes the "best" trout fishing in South Africa. One group contends that the wild rainbows and a few browns that inhabit the highland streams in West Cape, and three or four hours north and east of Cape Town, offer the finest angling experience. West Cape rivers tend to be clear, freestone streams with the exception of 4 miles or so of the spring-fed Olifants. While most of the rivers in this area are definitely rainbow water, the Olifants and the Witte carry healthy populations of browns. These streams see regular hatches of mayflies and caddis, and even some species of stone fly. But most exciting are the massive termite hatches – flying ants – after the rains in fall. The best times to fish the rivers of

West Cape are on the shoulders of summer: mid-September to November and mid-March to May. Much of the water here is open to the public, but the better mileage is reserved in the European tradition. A number of guide services are available, among them Trout Adventures Africa run by the able Tony Biggs.

Larger trout are found in the streams in the mountains of Mpumalanga and they are carefully nurtured. The idea is to sustain a viable sport fishery – largely stream-bred rainbows and browns – that will complement game viewing in Kruger National Park and other tourist pursuits. That's not at all bad. Not even in New Zealand can anglers be guaranteed that they'll play half a dozen trout in the 4 to 6½ lb range, and some up to 11, in a morning's outing. Trout fishing in this region is centered on Lydenberg, where Fishy Pete's

supplies flies, tackle, and information, and Dullstroom, about 37 miles to the southwest. Trout rivers in this area are small, not much wider than 13 to 16 feet, fast and high up in the hills. Among the better streams are the Whiskey, Kliprots, Steenkamp, and Spekboom. Dries and nymphs fished upstream carry the day. By and large, the best water is controlled by syndicates or clubs, but access is possible by booking a guide or accommodation in one of a number of lodges. One of the finest in the area is Mt Anderson Ranch, which sits within 8,000 mountainous hectares that encompass the headwaters of five rivers that contain healthy populations of rainbows and browns. Trout fishing is available throughout the year with summer's low flows being better suited for dry flies and winter for nymphs.

While trout attract most of the attention, not to be overlooked are largemouth yellowfish which inhabit lower reaches of the trout streams. These fish feed aggressively and attain weights up to 22 lbs. Among the best waters for yellowfish are those of the Vaal River system. Largemouth and smallmouth bass have been successfully stocked in many impoundments. To the south, in the tidal estuaries of the rivers draining KwaZulu-Natal, is excellent saltwater fly fishing for garick, skipjack, and grunter.

Traveling to Africa

Africa is very much a continent of developing nations, a condition that is particularly true of the countries of eastern and southern Africa. Political structures are moving toward democracy but not without some disruption and civil strife. Crime, often used as a political tool by contentious factions, is always a present possibility. Security forces may be more edgy in some areas than they are in others. The best advice for planning a trip to an African country is to check bulletins and advisories posted by your own government regarding travel to the country in question and to obtain similar bulletins from that country's embassy in your country. Those are the best possible sources of information.

That said, anglers traveling to Africa should encounter no untoward problems if they use a reputable booking agent to make arrangements for fishing with an experienced guide and or accommodations at an established fishing lodge or

Left **Sportfishermen carry anglers offshore for sailfish.**

Below **A gentle release returns this battler to fight again.**

Trout This is probably the only fly-fishing venue in the world where the six-weight is too much rod. Three- and four- weights are perfect. Streams are not heavily brushed so rod length is not a problem.

Dries Adams, Blue-winged Olives, Elk Hair Caddis, Royal Wulffs, 14-20. **Terrestrials** Black Ants 14-22, and Hoppers in 10-16. **Wets** Woolly Buggers (black, brown, and olive) with and without cone or bead heads, 10-14. **Nymphs** hare's ear, pheasant tail, black stonefly, 12-18.

Tiger fish Though they provide terrific sport on three- or four-weight rods and several veteran fly fishers use them, the tiger fish for all its initial ferocity is a fairly fragile creature. They exhaust themselves in fight and take a longish time to revive. Using a six- or seven-weight, equipped with a sinking tip or full sinking line, will do the job and protect the fish. Reels should be spooled with 100 yards of 22 lb backing. Fine wire tippets of ¾ inch or so have been standard, but some anglers are finding they lose no more fish using shock monofilament tippets of 22 lb test.

Flies Bright and gaudy streamers.

Yellowfish/bass Six- or seven-weight with floating line.

Yellowfish flies Shrimp 6-10, Mouse, 6. **Bass** poppers, 4-8; Black-nosed Dace, Zonkers, Woolly Buggers, 6-10.

Saltwater Seven- or eight-weight rod, with weight-forward floating line and 100 yards of backing for flats fishing.

Flats flies Shrimp, Crazy Charlies, Crabs, 6-10.

Sailfish 10–12-weight rod, floating line, 150 yards of 33 lb backing.

Flies bait fish patterns of 4/0 to 7/0.

camp. Game-viewing safaris are big business and many operate from luxurious lodges that also serve angling clientele. The agents mentioned below know both the fishing and tourism.

Health hazards in Africa are numerous. Yet careful attention to health bulletins posted by the government of your country or the country you intend to visit can minimize your exposure. Water, fresh foods, insect bites, cuts, and abrasions can all pose serious health risks. However, following the advice of your host or guide can save you from lots of discomfort and, perhaps, serious illness. Be aware that conventional medical insurance may not be valid in African countries and that most doctors, hospitals, and clinics expect payment in cash when treatment is rendered. In some countries medical supplies and drugs may be limited. It is wise to bring ample supplies of all medications you take routinely and to bring copies of the prescriptions as well.

Visa requirements differ from country to country. It is wise to secure all the necessary documentation from the country's embassy or consulate before you embark on the journey.

You'll save much time and expense in so doing. Again, your booking agent can be of tremendous help here.

While capital cities may have ATM machines that disperse local currency or travelers checks, and hotels, restaurants, and shops that serve international clientele may accept major credit cards, the further into the bush you go, the less you'll be able to use plastic money. The only option is to cost-out your trip and plan to carry enough cash to cover those expenses requiring currency.

Everyone who goes to Africa wants to return with good photos. While there's generally a good photo shop on each capital city, chances of finding a selection of print and almost any slide films in small-town shopping centers is almost nil. Double ditto for batteries. Bring what you need with you and consider packing the film in an X-ray-proof bag. Arrive at airports early so that security personnel can hand-check your cameras and related gear.

Asia

Around the world, places to fly fish are generally similar. Fly fishing in South America is similar to streams in the western United States; salmon fishing in the United Kingdom is not too different from that of Canada's Maritimes; bonefishing in the Caribbean is closely akin to fishing the lagoon at Christmas Island. Sure, landscapes and cultures and climates vary a bit, but the tackle and tactics are very much the same no matter where you go.

That's not the case in Asia. Rivers in the Himalayas carry browns, rainbows, and mahseer, a cold-water carp that is the size of tarpon. Nuwara Eliya, the peaks of Sri Lanka, also offers trout. In Mongolia, taimen up of 55 lbs, are reasonably common. And the tiny streams of Japan hold native trout, as well as stocked rainbows and browns. Of all the countries, only Mongolia is a destination country. A week fishing the Bator River is some of the most primitive angling in the world. Otherwise pack a rod for Asia and a box or two of flies, and when there on business or vacation, slip away and fish a stream or two.

India, Bhutan, and Sri Lanka

Along the sweep of the northwestern Himalayas, Arunachal in the far northeast, and Mysore in the southern part of the country, mahseer inhabit the rivers. You'll find them as well in Bhutan, which is just north of Bangladesh. Best taken during breeding periods in May through September, they spawn in shoals and fall prey to streamers imitating minnows. Among the best rivers, according to *Where to Fish*, are the Jhelum just

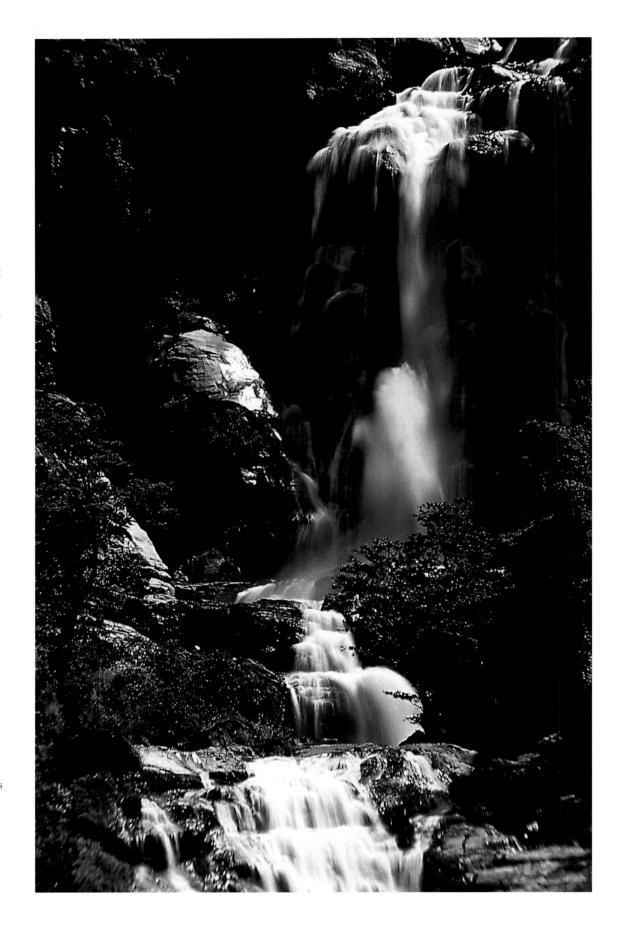

Opposite left **Streams in high Sri Lankan foothills carry catchable trout.**

Right **Huge taimen lure anglers to the wilds of Mongolia.**

west of the border with East Pakistan northwest of Srinagar; the Beas near Pong Reservoir in Himachal Pradesh, the Ganga, about 150 miles north of New Delhi above to Tehri; the Manas upstream from Jogighopa and into Bhutan; and the Bhoroli 56 miles due north of Tezpur. Way south, below Bangalore and east of Mysore, is the Kaveri, which can be fished for the huge mahseer, and fishes well in the water upstream of Stanley Reservoir. Mahseer are not traditionally thought of as suitable for fly fishing and the scrub along rivers such as the Kaveri is the habitat of wild elephants. Fishing for mahseer with a fly rod, and a guide who knows both the river and fly fishing, can provide sport of the highest drama. The Kaveri fishes best from January through April. Numerous freestone streams in the Jammu and Kashmir and in Hamichi Pradesh contain brown and rainbow trout.

So too do Nepal, Sikkim, and Bhutan, where Ernest Schwiebert fished for trout years ago. His principal rivers were the Paro at the town of the same name near the country's western border and the Mochu and the Phochu far to the north of Thimphu. Other streams include the Sankosh, Tang Chu, Panakha, Yamtso, Wang Chu, and Jamatso. The waters beneath the Himalayas here – the tallest peak is the 23,360 foot Ghomo Lhari – resemble those of the area surrounding Yellowstone in the American West. Anglers stay in tent camps on the Mochu or in hotels in Paro.

While the browns and rainbows of the central plateaus of Nuwara Eliya and Horton Plains, lying below the 8,200 foot mountain of Pidurutalagala in the center of the island, tend to be on the

smallish size – 8 to 15 inches – larger fish up to 24 inches have been taken. Streams such as the Ambawela, Bulu Ella, Agra Oya, and Gorge Valley flow through a mixture of grasslands and jungle. Sri Lanka is buffeted by monsoons during most of the year. The wettest months in the highlands are November through May; fishing is better when the rivers are lower. Average temperatures here hover around 70°F. Anglers stay in guest houses in the mountains, and fishing is controlled by the Nuwara Eliya District Fishing Club, which has undertaken some stocking. Permits are available from the club.

Mongolia

Taimen, a close relative of landlocked and Atlantic salmon, prowl the rivers of Mongolia. Tipping the scales anywhere from 33 to 220 lbs – though average sizes tend to fall into the 44 to 77 lb range – taimen are huge members of the salmon family. The taimen of Mongolia are reportedly a different strain from those found in the Danube and other rivers of Eastern Europe. And while Mongolian taimen readily take flies, their preference is not for those of normal pattern. They feed on other fish to be sure, but they prefer furred or feathered creatures that enter their territory. Ducks, lemmings, muskrats, prairie dogs, and weasels are all fair game. Taimen are found in many Mongolian rivers, though the Bator and the Aryol in Hüvsgül Province up near the Russian border, a half-day chopper ride northwest of Ulaanbaatar, the capital city, are among the best. Flowing through broad treeless valleys, the Bator and the Aryol look for all the world like big, wide shallow rivers from the US West. Yet don't be deceived: these rivers also course through gorges where angling can be very difficult, but the results – 25 inch taimen – can make it worthwhile. Most anglers who fish Mongol rivers float in flat-bottomed johnboats, pulling ashore at suitable riffles and runs of fast water where big taimen lie. The idea is to cast the fly across the fast water and let it work down into the taimen's lie. The take can be explosive. Fishing is best in late summer and early fall, after meltwater has cleared from the river systems. Fishing lodges are in complete absence here; anglers stay in camps

Right **Amago, a delicate cousin of Pacific salmon, inhabit streams in Japan.**
Below **Tradition dates fly fishing in Japan from the 1600s.**

comprising the round felt gers favored by nomadic herdsmen or in modern tents. While Mongolia is bitter cold in winter, temperatures average about 64°F in summer, and rainfall, even in the mountains, is minimal.

Japan

With lofty volcanic mountains as the core of this archipelago nation, it would seem a natural for fly fishing. And, to some degrees, so it is. Fly fishing in Japan, like so much of the country, is both very new and very old. In a story attributed to Kazuhiro Ashizawa, the Japanese discovered their own fly-fishing method – *ke-bari-tsuri* – by the 1600s. Among other species they fished for the lovely amago, its sea-run cousin the sakuramasu, and yamame, all diminutive relatives of Pacific salmon. Yet it wasn't until the turn of the last century that brook, brown and rainbow trout were introduced into mountain rivers. The decades following World War II opened up fly fishing and it, along with other forms of the sport, particularly Tomozuri for highly prized aku, has become something of a national pasttime.

Both amago and yamame tend to be small – 8 to 12 inches cm on average. Amago are more likely to be found in waters that flow down to the west into the Sea of Japan. The yamame is found predominantly on the country's eastern-flowing rivers. Most of Japan's trout streams are of the freestone variety with only a few that might be classed as spring creeks. In the main they tend to be narrow and delicate as befitting their native trout. Access to rivers is controlled by private cooperatives, *gyokos*, and they are also responsible for its stocking. Cooperatives have exclusive

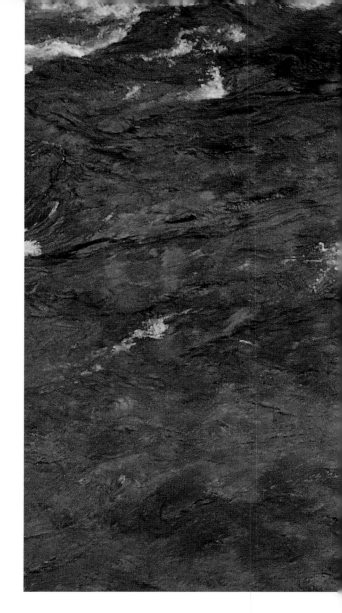

controls of sections of streams, so you may need permits from more than one to fish the mileage you desire. The open season is generally from the first weekend in March to the last weekend in September.

Overall, the best fly fishing is found on Hokkaido with its high mountains, vast forests, numerous lakes, and limited population. As the furthest north of the main islands, Hokkaido enjoys cool summers. Otherwise many of the streams in the narrow valleys of the mountains surrounding Tokyo to the north as well as east contain trout. Of particular interest are the Neb in the Nagano Prefecture, Yukawa near Nikko, and others in the Akika Keikoku region just two hours from Tokyo.

Traveling to Asia

All of the countries in this region boast reasonably stable governments and, at present, are safe from civil strife. Yet, with the exception of Japan and possibly India, most would be considered to be nations engaged in the process of political evolution. Before traveling, read and heed advisories and bulletins issued by the foreign ministry or department of state in your country.

As is the case in Africa, medical insurance may not be valid in these countries. Hospitals, clinics, and doctors may demand payment in full when services are rendered. Normal cautions about consuming fresh vegetables and fruits in rural areas also apply.

A bank in the capital city, in the case of Bhutan, Mongolia, or Sri Lanka, is the best place to obtain local currency. And with the exception in Japan, where fly fishing is big business, it will be difficult to find tackle and flies in these countries. Plan to bring what you need.

A great deal of time – at least two months, sometimes more – is required to obtain visas from Bhutan and Mongolia. Make plans well in advance.

TACKLE AND FLIES

Mahseer and taimen Weight-forward floating or sinking tip lines on nine- or ten-weight systems.

Flies Bunny, Clousers, Deceivers, Dhalbergs in bright, baitfish, and dark colors, size 1/0-2; also lemmings and mice, size 2 or bigger.

Trout A five-weight system with weight-forward line and an optional sinking leader system is more than adequate in most cases. In Japan, use a three-weight about 7 feet in length.

Dries Adams, Ants, Blue-winged Olives, Caddis, Hoppers, Humpies, Royal Wulffs, 10-16.

Nymphs & streamers Gold-ribbed Hare's Ear, Pheasant Tail, Woolly Bugger, 8-14.

Australia

With its crocodiles and koala bears and seasons turned upside down, Australia is a place of fascination as vast as its central plains and deserts and great offshore reefs. It is the world's smallest continent but its sixth largest country. Rimming the eastern coast is the Great Dividing Range with peaks up to 7,200 feet in the Australian Alps between Melbourne and Canberra. Though the country has a population density of only two persons per square mile, most of the country's 19 million citizens live between the mountains and the sea. Despite its laid-back image, nearly two-thirds of the Australians live in cities. They are among the most urban people on earth.

The northernmost tip of Australia lies about the same distance from the equator as the north coast of Venezuela, and Tasmania – 150 miles south of Melbourne – is situated at the same latitude as Northern California. The climates are similar, but reversed: spring begins in September and fall in April. Australia's tropical north is divided into two seasons: hot and wet in February through March and warm and reasonably dry the rest of the time. Southern Australia boasts moderate winters and warm, but not hot, summers. Prevailing winds bring rain to the lowlands east of the Dividing Range, and in the winter, Mt Kosciusko and its neighboring peaks in the Australian Alps can receive heavy snowfall. In Tasmania precipitation falls mainly as heavy rains in the winter and from cyclonic cloudbursts in summer.

Once part of the ancient supercontinent Pangaea, Australia has long been isolated by the Pacific and Indian Oceans for nearly 200 million years, ample time for evolution of wonderfully diverse animals and plants. In fact, nearly 70 percent of the birds and 88 percent of the reptiles are unique to Australia. Here you'll find primitive flightless emus and cassowaries and fan-tailed lyrebirds so named for their skilled song. In the southern rivers lives the platypus with its fur of a mammal, bill of a duck, and poisonous spurs. Marsupials abound – the kangaroo and lovable koala, but also the Tasmanian Devil, a scavenger that lives on carrion and rodents. Vermilion banksias and firewheel and waratah trees blaze like bonfires in northern forests. Traveling anglers will know the trout – mainly browns and rainbows – and some of the saltwater species will be familiar as well, particularly big-game species and tarpon. The fishing is quite good on the mainland as well as on Tasmania, and the flora and fauna are unlike any on earth. Australia and its island to the south almost demand a visit.

The Southeast

Rising to the east of Melbourne, the Great Dividing Range contains the Australian Alps, with several peaks topping 5,900 feet. From their slopes flow myriad streams feeding the headwaters of rivers like the Owens and Goulburn. Brown and rainbow trout of 2 lbs or so are fairly common in these stocked waters. Further east and north, in the heart of the Snowy Mountains of New South Wales, is the mainland's premier trout fishery. Here in the Monaro area, about 60 or so miles southwest of Canberra, are a number of streams – Bobundra Creek, Eucumbene River, Kybeyan River, MacLaughlin River, Mowamba River, Swampy Plains River, and the Thredbo River – that offer good fishing for rainbows and browns. The season runs from Labor Day Weekend in October to the Queen's Birthday Long Weekend in June. Lake Eucumbene, roughly 80 miles from Canberra, holds good stocks of rainbows and browns of 2 to 4 lbs. Sight-fishing for browns along the shore is a favored game among Australian fly fishers. Also work the mouths of the creeks that feed the lake. And while in the vicinity, don't

overlook the Murrumbidgee for trout of 12 inches or so, or the Yaouk with slightly larger fish. Accommodations are varied in the Canberra area. Fly fishers will feel right at home at the Dave and Judy Churche's Bed & Breakfast in Latham, a suburb of Canberra.

Queensland

The Cape York Peninsula, the northernmost tip of Australia, fishes like the Everglades in the USA's Florida. It's low and swampy and flushed with tides, and flats of sand and mud are cut with channels and dotted with mangrove. Cape York is a land of large crocodiles, exotic tropical birds, and fish to make a saltwater fly reel sing. The star is barramundi, that close cousin of the snook. Lurking beneath snags and twisted clumps of mangrove root, barra will slam flies that resemble finger-sized mullet. Also present are fingermark bream, long-tailed tuna, queenfish, small tarpon, and trevally. Summer is the wettest season and fishing is not good. But in spring – September and October, particularly during a quarter-moon –

fishing in the mouth of the Jardine River and in the channels of Jackey Jackey Bay on the east side of the peninsula can be excellent. Winter, when temperatures fall to about 79°F, puts the fish off their feed. And in summer, monsoonal rains cause extensive flooding. April puts an end to the rainy season and fish become aggressive in their feeding. The point of departure for fishing Cape York is Bamaga, across the cape from Jackey Jackey. Angling Adventures of Geelong or Frontiers can handle arrangements to book air travel to Bamaga, lodging at the Bamaga Hotel, and guides.

Northern Territory

Lefty Kreh, a guru of saltwater fly fishing who lives in the US, has called the western coast of Australia from the Kimberly area north to Darwin a "new frontier" for anglers. Indeed it is. Offshore are sailfish, wahoo, and tuna. On the flats and in the mangrove shallows are barramundi, trevally, queenfish, barracuda, and jacks. The only thing missing are maybe bonefish, but that shouldn't deter saltwater fly fishers who are looking for ultimate sport with lots of very good fish. The waters around Bathhurst and Melville islands across Beagle Gulf from Darwin are known for large numbers of barramundi – up to 200 have been caught by one angler in a single day. Barramundi can reach 55 lbs but most are in the 6 to 15 lb range. Two lodges serve anglers here: Barra Base Lodge on Bathhurst, and Jessie River Camp on Melville. Best fishing is found in the relatively cool months of April through October. To the south and west is the Kimberly Plateau, world famous for diamonds and other minerals. The coast is pocked with numerous shallow bays and just offshore lies a system of reefs, the Bonaparte Archipelago. This region has few towns, even for Australia. One fly-in lodge, the Alligator Camp, caters to saltwater anglers.

Tasmania

Lying about 150 miles across Bass Strait from Melbourne, Tasmania is a mountainous island of 26,200 square miles that holds undoubtedly the best trout fishing in Australia. It is a world-class fishery for a number of reasons. Forests and streams on this island receive little acid rain, yet ample precipitation throughout the year. The climate is moderate. Summers are warm, but winter finds snow on Mt Ossa (5,300 feet) which stands in a central plateau containing scores of lakes and rivers. Trout, particularly browns first stocked in

Opposite **Polaroid sunglasses are essential for sight-fishing Tasmanian lakes.**

Right **The lakes of the Central Plateau provide the best trout fishing in Tasmania.**

1864, abound. Most streams also hold some rainbows but browns are Tasmania's premier species. Attempts to introduce Atlantic salmon have largely failed, but a few fugitives from farm rearing operations show up from time to time. Mid to late summer tends to be the best period for dry fly fishing, while the fall is better for wets and nymphs.

Using fly gear to fish lakes is more popular in Tasmania than any other place in the world. The best lakes provide trout with a combination of deep, sheltering water, well aerated inflows from mountain creeks, and broad flats rich in aquatic life. When seeking large trout in the shallows, Tasmanian anglers employ bonefishing-like tactics – "tailing" or casting to fish whose fins rise above the water, or "polaroiding" using antiglare sunglasses to sight cruising fish. The most popular lakes are found in the Central Plateau: Arthurs Lake, Great Lake, and Lake Sorrell. The Compleat Angler Lodge in Miena provides fine accommodations and angling services for fly fishers vacationing in the lakes region. Fine technical fishing for trophy trout is found in Penstock Lagoon and Little Pine Lagoon. The western highlands between Great Lake and Cradle Mountain contains a number of small lakes and ponds with very viable fisheries. Tasmanian Fly Fishing in Deloraine provides guiding and instruction as well as information regarding accommodation.

Lakes, of course, are not the only fly waters on Tasmania. In the uplands, to the east of the lakes region, are the rivers favored by David Scholes, whose many good books, including out-of-print *Fly-fisher in Tasmania* and *Fly Fishing in Australia*, set the standard for trouting literature in Australia. The watersheds of the North and South Esk and their tributaries, the Meander, Liffey, St Patricks,

St Pauls, Elizabeth, Macguire and Break O'Day, offer very good sport. So too does Brumby's Creek, a tailwater in the Poatina power scheme. Other rivers of note include the Leven River near Gunns Plains in north central Tasmania and the Mersey near Mole Creek, a town due south of Davenport. And while salmon fishing is really nonexistent here, several rivers – the Derwert and Huon in the south, the Gordon, Henty, and Pieman in the west, and the Duck, Inglis, Leven, Forth, Mersey, and Foster in the north – carry sea trout. October and November are the best months for these saltwater feeding browns. Providing guide service in the southeast is Trout Fishing Safaris of Tasmania in West Hobart.

Traveling to Australia

A valid passport is all that's needed by visitors planning to stay in Australia for three months or less. More, and you'll require a visa. Customs are not particularly stringent as long as you're not carrying items on a specific list of products available from the local consulate. Tourists visiting Australia for a limited period may bring most articles into the country duty/tax-free, provided that they are for personal use and will be taken out of Australia on departure.

A six-weight system with a reel and a weight-forward floating line is all that's needed to fish for trout in most of Australia; a backup rod might even be a three- or four-weight. Sinking tip or sinking leader systems will fit the bill in those few cases where going deep is really necessary. Saltwater in the northern flats and mangroves is another matter. Here a nine-weight rod is preferable, and overlining with a ten-weight saltwater taper may help fight wind. Rods should have the backbone to horse barramundi out of mangrove thickets. Shock-tippet material is essential, so is insect repellent. In Tasmania, Victoria, and New South Wales, stores with good stocks of fly-fishing gear are reasonably accessible. Not so in Queensland, the Northern Territory, or Western Australia. If you aim to fish those areas, plan to bring what you need.

Trout *Dries Royal Wulff, Elk Hair Caddis, Iron Blue Dun, Adams, Compara Dun, 10-16; Griffiths Gnat, 16-20;* **Terrestrials** *(ants, 14-18; beetles 10-12; hoppers, 10-14); Muddler minnows.* **Wets** *Hare's Ear, Seal's Fur, Sloan's Nymph, Woolly Bugger (bead-headed and plain).*

Saltwater *Clousers and Deceivers in various colors, especially pink and white; the Pink Thing, and Giant Killers. Size 2/0 to 6.*

Canada *east*

Below **Swift rivers of Ungava teem with Arctic char.**
Opposite left **Labrador's brook trout are fuel for your dreams.**
Opposite right **The Southwest Miramichi is one of the finest Atlantic salmon rivers in the world.**

The sheer size of this vast land and the fly fishing opportunities it represents demands we divide it into two sections. From the gray, spruce-capped headlands of Canada's Maritimes north to the barren tundra of the Ungava and west to the multitude of glacial lakes of the prairie heartlands, the eastern portion of Canada tempts anglers with Atlantic salmon, fine native stocks of brook trout and char, leaping smallmouth bass, and big pike.

While the country's largest cities are here – Montreal, Toronto, Quebec, Winnipeg – the land around them soon fades into farms and then forest. Beyond the forest are vast regions of scrub wilderness that merge into treeless tundra favored by caribou and wolves and bear.

From Lake of the Woods on the Manitoba/Ontario Border to the mouth of the St Lawrence River, a band of shallow lakes and little rivers in the west grows into the five Great Lakes – Huron, Superior, Michigan, Ontario and Erie – and then into the St Lawrence seaway, demarking most of the boundary between Canada and the United States. Smallmouth bass and pike roam the lakes and rivers of the west. Bass, salmon, steelhead, and brown trout ply the shorelines and rivers feeding the Great Lakes and the St Lawrence. Muskelunge, the greatest of the predatory pikes, can be taken in the Thousand Island at the head of the St Lawrence.

Rivers that flow from Canada's eastern highlands into bays that empty into the Atlantic offer marvelous angling. South of the Gulf of St Lawrence are the Gaspe Peninsula, New Brunswick, Prince Edward Island, and Nova Scotia. In the mouth of the Gulf sit Anticosti Island and Newfoundland. To the north is the mainland of Quebec and Labrador. Rivers host continually improving runs of the king of game fish in the Northern Hemisphere – the Atlantic salmon, and runs of native brook trout in excess of 4 lbs.

Fishing has long been a staple of Canada's maritime economy. In recent years the focus has begun to shift from commercial fishing to angling tourism. The work of organizations like the Atlantic Salmon Federation, in cooperation with private and governmental fisheries managers, has resulted in a blossoming of opportunities for sporting anglers. Lodges are opening in increasing numbers. The number of shops selling fly-fishing equipment is increasing. Much of the better fishing water south of the St Lawrence is accessible by car. But to the north, the land is wild, rugged and

accessible only by airplane and boat.

Provincial governments set seasons and limits. They specify tackle and in some cases mandate that nonresident anglers must fish with licensed guides. Canadians are warm and friendly people; officials in tourism departments and agencies responsible for sport fisheries work overtime to accommodate the needs of visiting anglers.

Manitoba

The watery north of Manitoba is scored by thousands of lakes. Most contain healthy populations of northern pike, lake trout, and walleye. Some in the south hold smallmouth bass. And fly fishers can connect with all four species. In early June, northerns and lake trout will hit big, brightly colored streamers that leave a wake when retrieved. Walleye are difficult to catch with flies because their time near the surface is limited to the week or so before they spawn, and then at night near rocky reefs. Smallmouth in some of the southern lakes will hit minnow imitations. Increasingly, anglers who book into wilderness lodges in Manitoba bring at least one fly rod and a few big bass flies for the pike.

There is one river – God's River – in Manitoba that lures fly fishers from around the world. Brook trout range from 2 to 6 lbs and they readily take flies. Sam Healey, of Healey's Lodge at God's Lake Narrows, flies or boats clients to the headwaters of the river at the lake's outflow. Fishing is best in the second or third week of July during hatches of big mayflies and caddis. The God's is a crashing stream that flows over shelf-rock and smashes into pools. Wading is not generally possible. Anglers cast to rising fish from deep V- hulled boats. Distances are short – 65 feet or so. Unlike some other brook trout rivers, fishing on the God's tails off in the fall when the fish begin to spawn. The North Knife River, west of Churchill on Hudson Bay, also holds good brook trout. And there is some fishing for rainbows in the Pine River, which enters Lake Winnipegosis at Camperville.

Ontario

While the big game in this is the pike and walleye fishery, essentially the same as Manitoba's, two other species – smallmouth and steelhead – attract significant fly-fishing interest. In southern Ontario, many of the dark lakes with granite shores shaded by stands of spruce and birch hold stocks of smallmouth bass. Pound for pound, smallmouth outfight most trout, and only now are they getting the attention they warrant. Top water flies in summer and fall, and streamers in spring, cast to rocks near water's edge can produce violent strikes. Hawk Lake Lodge fishes some 15 lakes in the Kenora area that are known for good smallmouth.

Perhaps the most challenging fly fishing in the

province is found on the northern rim of Lake Superior. Here steelhead run in spring and fall and, though many rivers are accessible by paved road, angling pressure is lighter than you would think. Among the rivers recommended by Bob Linsenman and Steve Nevala in their book, *Great Lakes Steelhead, a Guided Tour for Fly-Anglers*, are the Old Woman, Michipicoten, and Magpie Rivers near Wawa; the Cypress, Jackpine, Nipigon and Wolf Rivers in the vicinity of Nipigon; and the McIntyre at Thunder Bay. These rivers are fast, full of rapids and falls that challenge anglers more than fish, and productive.

Quebec

The angling of interior Canada spills over the border into Quebec, but here it begins to take on the flavor of the Maritime Provinces. French is the dominant language. And while most anglers think of Quebec in terms of the great cities of Montreal and Quebec City, and the land that lies between, the province reaches far northward into the Ungava region just south of Hudson Strait. Several of the rivers that feed Ungava Bay teem with sea-run brook trout, Arctic char, and Atlantic salmon. The most famous of these are the George, the Payne, and the Tunulic. Camps on these rivers are operated by a small number of outfitters in cooperation with the Inuit, the native peoples. Accommodation is spartan at best, but the fishing more than makes up for the lack of comfort. Thirty to 50 fish days are fairly standard, and most of the fish are in the 2 to 6 lb range.

Further south, in interior Quebec, lakes and rivers hold numbers of pike, lake trout and walleye. Feeder streams and secluded lakes support populations of brook trout. Outfitters have established many lodges in the area. Some such as Oasis du Gouin on Reservoir Gouin are located on a single lake where walleye fishing is outstanding and pike and brook trout avail themselves of flies.

Air Melancon, on the other hand, flies anglers into the Sauterelle territory to fish for native brook trout in a trio of lakes and a maze of interconnecting streams and ponds.

Atlantic salmon makes its appearance in many of the rivers of the Gaspe Peninsula and on Anticosti Island. In July and August on the Jupiter River on Anticosti it's not unusual to hook and play three or four salmon a day. Access to this 40-mile watershed is strictly controlled. No more than 80 anglers can fish the river during the 10-week season. SEPAQ-Anticosti operates a few lodges on the river and they are first-class in every way. The St Paul's River in Quebec is also highly regarded for its Atlantic salmon from July to mid-September. And in the last month of the season, sea-run brook trout move into the river, an added bonus for fly fishers.

New Brunswick

No river system is better known for its Atlantic salmon than the Miramichi in New Brunswick. Studies show that about half of all the salmon caught in Canada's maritime provinces are landed from the Miramichi. In reality it is two rivers. The larger, longer stem is the Southwest, which flows from tidal waters at New Castle deep into the province before reaching its headwaters above Juniper. A small peninsula separates the mouths of the main stem and the Little Southwest, a shorter and smaller river. The longer stem receives most of the salmon, but the shorter stem gets less fishing pressure and offers more public water.

In May, kelts, those hearty salmon that have spawned, wintered over, and are now returning to the ocean, constitute the first run of the season.

Right **There is no time to fish that is better or as beautiful as autumn in Canada's Maritimes.**

Next, in June, come waves of the first bright salmon of the season. Fishing for them peaks in late July. The third season falls when leaves turn to burnished gold and there's a bite to the morning air. That's September and early October, the loveliest time to be on these waters. While the Miramichi receives the largest runs of Atlantic salmon – more than 1,000 salmon a day migrate through its pools – the Restigouche has a reputation for containing larger salmon. New Brunswick requires that all nonresident salmon anglers fish with a registered guide. As you would suspect, guides are plentiful and the best are usually associated with the many wonderful historic lodges along these rivers. Among the better lodges are Pond's at Ludlow and the Miramichi Inn at Red Bank.

New Brunswick rivers also contain good populations of brook trout and smallmouth bass. Smallmouth action spans the summer from May through September. Vaughn Schriver of the Chickadee Lodges fishes the St John's River and Lakes Harvey and Magaguadavic. A float on the Meduxnekeag River will produce an occasional brown trout as well as 4 lbs smallmouth.

Newfoundland/Labrador

Newfoundland and Labrador are a single province separated by the Straits of Belle Isle. Up the western side of the Island of Newfoundland run the Long Range Mountains. Many of the streams here support native brook trout and serve spawning Atlantic salmon. These waters are accessible by highway. Among the better-known salmon rivers are Harry's, near Stephenville Crossing, Grey River near the middle of the south coast, and the Gander in the northeast quadrant of the island. Salmon runs begin in June and

continue into September.

As good as the Atlantic salmon fishing is, the province's claim to fame is not fishing on the island. Rather, it's the huge brook trout of the Minipi and other Labrador fisheries pioneered by Lee Wulff. Deep red-bellied brook trout typically range between 3 to 5½ lbs. They rise readily to dry flies. Fishing opens in June and reaches its zenith in mid-August before tapering to a close in September. Camps and lodges are scattered on the

best water. Try Cooper's Minipi Campus or Matt Libby's Riverkeep Lodge on the Atikonak River south of Twin Falls.

Nova Scotia

Were it not for the narrow isthmus connecting Nova Scotia to New Brunswick, this land of low mountains, rocky inlets, and salmon-rich rivers would be an island. The northernmost portion of

famous of Nova Scotia's salmon rivers. Just more than 40 miles long, the Margaree is clean and swift flowing from riffle to pool to riffle again. Best runs occur in September, but fish enter the system as early as June. The entire length of the river is restricted to fly fishing only, public access is ample, and a guide is not required to fish the river. On the lower portion of the Margaree, is Ruth and Herman Schneeberger's Big Intervale Salmon Camp. With 3,000 feet of river frontage, you can angle for salmon from your cabin or use the inn as a base to explore the rest of the river, which also contains brook, brown, and rainbow trout.

On the east coast, about 75 miles north of Halifax, is the mouth of the St Mary's, perhaps Nova Scotia's most productive salmon river. Rising in the highlands north of the Lipscom Game Sanctuary, the river contains 25 miles of good water. Unlike the Margaree, the St Mary's fishes best in summer when it's running full. Water levels drop as fall approaches and the river becomes a bit too tepid for good angling. Among other outstanding rivers are the LaHave above Bridgewater, the Medway upstream from tidewater at Mill Village, and the Stewiacke between the hamlets of East Stewiacke and Upper Stewiacke.

Prince Edward Island

On this picture-book island province of white wooden churches, green fields and beaches of red and white sand, some of the rivers in the eastern portion do see limited runs of Atlantic salmon. They also hold brook trout. While PEI could never be classed as a destination for fly fishers, tourists who come to the island might be well advised to bring a rod and a few flies just in case.

the province is, in fact, an island. Cape Breton Island is separated from the mainland by the narrow Strait of Canso. Easily circumnavigated by road, Nova Scotia is a haven for tourists in summer and fall. Eddies from the Gulf Stream temper the climate. Yet cold water brings Atlantic salmon in from the sea, and they are found in most of the rivers.

The wonderful Margaree, about halfway up the west coast of Cape Breton Island, is the most

Rods for Atlantic salmon should be at least eight-weight, and increasing numbers of anglers are using ten-weight Spey rods. Spey rods offer a definite advantage on rivers where foliage is prone to grab one's back cast. The well-equipped salmon angler will carry weight-forward floating, sink-tip, and sinking lines on interchangeable spools. Reels must have smooth disk drags, and large arbor reels which gather more line with each revolution are increasingly popular. This same tackle will work for pike as well.

For trout and grayling, four- to six-weight systems are ample, the difference being size of the fish, size of the water, and wind. An all-round six-weight will serve quite well and can double up nicely for smallmouth bass.

Atlantic salmon Remember that the fuller the river, the fuller the pattern. Low autumn rivers demand fairly sparse or even the minimal "low-water" tie. Keep in mind also that when it comes to Atlantic salmon, there are no steadfast rules.

Dries Bombers (white, orange, blue), Royal and White Wulffs, Black Rat, Salmon Muddler, 2-6. Wets — Green Machine, Black Squirrel Orange Butt, Haggis, Cosseboom, Mickey Finn, Undertaker, Rusty and Blue Rats, Butterfly, Shady Lady, Hairy Mary, Blue Charm, Silver Doctor.

Trout *Dries Adams, Caddis, Royal and White Wulffs, Stimulators, Muddler Minnow, 8-12; Mosquito, Pale Evening Dun, Blue-winged Olive, 10-18.* **Wets/Streamers** *Mickey Finn, Black-nosed Dace, Woolly Bugger, Bead/Cone-head Woolly Bugger, Leeches, Hare's Ear, Gold Ribbed Hare's Ear, Scud, 8-10.*

Pike *Dahlberg Divers, 2/0-4; Rabbit Strip Diver, 1/0-*

Smallmouth *Poppers, 2-6; Hellgrammite, Crayfish, 4-8; Zonker, 4-10; Woolly Bugger, 6-10.*

Canada *west*

"Oh, Canada …" begins the nation's anthem and it could have been written by a fly fisher. Western Canada – Alberta, British Columbia, Northwest Territories, Saskatchewan and the Yukon – is a mother lode of wilderness fly fishing. Salmon course with the tides through the Discovery Passage, and steelhead, shiny as newly poured ingots of sterling, climb steep rivers to spawn in tributaries high in British Columbia's Coast Range. Furtive native cutthroats and bull trout lurk in the alpine rivers of the Canadian Rockies. Alberta's Bow River is one of the most prolific brown-trout fisheries in the world, and the deep lakes above the Arctic Circle in the Northwest Territories and the Yukon teem with record lake trout and char. In Saskatchewan, early and late in the season, northern pike will hammer big, shallow streamers.

While much of the best of western Canada's fishing is located far from cities in vast tracks of unspoiled wilderness, it is reasonably accessible. A highly developed network of fishing lodges, built to serve the European, Japanese, and American markets, spreads across the country bordering the Arctic Circle. Lodges can be plush affairs with near-gourmet cuisine, or they may be do-it-yourself outposts where anglers stay in plywood cabins and do their own cooking. And there's everything in between. Guides and outfitters are plentiful on Canada's western waters. And because sport fishing is a major element of the country's economy, provincial tourism boards are particularly helpful, as are the game and fish authorities, in providing traveling anglers with helpful and accurate information.

Major cities in the region – Vancouver, British Columbia; Calgary, Edmonton, Alberta; Saskatoon, Saskatchewan, Whitehorse, Yukon; Yellowknife, in the Northwest Territory – provide the jump-off points for the interior. While coastal British Columbia and the Canadian Rockies can be quite cool, as can the northernmost areas along the Arctic Circle, much of western Canada experiences hot and somewhat humid summers. The plethora of lakes and ponds makes this a haven for mosquitoes and blackflies. Long-sleeved, loose, light-colored cotton or blend shirts and long trousers are generally all the protection that's required. That and the insect repellent of your choice.

Many of the guides in wilderness are native peoples. The apparent squalor of their settlements frequently appalls visitors from cities and towns of industrial nations. We shouldn't judge so harshly: the customs of native peoples are very different from ours. Native guides tend to be very generous with their knowledge about local fishing conditions and are eager to help their clients enjoy successful holidays. Anglers who learn a bit about the peoples native to the areas where they will fish will find their trip much more fulfilling than those who come for the fishing alone.

Alberta

Alberta is a land of transition. On its western boundary with British Columbia rise the spectacular Canadian Rockies, great beds of carbonate rock deposited in shallow tropical seas and now thrust to near vertical and jutting thousands of feet above verdant valley floors. These are the mountains of Canada's best-known National Parks – Banff and Jasper. Fishing is vastly overshadowed by the glorious mountains, but here the traveling angler can find high-quality sport. Many of the major rivers run white with rock flour ground by the glaciers that feed them. In late fall, they take on a lovely shade of turquoise, the clearest they ever get. These hold big bull trout (Dolly Varden) and they can be caught at the mouths of clear-water streams in late fall.

Better angling is found on rivers such as the Maligne in Jasper and the Bow in Banff. The Maligne holds rainbows and brookies. The river

fishes best in fall when brook trout spawn. In summer Maligne Lake is an outstanding fishery for rainbows up to 4½ lbs. But the most interesting action occurs in Medicine Lake, midway between Maligne Lake and the Athabasca River. Medicine Lake swells with meltwater in summer, but in the fall its level drops almost 65 feet to little more than 12 inches deep! Winding through the center of the lake is a narrow channel where rainbows as silvery as newly minted coin congregate. Readily they take dries and streamers dredged deep. Book into Jasper Park Lodge and fish with Loren Currie or try the Pine Bungalow Cabins on the Athabasca.

To the south of Jasper is Banff National Park. The park is drained by the Bow, Alberta's premier trout river best known for browns below Calgary about 75 miles east of Banff. Summer melt from the Bow and Crowfoot glaciers carries tons of rock flour, but it settles out in Bow Lake before feeding the headwaters of the river. The Bow above the falls at Banff supports a good population of cutthroat and brookies, and only a few knowledgeable anglers fish it. Among the best headquarters for anglers is the Post Hotel with its exquisite French restaurant on the bank of the Pipestem, a trout-bearing tributary. Lower down in the tourist town of Banff is a tumbling falls, and the slick pool beneath the cataract yields bull trout (Dolly Varden) and browns to bead-headed streamers. Guests at the grand old Banff Springs Hotel can walk to the falls and fish the trout-rich mileage below. Out of the park beyond Canmore the river's braided channels hold good-size browns.

But it is the 30-mile fly-fishing-only stretch of the Bow from Calgary to Carseland that attracts all the attention. With just cause: Anglers who fish this famous section usually catch several browns in the 20 inch class. The season is open all the year round, but the river is at its peak from mid-June into October. Scores of guides offer float trips on this section of the river and at some places, such as Policeman's and McKinnon Flats, one can wade and fish without a guide.

British Columbia

Imagine yourself an eagle soaring over Vancouver Island. To the west are craggy headlands and tight inlets fed by small rivers into which salmon swim to spawn. To the east are the Straits of Queen Charlotte and Georgia and in between them, the Discovery Passage, a coursing thoroughfare for migrating salmon. To the east, beyond the passage, climb the peaks of Coast Range capped by the 13,000-foot Mt Waddington. Streams on Vancouver Island, particularly Campbell River, provide fly fishing for chinook and coho salmon as well as for steelhead. There is some fly fishing for cohoes in the Passage itself, but the best angling in the westernmost section of the province is on the Skeena River system and its tributaries like the Babine and the Bulkley for steelhead. Fishing shines in the fall when aspens and birch leaves turn yellow. Numerous lodges serve the region, but none better than Frontiers Far West in Telkwa.

In central British Columbia are a number of waters which the most popular of all North American trout – the rainbow – calls home. Rainbows thrive in most rivers and lakes, and they are numerous. Among the better rivers are the Blackwater and the Dean, but there are many more. Fishing is good on these waters from mid-June on, peaking in late summer and early fall.

Also, along the rugged border with Alberta are two small National Parks, Yoho and Kootenay. The Kootenay River above its junction with the Vermilion is a wonderful cutthroat stream that is generally unaffected by the glacial melt that plagues other rivers in these parks. Scores of alpine lakes have been but are no longer stocked with rainbows and cutthroat and provide outstanding fly fishing for anglers willing to hike. Headquarters for fishing these waters has to be Kootenay Park Lodge, a quaint cluster of 1920s cabins originally built by the Canadian Pacific Railroad in the woods by the Vermilion River.

The Yukon

The Yukon conjures up images of the Klondike gold rush of the late 1800s when the river carried hoards of prospectors into neighboring central Alaska. Then, as now, chinook, chum, and cohoes spawn in the upper Yukon and its tributaries, traveling more than 1,100 miles from the river's mouth on the

Below **Sheltered by the soaring Canadian Rockie, Maligne Lake holds large rainbows and brook trout.** *Opposite right* **Behind each rock lurks a cutthroat, bull trout or maybe a wild rainbow.**

Bering Sea. Grayling and lake trout are also found in the river. Perhaps the most fertile fishery in the Yukon is the Ales River which drains the southwest corner of the province, which includes portions of Klan National Park. Along with grayling and lake trout, the Ales and its tributaries host kokanee salmon, chinook, sockeye, coho salmon, rainbows and steelhead, Dolly Varden, and cutthroats. Lakes abound in the province, of course. Some, like Tincup offer fly casters good fishing for lake trout in mid-June, just after ice-out. Later in the season, there's action on grayling in the mouths of the small streams that feed them.

Northwest Territories

Two huge lakes – Great Slave and Great Bear – present anglers with unparalleled shots at world-record lake trout and pike. And north of the Arctic Circle, the Coppermine and Tree Rivers tender superior fishing for Arctic char with colors as bright as flaming sunsets. Chummy Plummer's camp on the Tree puts anglers over char up to 6 kg. Fish the pool below the rapids in front of the cluster of cabins or ride with an Inuit guide to other pools in where the fish are feeding. Great Bear lake is shallower than Great Slave Lake.

Thus, lake trout up to 44 lbs are within reach of fly-rodders throughout the season. Among the best lodges in this neck of the woods, where accommodation is scarce, is Plummer's main lodge on Dense Arm but the season here is very short, only two months: July and August. About 155 miles to the southeast is Great Slave Lake where northern pike and lake trout grow to exceptional size. Fly fishers have good opportunities when the season opens in June. Later these fish head for deeper waters. However, small feeder streams are thick with Arctic grayling to 3½ lbs, and lots of fun on a three-weight system.

Saskatchewan

The grassy prairies of the southern Saskatchewan become more heavily forested to the north and the number of lakes becomes greater. Lake trout are found in many of the cold, deep lakes of the northernmost zone of the province. And the dashing rivers that interconnect the lakes often hold large populations of grayling. Northern pike are ubiquitous throughout Saskatchewan waters, as are walleye and, to the south, yellow perch. Walleye can be caught on Clouser and other minnow-pattern flies before they spawn in the spring.

The best sport, and it is truly awesome, is the pursuit of 40 lbs or larger northern pike and lake trout on a fly rod. Fishing begins soon after ice leaves the lakes in May and early June. Large, brightly colored streamers worked through shallows will elicit thunderous smashes by pike and lake trout. Because this country is known for warm summers, big pike and lake trout soon abandon the shallows for deeper, cooler water. But grayling always play in the rivers, and the angler with a three- or four-weight rod and a fly box loaded with dark dries and nymphs will have endless sport, particularly early and late in the day. Camp Graying on Fond du Lac at Stony Rapids is a very comfortable camp where there's good fly fishing for pike in early summer and where the grayling are always ready to play.

Traveling to Canada

Canada has placed high emphasis on the economic benefit of tourism, and each province has a very helpful agency that works with tourists to ensure that all find the vacations they seek. Generally,

TACKLE AND FLIES

The salmon/steelhead rivers of British Columbia, Arctic char of the Northwest Territories, and pike and lake trout of northern Saskatchewan all require an eight-weight or nine-weight rod. Lines vary. For salmon, steelhead and char, bring both floating and sinking weight-forward lines spooled with at least 100 yards of backing.

A sinking leader system should be added to your kit. For pike, all that's really required is a weight-forward floating line. Bass and saltwater tapers will help throw the big flies required to attract monster pike and lake trout. For pike, a 12-inch section of steel tippet will result in fewer lost flies. All that's needed for grayling is a spry three-weight. Rainbows require a typical 6-foot six-weight system. Steelheading in British Columbia is arduous to say the least. Good waders and wading shoes are a must. They'll also serve well on the Bow, Tree, and Coppermine. Wet and cold weather is also part of the picture; breathable, waterproof shells over thick polar fleece sweaters provide maximum warmth. Waders can double as rain pants when you're fishing from a boat.

Steelhead Dries *Bulkley Mouse, Telkwa Stone, Steelhead Stone, Bombers, 2-6.* **Wet** *Brad's Brat, Blue Bruce, Polar Shrimp, Purple Peril, Muddler, Silver Hilton, Black Gordon, Blue Max, Prizm, Flash Dancer, Egg Sucking Leech, Woolly Bugger, Steelhead Charlies, Teeny Nymph, 2-8.*

Bow River Trout Dries *Adams, 14-18; Blue-winged Olive, 14-20; March Brown, 14; Elk Hair Caddis, 10-18; Crystal Green Drake, 8-10; Yellow Stimulator, 6-10; Trico, 18-20; Pale Morning Duns, 14-16; Hoppers, 6-12.* **Wets/Nymphs/Streamers** *Olive, black, and crystal buggers, 8-12; Gold-ribbed Hare's Ears, Prince, Pheasant tail.*

one or more members of the staff are knowledgeable about sport fishing. And all provinces maintain extensive lists of fishing lodges.

Air services are highly developed with Air Canada and Canadian Airlines providing primary service to major metropolitan areas and a number of regional carriers flying to remote areas. Canadian airlines are very conscious about the size and weight of both checked and carry-on baggage.

And regional airlines often allow less baggage per passenger than major carriers. Check baggage allowances with each carrier before you travel.

Passports requirements vary greatly depending on the country of origin of the traveler. The best advice is to check with the closest Canadian consulate or the Canadian embassy for current requirements. The Canadian dollar is a stable currency.

Caribbean Basin

Below **To fish the Bahamian bonefish flats is like wading a desert.**

Opposite left **Not only bonefish, but barracuda, prowl the flats.**

Opposite right **The runs are done; now to release the bone so it fights another day.**

A faint zephyr ripples across the flats, amber in the afternoon sun, disturbing, but not much, the fronds on the palms that line the shore. Beyond the palm and a string of pastel houses rise green hills that turn purple with distance. Bonefish and permit prowl the flats. Mangroves stud the delta of the river. Here snook lie in the shade and tarpon in the shallows in the sun. Offshore in the blue water sailfish and marlin play. For fly fishers, the Caribbean is a most sensual land. Anglers from winter climes dream of these velvet waters in winter, yet in most cases the better fishing occurs in spring, summer, and fall.

Fishing these waters is about four-tenths angling technique and six-tenths hunting stealth. Flats fishing requires wading or poling the boat quietly to get in range. Waters are frequently clear. Fish can see you as well as you see the fish. Dress in neutral colors – tans, light greens, sky blue. Sun screen of SP 30 is essential, but don't get it on your flies. Fish can smell it. Long casts are often, but not always, required. More important is the ability to spot fish through polaroid glasses from beneath the long-billed cap that shades your eyes. Then play the wind and current to your advantage. Get as close as you safely can.

The Caribbean Basin includes the countries of Central America; those, with the exception of the United States, that border on the Gulf of Mexico; and those in and bordering the Caribbean Sea. It is the region of discovery: Christopher Columbus and his caravels sailed into these waters in 1492, the first of legions of Spaniards and Portuguese who entered this cul-de-sac thinking it was the new route to Cathay. Pirates soon plied these waters seeking homeward-bound vessels laden with gold. The British, Dutch, and United States staked their claims here too. All collided with native cultures – the Tainos, Mayas and Aztecs – to the benefit of none. Today, the cultures of the Caribbean Basin form a rich and occasionally volatile broth demanding sensitivity on the part of traveling anglers.

Bahamas

Stretching more than 590 miles from Abaco on the north to Great Inagua, the string of 3,100 islands and cays known as the Bahamas is one of the richest sport fisheries in the world. The blue-water Atlantic lies a few miles to the east. To the west, off the east coast of Florida on the US mainland, courses the warm and fertile Gulf Stream. In between are hundreds of square miles of sandy flats. The Bahamas are famed for their schools of bonefish, for gentle water that is easy to wade, for native guides who know their stuff, and for laid-back hospitality.

Bonefish clubs are numerous. You'll find them on every island where there's a nearby flat.

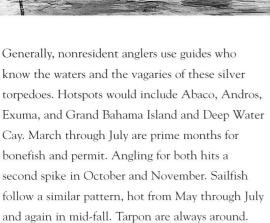

Generally, nonresident anglers use guides who know the waters and the vagaries of these silver torpedoes. Hotspots would include Abaco, Andros, Exuma, and Grand Bahama Island and Deep Water Cay. March through July are prime months for bonefish and permit. Angling for both hits a second spike in October and November. Sailfish follow a similar pattern, hot from May through July and again in mid-fall. Tarpon are always around.

Belize

An extensive barrier reef which runs almost the length of Belize creates a mosaic of lagoons, flats, and inlets that harbor an incredible sport fishery. Tarpon of up to 110 lbs, snook to 13 lbs, permit up to 22 lbs, bonefish in the 4 lb range, and barracuda of 22 lbs are the mainstays here. Tarpon and snook hold in the mouths of the Belize, Sibun and Manatee Rivers and in scores of shallow bays and channels through coastal mangrove thickets. Tarpon fish best in winter and snook in summer, and permit have a solid lock on August. Bonefishing is all year round. Among the most pleasurable modes of fishing these waters is to rent a cabin cruiser with a skiff in tow. The captain is your guide. You'll motor down the coast, launching the skiff to get into the fish. Belize River Lodge offers a number of such packages.

A more traditional approach is to book into Turneffe Island Lodge, on the atoll about 28 miles east of Belize City. Flats here run with large schools of 2 to 4 lb bonefish and smaller schools of bones in the 4 to 6 lb class. You'll also find tarpon and permit and your chances of hooking a grand slam – permit, bonefish, and tarpon – are reasonably good in September or early October.

Caymans

While highly regarded as a destination for divers and those who enjoy snorkeling, the flats inshore of the reefs surrounding the islands do hold schools of bonefish, and canals that penetrate the islands have populations of small tarpon. Serious

fly fishers are better off heading for other locales in the Caribbean, but the visitor who aims for the Caymans to dive or sail would be well advised to pack along an eight-weight system and a box or two of flies.

Costa Rica

The Gulf of Papagayo, near the very northwestern tip of this small country, has a big reputation for Pacific billfish. Sailfish frequently top 66 lbs, and their best months are May through September. Black marlin run from May into July, and blue marlin ply these waters through the winter. Here, too, most angling for these big-game species and for roosterfish and tuna is with conventional tackle. However, interest and expertise is growing in fly fishing, and El Octal, a lodge in Guanacaste, caters to fly-fishing anglers.

The core of the country is a range of high mountains covered with lush tropical forest. On

Below **Beneath the lush vegetation lurk snook of line-searing size.**
Opposite left **Bonefish often tail at the edge of the flats.**
Opposite right **Permit are fine quarry for fly rods.**

the Caribbean side stretches a lowland that terminates in watery jungle. The rivers that drain the jungle are heavy with snook and tarpon, and none is more famous than the Rio Colorado. Tarpon average 44 lbs, and snook 13 lbs February through May and October are the best months to fish. Inshore angling is done from 20 to 23 foot skiffs and fishing in the Caribbean for wahoo, yellowfin tuna, sailfish, dorado, and marlin is from a 40 foot sportfisherman. Rio Colorado Lodge and Silver King Lodge are headquartered at the mouth of the river and provide boats and guides for flyfishers.

Cuba

Off limits to anglers from the United States, but fair game for anyone else, Cuban waters hold large schools of bonefish, particularly in the islands known as the Jardines de la Reina Archipelago or Garden of the Queens. Separated from the mainland by the Golfo de Ana Maria, this string of tiny islands and mangrove cays provides a near-perfect environment for bonefish. Typically from 2 to 4 lbs with a good fish running 5½ to 6½ lbs, the numbers are very high and it's quite reasonable to expect to hook 20 or more in a day. It's always windy here, it seems, but despite the weather fishing is fairly good. Here you'll find tarpon as well, but they are small, in the 10 to 20 lb range. And the clarity of the water in these broad flats makes them spooky as trout. Precise casting is a must. Some permit also frequent this area. The best bet for fishing the Garden is a live-aboard houseboat which can be booked through Canada-Cuba Sports and Cultural Festivals in Toronto.

Other promising spots in Cuba include the Bay of Pigs and Zapata Safari Lodge at the million-plus-acre national park.

Reports on angling in Cuba are mixed. The economy of this country is a shambles and tourist services may not be up to par with those of Caribbean nations with more enterprising governments.

Many residents of coastal communities rely on what would otherwise only be considered game species for food. Still, good angling can be found in areas where population is limited. And no hosts are more outgoing than the good people of Cuba.

Guatemala

What this Central American country lacks in terms of a fishery on its short Caribbean coast, it more than makes up for with billfishing on the Pacific side. Porto de San Jose is the center for big-game angling and sailfish – from October through January – are most common. An angler can expect more than a dozen strikes during a day's fishing from a 30 foot plus sportfisherman. Among the better places to stay in the area is Fins 'n' Feathers Inn at Iztapa.

Honduras

Northeast of the town of La Celba on the Honduran coast lies a group of little islands, now largely national parks, which was the anchorage of Columbus during his final and saddest voyage. The islands – Rotan, Utila, and Guanaja – are joined by an expanse of flats that contain some very good bonefishing grounds. Fish, averaging 2 to 4 lbs, are not large, but they are plentiful. Most anglers hook and play between 10 and 20 bones per day. Permit frequent these waters, and the mangrove shoreline and tiny cays shelter a few snook and tarpon as well. Lying at the base of the mountain core of the island, Posada Del Sol is a lovely little resort that provides a base with lodging, tackle and guides for anglers.

Mexico

Jutting eastward toward Cuba, the Yucatan Peninsula separates the Caribbean Sea from the Gulf of Mexico. Along the coast lies the 1.4-million-acre Sian Ka'an Biosphere Reserve, home of the rare Jaribu Stork. Just offshore is a barrier reef and series of atolls that reach down past Belize. These warm waters – a wealth of bays, flats, and mangrove swamps – nurture some of the finest bonefish, tarpon and permit in the northern hemisphere. Schools of small bonefish in the 2 to 4 lb range are so plentiful, that novice anglers will have ample opportunity for practice before stalking really big bonefish of 8 lbs and more. Permit, too, are abundant. They feed on young spiny lobsters, the only commercial fishery permitted in the reserve. Tarpon, though generally no larger than 40 lbs, are also in good supply. The odds of hooking a grand slam are quite good in August. Among the better lodges in the area are Ascencion Bay Bonefish Club and Casa Blanca, which also operates a smaller satellite lodge on Espirito Santo Bay.

On the Pacific side, the tip of Baja California is a world-renowned center for billfish – blue, black, and striped marlin and sailfish – and more than 50,000 are hooked each year off Los Cabos. Most charter captains use conventional big-game tackle, but a growing number are switching to lighter gear. Some, such as Baja on the Fly, also seek billfish on fly-fishing gear. Most angling is done from 30-foot plus sportfisherman or from seven-meter pangas with one or two anglers per boat. Roosterfish, jack cravalle, and sierra are often caught from the beach. Cabo San Lucas is a tourist Mecca. Best months for billfish are May through October.

Panama

The absence of significant flats pretty well rules out bonefish and permit, though some are found off the north coast. Also rivers on this, the Caribbean, side contain a few snook and tarpon. But the best fly-rodding in Panama is on the Pacific or south coast at Pinas Bay toward the eastern end of the isthmus and near Coiba, the large island just off Peninsula de Azuero. Sailfish, small black marlin, and striped marlin are the quarry. In both locales, seamounts rise from 100 or more fathoms coming reasonably close to the surface. They hold bait fish on which billfish feed. While most lodges stress conventional big-game tackle, one, the Tropic Star at Pinas Bay, is very

Below **Flamingoes race past a flats boat.**
Opposite **The shallows off Los Roches, Venezuela, offer excellent fishing.**

comfortable with fly fishing. Black marlin appear in December and striped marlin follow in March. Sailfish are year-round residents but the heaviest concentrations occur in March and April.

Venezuela

Beginning in the west with Aruba, the Lesser Antilles shadows the Venezuelan coast in much the same manner of a barrier reef. About 80 miles north of Caracas is an atoll, Islas los Roches. This

handful of islands with its scores of tiny mangrove-capped cays rise out of flats that teem with bonefish and small tarpon. These flats are not the broad expanses found in Belize or the Bahamas, but narrow shoals that rim the islands. Bonefish here in the 4 to 6 lb range readily take flies. While some of the flats are marl others are sandy and offer good wading. May through August is considered the prime period here. Permit are also available, particularly over the corals to the northeast of the islands. Tarpon are year-round residents in these waters though fishing for them is overshadowed by the numbers and quality of the bones. Some permit are also found here. Included in the Venezuelan National Park of Archipelago los Roches, these islands are virtually undeveloped. Macabi Lodge, operated by Chapi Sportfishing, provides accommodation and guides.

While tarpon frequent the channels around the main island, El Gran Roche, a better tarpon fishery can be found about 80 miles east of Caracas at Rio Chico in Tacarigua National Park. Lying in the shallow waters of a lagoon, these tarpon provide excellent top-water action with the best coming in fall from September through November. Tarpon do not grow huge here – a 44 lb fish is a very good one. But an angler will hook and play two dozen fish a day and that's good sport. And snook, also called robalo, inhabit these waters as well.

Traveling to the Caribbean Basin

Owing to the economic importance of tourism in these countries, travel infrastructure is highly developed around major cities and resorts. And most lodges make arrangements to ferry their guests from urban airports with regularly scheduled commercial services to the lodge itself. But be prepared for severe baggage-weight limits. In some cases passengers on charter or regional flights may be restricted to no more than 25 lbs. That's not much, especially if you include camera and tackle. Baggage that exceeds weight limits will, at best, cost you extra. But more likely, it won't be carried on your flight. That greatly reduces your odds of seeing it again. Pack frugally, remembering that you can wash clothes at the lodge.

Documentation required for entry into each country varies with the citizenship of the angler. Each country may also require visitors to demonstrate enough financial resources to maintain them during their visit and to pay for the flight out of the country. Policies on duty-free goods also vary for each country. Anglers who use agents to book their fishing trips can usually rely on details provided by the agent. But to be safe, check current requirements and policies with the embassy or consulate of the country you intend to visit. Ask about and heed travel advisories.

In terms of rods for fishing waters of the basin, a 10-foot eight-weight is ideal for most bonefishing and it will serve well for other inshore species such as snook, roosterfish, and juvenile tarpon. Some anglers prefer six- or seven-weight systems, which provide enhanced sport under ideal conditions. Weight-forward floating lines, tapered for saltwater and colored white or light gray, are all you need. For windy conditions, it's wise to carry along a weight-forward line one level heavier than the rating of your rod. Reels should be constructed for saltwater use, equipped with an excellent drag system, and spooled with 100 yards of 15 lb backing. For all but the biggest tarpon, a ten-weight rod will suffice, but if you're going for those behemoths of 60 lbs plus, you'll want a 12. And the 12 will serve adequately for billfish.

It's not necessary to use weighted lines or leaders to get flies down to fish, but it is important to include flies of various weights, sizes, and colors in your box. Probably the most effective all-round patterns are Clouser minnow, deceivers, Crazy Charlie's, crabs, SeaDucers, and big-eyed tarpon flies. Snook also respond to poppers fished in the mangroves. Of these patterns, the better fishing lodges offer local versions that have proven effective. But in the more out-of-the-way locales, you'll need to fill your fly boxes and purchase saltwater leader material and so forth before you arrive.

Continental Europe

Mention Europe and the mind fills with visions of great cathedrals, museums replete with Impressionist paintings, of food and wine, and, yes, of wars. Grand images of the great cities of Paris, Madrid, Lisbon, Brussels, and Berlin compete with equally romantic views of narrow country roads winding past whitewashed stucco farmsteads. Marvelous resorts on the Mediterranean coast and ski slopes of the soaring Alps present pictures of Europe as a playground. And because of its limited landmass and relatively large population in excess of 600 million, Europe is perceived to be somewhat crowded.

While population densities are high in cities and suburbs, much of the land is rural. Europe is a tableau of broad glacial plains and highlands of low relief. Several major mountain ranges – Alps, Apennines, Black Forest, Carpathians, Jura, Pyrenees, and Vosges – are drained by freestone rivers. From the low countries to the Adriatic, Europe's coast is extensive and varied. Opportunities for fly fishers are abundant, though they are not of the same ilk as those on Scandinavia's salmon streams, the trophy rainbow waters of New Zealand, or the trout-rich streams of Yellowstone in the US. Only the esoteric angler would plan a trip to continental Europe just for the fishing. But anglers who plan on spending a week or more on the continent will miss out on some potentially wonderful experiences if the rod is left at home.

Of course regulations vary from country to country and, within countries, from province to province or region to region. Tourism offices can

Opposite **Draining the eastern Pyrenees foothills, the Ter carries good trout.**

Right **Public water is found in Spain's national parks.**

be very helpful as sources of accurate information, and in some cases, they sell licenses. The angling infrastructure – networks of fly shops and guides – is generally not as well developed as it is in England or Ireland, but there is a thriving and vibrant virtual community of continental European fly fishers. They are linked by the World Wide Web, and anyone (even those who are monolingual) with a modem-equipped computer can find a wealth of information online.

Portugal

Mountains make up more than half of this country on the western edge of the Iberian Peninsula. While Portugal's Atlantic coast is relatively extensive, the country lies at the southern edge of the range of migrating Atlantic salmon. Still, a few enter the River Minho which forms 37 miles of the border with Spain. Sea-run browns also frequent this river as well as the River Lima at Viana do Castelo about 15 miles to the south. This region is about 190 miles north of Lisbon and well off any beaten tourist path.

Spain

Pamplona sits beneath the northern foothills of the Pyrenees, that unbroken stretch of mountains that runs some 270 miles from the Bay of Biscay to the Mediterranean Sea and forms the border with France. Throughout the mountains are wonderful streams – the Segre, Garona, Aragùn, Cincia, Gállego, Noguera-Pallarsea, Arga, Esca, Riera de

Alp, Ter, Rigat, and Fluviê – all with good populations of trout, both browns and rainbows.

In addition to the Pyrenees, good trout fishing and the country's best salmon are found in the rivers and their headwaters that rise in Cantabrian Mountains and flow north into Bay of Biscay. Among the better rivers is the Cares and its tributary the Deva, which joins the main river near Panes. Salmon fishing peaks here in June. Another good river is the Narcea about 12 miles west of Oviedo. The Narcea's best fishing is found in its deeply incised canyon near Cornellana. Further west is the Navia, which courses through a very narrow valley and a chain of little lakes to the sea. In Galacia, about 50 miles of the Miño, called the Minho over border in Portugal, is considered good salmon water, as is the Ulla River

near Santiago about 37 miles south of Coruña.

While most of Spain's best trout fishing is concentrated in the rugged north and eastern mountains, the Tormes drains the western regions of the great central plateau, called the Meseta, and is considered a very good river for trout.

Andorra

The headwaters of one of Spain's most famous trout rivers, the Segres, rises in this tiny country of towering mountains and tranquil valleys. Here the river is called the Valira and its primary species is brown trout. Tourism and duty-free shopping have caused Andorra to develop an excellent highway system, but there is no airport. The best route is to drive from Barcelona.

France

France is France and one goes to France to taste the wine and sample the cheese, not for the fishing. The fishing is a bonus, something extra, something unexpected. France contains more trout waters than any of the other countries of continental Europe. Massive ranges of mountains – the Alps and Jura on the border of Italy and Switzerland, and the Pyrenees along the Spanish frontier – contain headwaters of hundreds of streams many of which contain trout. The Massif Central, separated from Alpine regions to the east by the Rhône River, is a highland of irregular relief drained by a vast net of trout streams. Normandy, that great plain an hour north and west of Paris, is geologically similar to Hampshire across the Channel. Here are a number

of clear cold spring creeks where brown trout hide in the cresses. To the west in the peninsula of Bretagne (Brittany) are short rivers that carry salmon and sea-run brown trout.

Among Ernest Schwiebert's favorite streams in Normandy is the Risle above Pont Audmer. Its tributary, the Charentonne above Bernay, is also highly regarded. The Eure, and particularly its headwater feeder, the Avre, also has a good reputation, as does the Andelle, which enters the Siene at Port Mariniere. Most of these rivers are strictly reserved, though it may be possible to obtain tickets through local tackle shops.

Access to trout and salmon water is better in Brittany. The Elorn gathers its waters in the Monts d'Arree and circles north, then west, before entering the estuary at Brest. Le Clos des Quatre

Saisons in Sizun holds fly-fishing schools and can provide river access and guides. Fishing for salmon, sea-run browns, and riverine trout is best from March to June and again in September. To the north, on the Jaudy, which flows into the English Channel, sits the charming stone Château Hôtel de Brelidy with its mile-long stretch of private water for browns, trout, and salmon. The nearby Trieux, a more open river, is also quite good for salmon and trout in early summer and again in early fall. Other rivers in Brittany that are worth a look include the Doufine, Odet, Elle, and Lata, all rivers that flow into the Atlantic. At Lannion on the Legner there is an excellent tackle shop.

In the French Pyrenees, salmon work their way up the Nivelle. Snow melt fills the river until the end of May, then fishing for trout begins in

Opposite **Fishing the streams of France can be as technical as those of England.**
Right **Browns are found in the high mountain streams of Switzerland.**

earnest. The best time for salmon is from mid-June on. Hôtel Bichta-Eder in Quartier Cherche-Bruit has access to a "no-kill" stretch of a mile and a half reserved for a maximum of six rods. This hotel is also within a few miles of the Nive, another good trout and salmon fishery. About 45 miles west of Bayonne near the Atlantic is the watershed of the Orolon, which contains the Gave d'Ossau and Gave d'Aspe, both very good trout streams. Au Relais Aspois at Gurmenìon is a comfortable headquarters for fishing this region, and staff at the hotel can arrange for guests to attend fly-fishing schools as well as guides. The upper Gave d'Orolon itself is one of France's finest salmon rivers, and the delightful Hôtel du Vieux Pont overlooks the river.

Among other productive fly-fishing rivers in France are the Allier above Broude and the upper Loire just to the east in the Massif Central. Further east and north in Franche-Comte are the Ain, Doubs, and the Loue.

Belgium, Luxembourg and the Netherlands

None of these three countries offers visiting anglers much in the way of fly fishing. The streams of the Ardennes, a land immortalized during both World Wars, contain trout and grayling. Local angling associations control access. In Holland there are no salmonids of note, but good sport may be had with pike on a fly.

Germany

Fly fishing in Germany is pretty well concentrated in the mountains of the Schwarzwald (Black Forest), which runs from the Swiss border at Basel north to Pforzheim. Among the best rivers here is the Kinzig, which rises near 3,000-foot Brandenkopf. Reserved for fly fishing is 3 miles of the river, which carries browns and rainbows up to 2 lbs. The Elz with its trout and a few grayling is the next watershed to the south, and beyond near Freiburg is the Wiese. Here 4½ miles are set aside for fly-fishing only and browns occasionally surpass 4 lbs. On the east side of the mountains is the Wutach, which has some fishing for browns and rainbows. Streams in Bavaria and the Harz Mountains also provide some trout fishing. The Germans are working diligently to restore a trout fishery that has been degraded by pollution and overharvesting. Regulations are stringent, but the fishing can be very good for those willing to invest the effort. Seasons generally run from early March to October for trout.

Switzerland

The collision between the African and Eurasian continental plates bucked up the Alps, which run almost due east–west from Switzerland through Liechtenstein into Austria and south into Slovenia. Angling in Switzerland is pervasive – most of the streams in high mountain valleys carry stocks of brown trout and some of the streams see hatches of mayflies. Lower in the headwaters of the Rhine and Rhône are bigger brown trout. Snow melt can be a problem. In the lower elevations, rivers become difficult to fish after mid-April. In summer, high mountain streams may see rapid rises of water as the midday sun accelerates snow melt. Still, there is much fly fishing in this country, and a small pack-rod would be a valuable addition to a visitor's baggage.

Austria

An abundance of swift rivers and their clear and cold freestone tributaries, earn Austria top marks as a destination for anglers. The fish – predominantly brown, brook, and rainbow trout, as well as grayling – are not large here, though some of the rainbows that leave their lakes only to spawn can top 4 lbs. But the sheer number of trout streams, their reasonably good access to visiting fly fishers, and the deep and effective commitment of the Austrian government to improving the quality of fly fishing combine to offer lots of high-quality opportunity.

Right **The larger the river, the larger the Swiss trout.**
Opposite left **Highlands south of Berne offer tranquil pools.**
Opposite right **Climb higher and you will find waters like the crashing Saxet.**

Perhaps the best known of Austria's trout streams is the Traun, which rises in the Salzkammergut range, about 25 miles east of Salzburg. Above a large lake, Traunsee, the river twists around boulders and plunges into little pools with all the wonderful qualities of a mountain fishery. Below the village of Gmöden, the Traun comes into its own. Trout of 16 inches plus are not uncommon and sometimes, but not often, they will go as large as 15 lbs. In addition to browns, grayling inhabit the river.

The Waldhotel Marienbröcke in Gmöden caters to anglers, offering packages that include lodging, access to private sections of the Traun, and ghillies.

Most, but not all, of the quality trout waters are found in the provinces of Steiermark, Kärnten, Salzburg, and Niederosterreich. The headwaters of Enns and its tributary the Salza, Mur, Drau, and the Traisen, Erlauf, Ybbs and Lammer all carry good fish.

Slovenia

A remnant of the former Yugoslavia, Slovenia has escaped the tortured civil wars of Croatia and Bosnia-Herzegovena, and offers some of the finest fishing in Europe. Rich limestone valleys and high mountains, coupled with a moist climate, creates an outstanding habitat for brown, brook, rainbow, and marble trout as well as grayling and taimen (Danube salmon). These waters are generally well managed and many are reserved for fly fishing only. Staff of the Fisheries Research Institute, which issues licenses, seems to be doing a superb job. Rising in the Julian Alps near the border of Austria and Italy is the Soca, definitely a big-fish river. Marble trout (*Salmo marmoratus cuvier*) weighing 6½ to 9 lbs are taken annually. Browns are also present. While some of the river flows through inaccessible gorges, much of it is fishable. Best angling occurs in August and September, following heavy snow-melt run-off in June and

July. If the weather cooperates, good sport may be had in April and May before run-off begins.

Also forming in the Julian Alps are the upper reaches of the Sava, the longest river in Slovenia. The best fly fishing is centered near the town of Bohinjska below the Lake Boinj. The lake mitigates the impact of snow run-off so water levels in the upper Sava are fairly consistent. Among the best time to fish for browns is during the mayfly hatches of June. As summer progresses, water levels fall and the fish can become spooky.

Further south in the Karst region near the little town of Cerknica is the Uncia, a lovely chalk stream. Gathering its waters from the Malenscica and the Pivka, the Uncia was once among the most productive of Europe's streams for large trout. Now, however, the Uncia is primarily a grayling fishery, though the Fisheries Research Institute is working to strengthen the trout fishery. Hatches begin with Mayflies toward the end of that month and continue throughout the summer. Another chalk stream, and

one fly-fishing-only stretch.

South of the great Po Valley and rising in the northern terminus of the Appenine Mountains north of Genova and a pair of nice trout rivers: the little mountain river Aveto which is regarded for its grayling and a few browns, and the Trebbia, a long grayling river with a fly-fishing-only stretch. Piacenza is the town closest to the best fishing on these rivers.

About 43 miles south of Rome is the town of Frosione where the Fibreno, a chalk stream, attracts anglers seeking a local trout – the macrostigma. According to Osvaldo Velo, the chalk stream is wonderful to fish but impossible to wade. Trout here grow big for Italy, up to 4 lbs. Further to the south, near Napoli, is the Volturno, a large river with large brown trout.

this one with a better fishery for browns, is the Kirk, which rises east of Grosuplje about 12 miles west of Slovenia's capital at Ljubjana. Local anglers know the Krka for its prolific sedge or caddis hatches and trophy-sized trout.

Italy

While not known for large numbers of high-quality fly-fishing waters, many of the streams in alpine regions north of the great Po Valley carry stocks of trout. In the Valle D'Aosta is one trout stream – the Dora – where one can fish during the closed season from October through February. The river also contains two fly-fishing-only sections. The upper part of the River Po near Carmagnola, about 18 miles from Torino, has all the look and feel of a chalk stream and in addition to a small charge of trout holds nice grayling.

The River Adda above Milano is also very good. The 30 miles above Lake Como is a mid-sized mountain river. It too is known for its grayling, but there are some trout and a special area has been set aside for fly fishers. Below the lake is another fly-fishing-only section of the river, this one near Spino D'Adda, but fishing here is complicated by large numbers of pike and whitefish. Further west the region of Trentio-Alta Adige takes the last part of its name from a large river with good grayling and marble trout. The best section of the Adige flows in the vicinity of Rovereto. In the same region is the Piave, a medium to large river that is one of Italy's best. Here are excellent grayling and trout and at least

Traveling to Europe

Creation of the European Union has facilitated travel on the continent for residents of these countries and travelers alike. Generally passports are all that are needed unless one plans an extended stay in any country. There is much interest in fly fishing, and in every major city one should find sources of tackle and information. Travel agents, however, are generally not knowledgeable about fly-fishing opportunities on the continent, and larger booking agents – Frontiers, Orchape, and Roxton Bailey Robinson – are more attuned to putting clients over huge trout and salmon in exotic places than they are to finding a secluded lodge in the Juras where one can fish a bit in the morning.

TACKLE AND FLIES

With the exception of salmon in Spain and France, the angler traveling to Europe should need nothing more than a light rod of four- to six-weight and a reel with a floating, weight-forward line. Salmon are not large, generally speaking. An eight-weight system with a rod of 9 to 10 feet should suffice. Weight-forward, floating lines with a loop-to-loop leader connection to allow adding sinking tips will meet virtually all of your needs.

The salmon angler should bring standard patterns – Silver Doctor, Undertaker, Peter Ross, Blue Charm – in sizes 6–12. Tube ties should be included, as should sparse patterns for low-water.

Trout fishers whose boxes contain Adams, Elkhair Caddis, Royal Wulffs, and Blue-winged Olives in sizes 8-16; Hare's ear, Prince and Pheasant-tail nymphs, 8-10; and Woolly Buggers (various colors and some beadheads too) and Mickey Finns, 6-10, will be successful. Plan on buying local patterns.

Denmark and Greenland

Denmark is the smallest country in Scandinavia, but it boasts the second largest population. Most of the population is concentrated on Sjælland around the capital København (Copenhagen) directly across a narrow sound from Malmo, Sweden. The western reaches of the country, the low and verdant Jylland (Jutland) peninsula, is largely agricultural dotted here and there with small towns. The peninsula itself is a gentle rise of sedimentary rock, nowhere higher than about 560 feet. This, the Danish mainland, is indented by fjords on the east where the land is highest. The west coast faces the North Sea, and sandbars capped by high dunes separate the sea from a series of in-shore lagoons. Surrounding the peninsula are more than 400 islands, only 20 percent of which are inhabited. All together Denmark has 4,600 miles of sea coast.

Denmark is virtually surrounded by the sea, which moderates its climate. Temperatures in winter average 32°F and in summer, 61°F. Rainfall is generally less than 1½ inches per month and is fairly even throughout the year with June, July, and August seeing slightly more than January, February, and March. Denmark does not experience the midnight sun of other Scandinavian countries, but daylight lasts long into summer evenings, which, as night falls, opens the curtain on the best fishing for sea trout.

Denmark

Unlike Iceland and Norway in Scandinavia, Denmark is not, generally speaking, a "destination" country for traveling anglers. Yet fishing here can be quite good and very different from that which is experienced in most other places in the world. Anglers who are planning a holiday or business trip to Denmark should consider bringing along a traveling tackle kit – rods, reels, waders, and shoes – and plan to spend a few days sampling the unusual sea-trout fishery.

Sea-run brown trout, averaging from 2 to 10 lbs are almost ubiquitous along the coast where currents swirl over rocks, sandbars, and banks of aquatic grasses. They feed throughout the year on shrimp, fry, small fish, and eels. Some of the finest angling for sea trout is found around the islands – Fyn, Lloland, Falster, Møn, and Sjælland – east of the peninsula, which contain saltwater pike that are a real challenge on a fly rod.

The season for sea trout begins on those balmy days (or so it feels) in January when the wind abates and the sun pushes the thermometer up a few degrees. Through February and March, one can find action throughout the day, but as the sun climbs higher in the sky, the fish begin to restrict their feeding to evening and morning hours. During the hot days of midsummer, night fishing is best because the water is cooler. Try fishing muddlers on top then, or working shrimp patterns or streamers through the eddies behind rocky reefs or bars. In summer, and in the other months as well, a sea wind will stir up the waters, discoloring it slightly and lifting food from the bottom. Fishing bright red or orange streamers with a bit of flash can provoke strikes from the biggest trout.

While night fishing offers fine and very unusual sport, the fall months are the best time to fly-fish for sea trout. They are on their last feeding binge before going on the spawn. While the romance of top-water fishing at night fades with falling temperatures, the chances of catching heavier fish increases as autumn reaches its peak. In late September they begin to concentrate near the mouths of estuaries – where fishing is tightly regulated – in preparation for the spawn.

Though sea trout have moved into the rivers by October, the number of really stellar rivers for sea trout is few. Most of the best sea-trout angling is found in waters along the coasts. However, the Karup Å, a tributary of the Skive Å, has a reputation for being among the best sea-trout rivers in Denmark, and perhaps in Europe. About 30 miles in length, the Karup Å rises near Engesvang in the center of the peninsula before joining the Skive Å east of Harderup. The waters then flow north entering an arm of the Limfjorden at Skive. The upper river carries brook trout. The best water for sea-run browns is found between Vristed and Resen. In summer, one fishes for the Karup Å's sea trout after dark. Wading the river after dark is dangerous. In places the river is deep and others it is swampy. It is best not to fish alone. Local anglers prefer two-handed rods to better control hooked fish without having to race down the bank in the dark.

Salmon also run in the Skive Å, but their numbers are not large. You can also find salmon in the Storå which flows through Holstebro on its way to Nissum Fjord 12 miles west. Further south the Skjern Å enters Ringkøbing Fjord. Neither of these two fjords fits the classic Norwegian style; both

Right **Quaint seaport villages in Denmark host anglers who fish for seatrout.**

might be classified more as almost totally enclosed lagoons separated from the sea by wide, sandy beaches. Other salmon rivers include the Varde Å, which feeds into Ho Bugt north of the island of Fanø, and the Ribeå, which enters the sea due east of the tip of the same island.

Salmon fish best throughout the peninsula from April through June and again in September.

During the winter, small sea trout called "Greenlanders" enter the rivers when near-shore saltwater becomes too cold and saline. These small fish feed aggressively and provide good sport on very light tackle. These rivers are not large by any means and most are easily fished after obtaining permits from the resident angling associations as well as a country license. Numerous other small rivers and streams hold modest populations of nonmigratory browns and grayling. In addition, rainbow trout, reared in saltwater pens for the commercial market, escape and occasionally wander into the rivers.

Greenland

While still a protectorate of the Kingdom of Denmark, Greenland achieved full internal self-government in 1981. The largest island in the world, Greenland is perceived to be nothing more than a huge icecap. That's not entirely the case. Sea-going Arctic char inhabit the fjords and feeder rivers of Greenland's west coast from Qaanaaq/Thule south to Kap Farvel. Such rivers as the Robinson and Paradise Valley host seagoing char up to 13 lbs in late summer. In other rivers near Narsarsauq, Nuuk/Gothåb, and Kangerlussuaq/Sønderstrømfjord, fish of 4½ to 6½ lbs are more the case. Rivers on the west coast see smaller fish.

Angling in Greenland is very much a frontier, and fishing here is a chancy business unless one books with tour operators of proven experience. Although Greenland is beginning to protect the migratory fish in its waters, the population relies heavily on fishing for both subsistence and cash revenue. Rivers that once contained good runs of char may be depleted by commercial fishing. Little infrastructure, aside from a few tourist operations, is available to support visiting anglers. Still, the thrill of casting to schools of char in clear waters where few other anglers have ever fished has a certain allure. Angling Travel in England book trips to Greenland.

Traveling to Denmark

Passports are required of all non-Scandinavian tourists, and visas are needed for stays of three months or more. Citizens of non-European Union countries may import the equivalent of 1 liter of liquor or one carton of cigarettes. The krone is the standard monetary unit, and prices are generally a bit lower than Norway or Sweden. Prices are noticeably lower in Jylland (Jutland) where the fishing is best.

Because Denmark is not well known as an angling destination, lodges that provide full services to anglers are few and far between. Indeed, it's best to rent a car and drive (on the right) to places where you want to fish.

Big gear is not always needed here, though Danes do prefer two-handed rods of ten-weight for long casts across the marshy Karup Å. A 10 foot, single-handed eight-weight rod should handle most fresh and saltwater angling. Weight-forward floating and sinking lines with reels loaded with 100 feet of backing are ample. Sinking leaders of various densities will have some application. Anglers traveling to Denmark in winter might stow a light multi-piece five-weight in their carry-on in the off chance that they'll have a go at "Greenlanders," those immature sea trout that enter the rivers. Similar outfits will meet the needs of fly-fishers traveling to Greenland, but remember to take along duplicates of everything. There are no tackle shops on the world's largest and coldest island.

Flies for salmon should include traditional patterns – Peter Ross, Blue Charm, Medicine, Bloody Butcher, March Brown Silver, General Practitioner, Undertaker – somewhat sparsely tied; and modern patterns like the Temple Dog in sizes of 6–12.

Sea trout *Moor Fly, Idiot, Muddlers, Glitter-shrimp, Woolly Bugger (white and flash as well as gray, brown, and black), Magnus, Bjarke, Scuds, 6–10. These flies should work in Greenland as well.*

England

If anywhere there is a spiritual home for the fly fisher it must be the spring creeks that rise from the chalk beds in the gentle green plains of Hampshire. Endless fascination with the ways of rising trout and meticulous documentation of experiment after experiment gave birth to the literature of Frederic Halford and G. E. M. Skues. Halford told us how to make dry flies that imitated insects, and Skues gave us the wets and nymphs that comprise the larger portion of trout diet. Halford's correspondence with Theodore Gordon in the American Catskills of New York State reveal yet another evolution in the dry-fly code. To fish these waters is to cast in an angling

tradition that spans nearly half a millennium.

While virtually all of the good trout and salmon water in England is "preserved," that is carefully managed by angling associations or estates for the pleasure – and yes, sometimes profit of members and owners – beats on even the most famous rivers are available to traveling anglers. Fees in the form of season, monthly, weekly, or daily tickets are charged, of course.

Numerous agents book anglers on prize beats. Relatively speaking, one pays about the same to fish the blue-ribbon waters of England with a ghillie as one does for a guided day in New Zealand or the American West. But were it not for the proprietary interests of private ownership and the cost of tending the fish, the waters, and the lands through which the streams flow, most would have been consumed by the country's growing population. And private stewardship of its best fishing preserves it for posterity.

In England, how one plays the game is much more important than the catch. In the main, the fly fisher will walk the beat on a path keeping well back from the stream so the trout, wary browns of both sea-run and residential stripe, be spooked. Rather than prospecting with an attractor pattern, so common on many American waters, the drill here is to spot a rising fish, select an appropriate fly, and cast to the fish from below. Wading is usually not done and in some cases prohibited.

In addition to an abundance of streams and rivers, England boasts hundreds of fee-fishing lakes that are stocked, sometimes daily, with rainbow and brown trout. Fly fishing for trout and salmon

is truly civilized: nobody rushes the sun to streamside. Nor do they need to. Daylight extends to 10 p.m. or later in the height of summer. However, angling for sea-run brown trout, called "sea trout" in the United Kingdom, is a solitary nocturnal affair – the blacker the night and the stiller the air, the better the fishing.

English weather is mild and somewhat damp. In July, the hottest month of the year, the average temperature is 61°F. Skies do tend to be overcast, particularly inland, and October sees more rain than any other month. Trout season in England is generally closed from October 1 to March 24, and

Opposite **On English streams, trout and fly were married and the tradition was born.**

Above **Angler plays a brown on the Avon near Kennett.**

Right **Prolific hatches of mayfly make the Test one of the most special trout rivers in the world.**

salmon is closed from November through January. Dates will vary a little on specific waters. Licenses are required and readily available from regional National Rivers Authority offices, lodgings, tackle shops, and other stores near the area where you wish to fish. England enjoys a wealth of tourist accommodations ranging from furnished rooms in castles and country manor homes to intimate hotels and bed-and-breakfasts.

Southwest

Stretching from Land's End, the westernmost point of England into the counties of Hampshire and Wiltshire, southwestern England begins as rolling tableau of coastal uplands which flatten across the Salisbury Plain and then rise a bit in the chalk hills north of Winchester. From springs in these hills rise England's two most famous trout rivers:

the Test and the Itchen. They have been severely damaged by the persistent introduction of Jumbo rainbow trout from stewponds which have largely destroyed their claim to be quality streams. At Longparish on the Test you can still fish for wild brown trout, no rainbows, no mown edges, and that is the place to aim for.

Hatches are reasonably regular: duns begin coming off about 10 am and trout feed on them for

Opposite **While main streams may be stocked, small tributaries carry wild trout.**

Right **Richly colored wild browns lurk in headwaters of English streams.**

three hours or so. The returning spinners begin falling on the water in the evening about 7 pm and trout rise to them until dark. On the Itchen, trout fishing is best above Winchester. On the Test, the really good mileage runs upstream from Romsey. Many organizations offer beats on these rivers, including Roxton Bailey Robinson in Hungerford, and Orvis in Andover. For local information and beats, try the Rod Box in Winchester.

Don't, however, be misled. Renowned as they are, the Test and the Itchen are not the only fine trout and salmon streams in the southwest of England. On the border of Devon and Cornwall, the Tamar River carries salmon, sea-run and resident brown trout, and grayling. About midway between its mouth at Plymouth and its source above Bridgerule is Endsleigh House at Milton Abbot, which offers guests access to 9 miles of Endsleigh Fishing Club sea-run brown and salmon water. The Arundell Arms at Lifton has more than 18 miles of excellent water on the Tamar and nearby Lyd, Thrushel, Carey, Wolf, and Ottery Rivers, a trout pond stocked with large rainbows, tackle shop and fly-fishing school.

There's good fishing too on the Torridge in the vicinity of Shebbear and Sheepwash. Licenses and permits are available from Devil's Stone Inn at Shebbear, and the Half Moon Inn at Sheepwash. The Fowey River gathers its headwaters in Bodmin Moor and flows south to its namesake town where its estuary enters the English Channel. From May to September, sea-run brown trout (averaging 15 lbs) use the river, and salmon (averaging 9 lbs) run in April and May and again in October and December. The Fowey suffers low water in late summer and fishes best when in spate. Above

Lostwithiel wild brown trout enter the picture.

Dartmoor National Park with half a dozen mountains over 1,600 feet gives birth to a number of rivers including the East and West Branches of the Dart. Best runs of salmon occur in March and April and in September. Sea-run brown trout fish best in the main river from July to September. The upper reaches of the Dart and its East and West Branches tend to be on the small size. Much of the water is owned by the Duchy of Cornwall, which restricts it to fly fishing only. Permits for fishing the Dart, and Wallabrook, Swincombe, and

Cherrybrooke are available from the Land Steward at the Duchy of Cornwall Office in Liskeard. The Forest Inn at Hexworthy offers guests services of a ghillie and instruction.

The Taw also has its headwaters on Dartmoor, but it flows north some 46 miles to enter the Celtic Sea at Barnstaple. Much of the Taw near Umberleigh and above is preserved, but daily permits may be acquired from the Rising Sun and the Fox and Hounds hotels at Eggesford. The Yeo, which joins the Taw above Lapford, also offers good trout angling. Flowing east from its source on

Dartmoor, the Teign abruptly turns south in its leisurely run to the estuary at Newton Abbot. As a salmon fishery, the river is quite good from the last weeks of May into September. Sea-run and resident browns also inhabit the river.

In Dorset, the chalk-stream-bred Frome and Piddle (Trent) Rivers enter Poole Harbour at Wareham and provide good sport for large salmon and brown trout of both sea-run and resident varieties. On the lower Frome, sometimes preserved waters can be accesses with landowner permission. Above Dorchester, wild brown trout prevail. For information, contact Specialist Angling Supplies in Dorchester. While the upper reaches of the Avon do hold some trout, the river's tributaries, particularly the Wylye at Warminster, make for a better fishery. Sutton Veny Estate at Bishopstrow manages more than 3½ miles of the river. Also, check out the Nadder, a tributary of the Wylye, which is gaining a reputation as a fine chalk stream.

Fishing for wild trout and salmon in the south of England declines rapidly once one goes east of Hampshire. Increasing numbers of salmon and sea-run browns brave the Thames, testimony to the good work of the Thames Angling Preservation Society, which got its start in 1838. Among the river's upper tributaries, the Coln, Evenlode, and Windrush are very good for trout, but opportunities for visiting anglers to fish them are few.

Central

The band of counties from the border with Wales to the North Sea, contains few wild trout and salmon waters. Among them is the lower half of the Wye River, one of the finest salmon rivers in the country. Rising about 18 miles from Cardigan Bay in Wales, the Wye crosses into England at Hay-on-Wye, climbs a bit to the north, then swings east to Hereford before turning south, rejoining the Wales boundary and eventually

entering the Severn Estuary at Chepstow. The better fishing is in Wales, but the Red Lion Hotel at Bredwardine in Hereford has access to 8 miles of English salmon, trout and coarse water. The story is the same on the Severn, England's longest river. Weirs in the Worcester area offer some angling for salmon from January into April and May. Salmon and trout fishing improves the closer to the headwaters you get.

North

Beneath Hadrian's Wall, which tracks east from Solway Firth to the mouth of the Tyne, lies a rugged range of low mountains known as the Cheviot Hills. Much of the area is preserved in Northumberland National Park and its neighbor to the west, Border Park. In these uplands rise a number of good trout and salmon streams. Among

them is the Coquet, carrying the waters of Corby Pike and Shillhope Law to the North Sea at Amble. The river sees a good run of spring salmon and sea-run browns in spring and fall. The Anglers Arms Hotel at Weldon Bridge in Morpeth has a mile of water at the middle of the river for three rods. Upstream, there's a good late salmon run in June and October as well as very good sea-run brown trout. Whitton Farm House Hotel can sell permits to visiting anglers and can steer them to other streams with heavy salmon as well.

The main salmon fishery in Northumberland is the Tyne. The North Tyne rises in the national park, and the South Tyne, in the hills where Durham and Cumbria come together. The two branches of the river join at Hexham and flow to the North Sea at Tynemouth. Once threatened by pollution, the Tyne has been enjoying quite a resurgence. There is a bit of salmon and sea-run brown trout fishing at Bywell, and the quality of the angling improves the further upriver one goes. But the better fishing is on its two branches and on the Rede, which flows into the North Tyne at Otterburn. Rods to let for tourists are somewhat limited.

To the west, the county of Cumbria accounts for a number of good streams in northern England. The Derwent has reasonably good populations of salmon and trout from its mouth at Workington on the Irish Sea to its origin in the outflow of Bassenthwaite Lake. July through October are the most productive months. The upper section is very clear and quite good. Fishing after sunset can be rewarding. The middle and upper sections of the Eden River are also worth a look. The Bracken Bank Lodge at Lazonby provides discounts on rod fees for the middle river with overnight accommodation. Guests at the

Sandford Arms in Sandford angle here for browns in the 3 lb class on dries. Grayling provide sport throughout the winter.

Traversing North York National Park from its headwaters on Westerdale More, the River Esk flows into the sea at Whitby about halfway between Middlesborough and Scarborough. The river has twice held English record sea trout and 1½ to 2½ lb. browns are plentiful. While much of the river is preserved, it's possible to fish in some areas. For more information and permits contact the Northumbria and Yorkshire National Rivers Authority. The River Lune offers good salmon, sea-run brown, and brown-trout fishing. August and September are the best months for salmon and sea-run browns. At Kirkby Lonsdale, angling for browns is very good, and anglers booked into one the area's hotels or bed-and-breakfasts can obtain permits through the tourist information center. Permits are also available to fish the upper waters of the river at Sedbergh, Low Gill, and Tebay.

On the Ribble, which flows from the Pennines to the Irish Sea near Southport, the best fishing is found between Settle and Great Mitton. The Settle Anglers Association holds about 6 miles of fine fly-fishing-only water for trout and grayling in the upper reaches. Permits are available through the Royal Oak Hotel.

One must not overlook the Isle of Man, what may be a jewel of an untouched English trout fishery. Little of the water is posted, and permission from the landowner is all that's usually required. Among the better rivers: the Neb and its tributaries for salmon in August; Silver Burn for trout and the lower Sulby for salmon and sea-run browns in August.

English rivers are not big, nor are trout and salmon of the size found in New Zealand or Alaska. And the style of fishing here is more delicate. A good four- or five-weight rod should be quite ample for these rivers, with three-weights favored for presentations on chalk streams. Floating lines, double-tapered is best for chalk waters and weight-forward for others, and 100 yards of backing will be ample. A sink-tip line may come in handy. Neutral colored lines spook fewer fish than those of brighter color. For salmon, the rod of choice is a two-hander or Spey rod of ten- to 12-weight in lengths to 13 feet plus. Floating and sinking-tip weight-forward lines with 150 yards of backing are typically employed.

Brown Trout *Dries* Itchen Olive, Dark Olive, Greenwell's Glory, Iron Blue Dun, Pale Waterys, Kite's Imperial, Hawthorn, Black Midge, Black Gnat, Blue-winged Olive, Medium Olive, Blue Dun, Olive Comparadun, March Brown, Dun Sedges in various colors from light to dark, Adams, Pale Morning Duns, Lunn's Particular, Sherry and Red Spinners, sizes 12-20. **Terrestrials** Beetles, Daddy-Longlegs, Ants (red, brown and black) 12-16.
Nymphs Gold-ribbed Hare's Ear, Pheasant Tail, Cased Caddis, Mayfly Emerger, Grey Goose, Damselfly Nymph, Cactus Damsel, 10-12; Waterlouse, Shrimp, 10-16.

Sea Trout Butcher, Medicine, Teal Blue and Silver, Tandem Sunk Lure, Peter Ross, 4-12; also (on very dark nights) Bombers and Muddlers, 4-10.

Salmon Thunder & Lightning, Willie Gunn, Ally's Shrimp, Hairy Mary, Silver Stoat, 4-12.

Traveling to England

Passports are generally required, but check the consulate in your country for variation and other specific regulations. Travelers from nations outside of Europe may bring the equivalent of 400 cigarettes and two liters of distilled spirits into England. For those arriving from EU members, the amounts are doubled, and for those residing in European states that are not EU members, the amounts are halved.

The British pound (£) is the standard unit of currency. Banks provide the most favorable exchange rates. While some angling destinations are served by rail, a rental car will provide more flexibility and allow you the option of poking about in the charming countryside. Driving is on the left and seat-belt and speed limits are rigorously enforced.

Finland

Below **Massive browns can make your day in Finland.**

Right **Rivers in Finland offer big water well suited for nymphs or streamers.**

Far right **Crashing torrents mean high dissolved oxygen content and healthy trout.**

A quiet country that is not much in the public eye, Finland's sport fisheries are just beginning to come to the attention of the English-speaking fly-fishing community. With rivers like the Teno, Torino-Muonio and Kymi (where salmon average 33 lbs!) and others in wild and inaccessible Lapland, Finland is primed to become one of Europe's major angling destinations. The chances of catching really big salmon, record-book grayling, heavy sea-run brown trout, to say nothing of Arctic char, brook and brown trout, taimen (a large, fast-growing salmon-like species but of a different genus), and salt-spirited pike are very good here. Most of the best fishing, but by no means all, is found above the Arctic Circle in that barren and beautiful land inhabited by the Lapps and their reindeer.

Lapland spans the northern reaches of the country encompassing a low range of mountains that cross northern Finland and extend about halfway down its border with Russia. To the east and south is a broad glacial peneplain that wraps around the top of the Gulf of Bothnia and, in a kind of "S" curve, follows the coast down to Turku and then around to Helsinki and up to Kota on the Gulf of Finland. The terrain climbs slightly a few dozen miles inland from the coast. This modest upland creates a divide that separates the waters that flow westward to saltwater from those that drain to the east into Finland's massive lakes district.

No one is really quite sure just how many lakes Finland has; estimates range between 60,000 and 185,000. And, while one is never far from a lake in Finland, the greatest concentration is found in the southeast. Here the peneplain has been scoured by the ice sheet, leaving a network of long, narrow, and shallow lakes that includes Samaai, the largest natural system of lakes in Europe. The lakes provide truly outstanding fisheries for pike, trout, and landlocked salmon. These can also be caught in the myriad rivers and streams that flow between the lakes.

Finland has not been spared the depredation of commercial angling. In some cases, river nets still inhibit the return of salmon to their breeding grounds. But the nets are coming off the rivers, and recent agreements with countries neighboring the Baltic and its major gulfs are limiting catches at sea. Industrial pollution, acid rain, and hydroelectric projects have taken their tolls as well, but efforts are under way to restore and enhance game fishing. The result is a cautious optimism that Finnish stocks of salmon will return in the numbers of yore.

There is no doubt that the fishing in Finland is better than good. Add to it vast unspoiled stretches of Lapland; a reasonably benign summer climate where daytime temperatures can climb into the mid-80°F, but not often; average precipitation of less than 2 inches per month; and the fact that in high summer, the sun never really sets. There is one caveat. Mosquitoes and blackflies grow large in Finland. Insect repellant is a must. Loose-fitting long sleeves also help, but headnets are generally not needed.

The North

The small city of Oulu sits astride the 65th parallel and 12 miles to the north at Haukipudas, the Kiiminkijoki enters the Gulf of Bothnia. Salmon, sea-run brown trout, grayling, and pike are found in the 70 sets of rapids on this 105-mile river, which contains Finland's highest waterfall. Due east across the country is Suomussalmi, a district where short rivers between scores of lakes hold brown and rainbow trout as well as grayling. To the south about 62 miles is Oulujärvi, Finland's fourth largest lake. Browns and rainbows can be caught in the center of Kajaani, where the Kajaanijoki enters the lake.

But the best fishing in this southern fringe of Lapland is to be found above Kuusamo about 78 miles north of Suomussalmi on the Russian border. Three rivers – Kuusamojoki, Oulankojoki, and the Kitkajoki – all host runs of "Russian Trout," browns that swim up these rivers from Lake Paanajärvi across the border. Most are of the 4½ to 6½ lb class, but some as large as 17½ lbs begin their runs in June. Rivers here flow through heavy forest, swirling over boulders, creating holds where fish lie. In addition to the main rivers, scores of tributaries offer small-stream alternatives to big water. Get-Lost Tours provides guided trips to the region, as does Rukapalvelu Oy Safaritalo.

Further north, at the head of the Gulf of Bothnia, is the Torinonjoki, which the Swedes,

who share its border waters with Finland, call the Torne. As more nets are removed from the river's mouth, the Tornio and its major tributary, the Muonionjoki, are revealing their potential as tremendous salmon fisheries. Average weight of fish caught in 1997 was 13 to 22 lbs and 44 lbs salmon were occasionally brought to net. This is really big water, ranging in width from 100 to 650 feet, and flow is swift. The largest salmon are entering the river when the season opens in mid-June as the last of the season's snow melt leaves the drainage. Fishing can be quite difficult, but the rewards are ample. Two-handed rods are an important ingredient for success here. Unfettered by hydroelectric projects and unsullied by industrial pollution, this 270-mile river drains the

center of Lapland. Few towns are found along its banks and accommodations and services for visiting anglers are limited to say the least. Bookings are best done through agencies such as Get-Lost, which offers regular trips to the Torino-Muonio.

Leading the list of superb salmon rivers in northern Finland is the Teno, which flows eastward along the Norwegian border before breaking to the north at Nuorgam in its dash to enter the Barents Sea. Similar to the much-vaunted Alta, the Teno is a huge fish river. Average catches range from 13 to 44 lbs. Quite wide – in places 650 feet – and occasionally deep, much of the fishing on the Teno is from boats. Harling, a technique similar to back-trolling where the fly is drifted down over salmon lies from a boat pointed upstream and moving at a speed a bit less than that of the current, is frequently employed here. Wading, and best done with the aid of a wading staff, is possible in the hundreds of sets of rapids. The good news about the Teno is the size of the fish. The bad news is that access to the river is severely restricted. As this is being written, anglers are permitted on the river for only four hours per day, and each is permitted no more than a single hour at a given pool. The fishing runs from mid-June to early August with the first two weeks in July being peak time. Get-Lost also runs trips in this area.

Anglers should not overlook Inarijarvi, a large lake system in the top of Finland. Inarijarvi is one of the few lakes in Western Europe with fishable populations of taimen. Found throughout the cooler climes of central and northern Eurasia, taimen resemble landlocked salmon, but they are a completely different species. They are aggressive feeders and grow quite large. Along with its taimen, Inarijarvi is known for its huge browns (13 lbs) and very big grayling. Fishing is best in late summer on the lower sections of tributary streams.

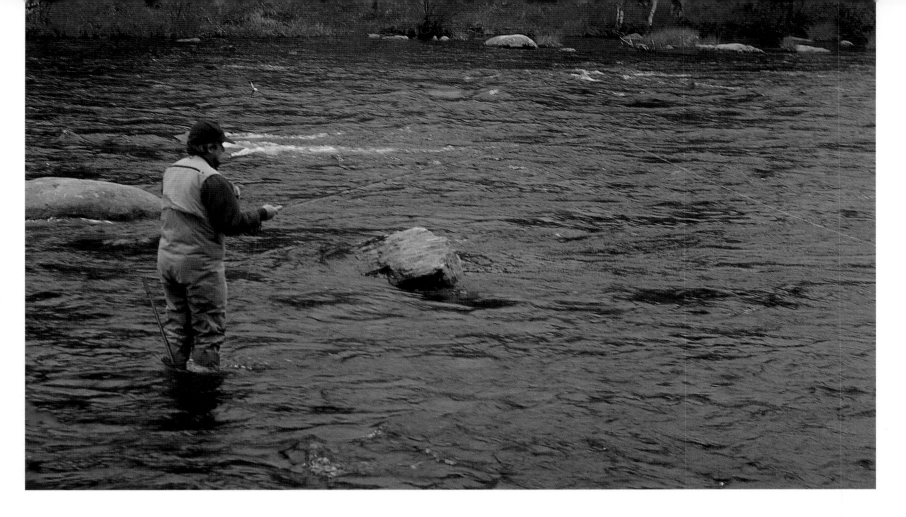

The South

Salmon waters are not restricted to the wilderness of the north. In fact the Kymijoki, one of the best salmon rivers in Europe and an outstanding example of how public private partnerships can restore a fishery, flows through the historic port city of Kotka where it enters the Gulf of Finland. Some of the best fishing can be found in the center of town at Langinkoski rapids where Czar Alexander III, a dedicated salmon fisher, built a lodge for his family. The lodge is now a museum, but angling in the river's braided channels studded with submerged boulders where salmon lie is amazingly good. These fish average 10 lbs during the peak season in mid-June and early July, but a number of 40 lb fish have been taken as well.

Kotka holds two additional sets of rapids: Siikakoski and Korkeakoski. The latter is at the base of a small power dam and angling is from a boardwalk over the river. In the midst of Keisarinkoski (Emperor's Rapids) at Siikakoski is Munkkisaari, an island where monks in the 1800s harvested enough salmon to pay for a new monastery at Valamo. Today, the fishing in the vicinity of this island is quite good. Kotka, a city filled with historic buildings, has spread from its original island in the river and now encompasses the estuary. In addition to wonderful restaurants serving Russian cuisine, the city is rich with attractive hotels. In Kotka, civilized living and salmon fishing go hand in hand.

Almost 190 miles north of Kotka, is the village of Viitasaari on a spit of land bounded by Lake Keitele. The village is the center of a large wilderness containing more than 300 lakes. The best fly fishing is on a river of just over 4 miles that connects a pair of lakes. Rapids in the river hold brown trout and grayling. Small lodges provide room and board for visiting anglers and the services of English-speaking guides are available. Check with Viitasaaren Kunta in Viitasaari. Less than 30 miles to the east near Tervo is a similar fishery, the Ayskoski, a set of rapids about 3 miles long that fishes particularly well from June through August. Nearby are several hotels that cater to anglers. And to the west, near the towns of Viirat and Ruovesi, is the heavily forested Green Heart region of central Finland. Here you will find two national parks – Seitseminen and Helvetinjärvi – that offer anglers easily accessible fishing on fast rivers containing landlocked salmon and trout.

The Islands

While saline, both the Gulf of Finland and the Gulf of Bothnia are better described as brackish rather than saltwater. The relative freshness of these coastal waters provides habitat for an interesting mix of species for fly fishers. Cast large white streamers for pike of 40 lbs or more, or fish shrimp or minnow patterns for sea-run brown

Opposite **The Ayskoski, near Tervo, is a marvelous fishery for trout.**
Right **Many towns along the Finnish offer angling for sea-run browns and pike.**

trout. Tyninyrakari OY lets an entire 4-acre island, Tynnyrkari, to fishing parties. The island, about 15 miles east of Kotka, comes complete with guide, boats, and a fully staffed lodge.

Extending from Turku almost to the doorstep of Sweden is an archipelago containing more than 600 islands. The waters of this region teem with pike in the summer, but in spring and fall, sea trout move in. Eland, the largest island in the chain, provides lodging, guides, and other angling-related services. Heading up the coast north of Pori is a tiny group of islands offshore of Merikariva, a very good location for sea trout, and further north, at Vaasa, is a small archipelago where the fishing for large pike locally known as "crocodiles" in the shallows is very good in August.

Traveling to Finland

Unless visitors plan on staying three months or longer, a passport is all that is required for tourists who live outside of Scandinavia. Tourists over age 22 can import one liter of alcohol and the equivalent of 15 packs of cigarettes.

With the exception of fishing in the Kotka region, most good fly fishing does not require a car – if you have booked with a travel agent or guide. Finland is a big country, and some of its roads in wilderness areas are unpaved. The country boasts a fine network of regional airlines. Unless attempting to fish freelance, there's not much to be gained by renting a car.

The Finmark is the standard unit of currency. Prices in Finland are a bit lower than in Sweden, Norway, or Iceland.

Finland does not have the network of fly tackle shops that one finds in Norway and Sweden. Consequently, bringing backup rods, reels, and waders is a very good idea. It's also a reasonable suggestion to stock up on little gear – leaders, floatant, and traditional fly patterns – before arriving. Guides will have local patterns for sale.

Gear for Finland really depends on the quary: salmon in the Teno and Tornio-Muonio almost depend on two-handed rods of four meters throwing ten-weight lines. One can get by with a three-meter single-handed rod of eight- to ten-weight. Using shooting heads (floating and sinking) will give anglers with single-handed rods considerably more reach. Because wading is somewhat limited on many of Finland's rivers, extra backing is important: consider 164 feet as a minimum. Large arbor reels are a plus here. And a high-quality disk drag system is a must.

Trout, both sea-run and nonmigratory, grow to impressive sizes. A seven- or an eight-weight rod is advisable, though a six-weight can work in a pinch. Here, too, reels should carry good drag systems and contain ample backing. A third rod also ought to find its way into the kit of anglers who visit Finland. This extra rod should be a three- or four-weight of 6½ to 8 feet weighing just an ounce or two. This is for grayling, for the fun of fishing after throwing a big rod all day.

Salmon *Traditional hair-wing patterns work well, as do tube flies and local ties such as the Punamusta, Silver Black, Paten Morottaja, Ormu; 4-10.*

Trout **Dries** *Caddis, Olives, Stoneflies, Adams, 8-12; Mosquitoes 12-18; Black Gnats, 14-18; Black midges, 14-20.* **Nymphs** *Gold-ribbed hare's ear, Caddis pupa, Prince, 6-10.* **Streamers** *Sculpin, Woolly Bugger, Mickey Finn, Grey Ghost, White Ghost, 6-10.*

Iceland

Often described as the land of fire and ice, Iceland is, indeed, an island of wild extremes. Here the Mid-Atlantic Ridge – that huge submarine rift valley caused by the pulling apart of the Eurasian and North American continental plates – breaks through to the surface producing stunning displays of the violent forces that give birth to terra firma. The island itself is only 25 million years old, a mere hour in the day of a world where the oldest surface rocks go back more than 600 million years. In 1783, a volcanic eruption reduced Iceland's population by a quarter, and in 1963, venting of molten rock from the rift produced the new island of Surtsey, an event watched by the world on television. Geysers, those plumes of superheated water, draw their name from Iceland; in fact much of the country is heated with geothermal power.

For all its internal heat, Iceland lives up to its name. Rifstangi, a peninsula on the northeast coast brushes the Arctic Circle, and the Vatnajokull and three other ice fields cover more than 10 percent of the land. Yet Iceland is an island of relatively moderate climate, thanks to remnants of the warm waters from the Gulf of Mexico that wash past the island as the North Atlantic Drift. In the height of summer, when fishing is best, temperatures normally range from 41 to 68°F. Precipitation varies with elevation and falls, not so much as downpours, but in a more steady, leisurely pace.

A steady supply of rain, plus snow melt, feeds more than 100 salmon rivers. They flow down from treeless mountains into gentle grassy valleys, spilling over ledges of basalt into pools where

Despite the fact that virtually every river in Iceland carries fishable stocks of salmon and sea-run browns, there is very little freelance angling available to nonresidents of the country.

North

The premier salmon river in Iceland is known, simply, as the "Laxa." Loosely translated "Laxa" means "river of salmon" and for geographic specificity – there are a number of rivers in Iceland named "Laxa" – the name of this most marvelous stream is the Laxa i Adaldal. Flowing from Lake Myvatn, the river enters the Denmark Strait at Husavik on the north coast. Hot springs and glacial melt feed the lake, the fourth largest in this tiny nation, and the outflow creates an incredibly fertile fishery of roughly 30 miles in length. The lower half of the river, with its falls, rocky rapids, and slick pools is the salmon water. The upper reaches hold brown trout which grow to 4½ to 6½ lbs in addition, a tributary, the Myrarkvisl, offers another 18 miles of salmon water. Both are gifted with fairly consistent flows and thus do not suffer the vagaries of high or low water.

Access to Laxa i Adaldal is limited to a dozen rods, and the Myrarkvisl to three. But here, as on most other salmon rivers in Iceland, rods may be shared. The fishing day is split into two shifts: 7 am to 1 pm and 4 to 10 pm. Between shifts, the river rests, the salmon recover, and anglers dine and nap. While some believe that morning is the best time to fish for salmon, those fishing the evening shift do as well. At the height of summer, during peak salmon runs, dusk lingers as the sun refuses to dip far beneath the northern horizon. There's ample light to see and cast to salmon in their lies

salmon and sea-run brown trout school. Salmon enter the rivers in May, and the season usually opens during the second week of June. Peak time is July but good fishing continues into September when the season closes.

Iceland, a nation long dependent on fisheries, understands the economics of high-quality sport fishing. It limits the number of rods on each river based on the size of the river and the relative strength of the salmon runs. The limits are small, generally at least two and no more than 12. Anglers who fish in Iceland seldom see others than those in their party. Not only is the solitude in such vast and gentle wilderness a real enticement, but so are the salmon. Hook-ups of three or four fish per day are not at all unusual. Fish average 11 to 13 lbs with a few of 22 lbs

taken each year. Sea-run browns enter the rivers in late summer and the season continues into October, a month after the season for salmon has closed. Averaging 4½ to 6½ lbs, these anadromous browns fight like steelhead but do not grow as large. Hundreds of lakes and small streams in the highlands hold populations of native brown trout.

Iceland is in the upper range when it comes to the cost of a visit. A day at a full-service lodge with guiding, three meals per day, and accommodation with private bath, can easily reach US$1,000 per day. A less expensive option is booking into a self-catered lodge where anglers do their own cooking and may or may not use a ghillie. Self-catering lodges are generally found on rivers that are limited to two or three rods per day, and fishing on those rivers can be quite good.

late into the evening. Henfish arrive in the Laxa earlier than males, and they tend to weigh less. Fish on the Laxa are apt to run larger than those in other flowages, but most range between 6½ to 15½ lbs. Occasionally fish will exceed 20 lbs, and the rare beauty will top 33 lbs. Numerous agents, such as Frontiers in the UK and US (and see a full listing on page13), book premium trips to the Laxa for seven days of guided angling.

While the Laxa i Adaldal is everyone's dream river in Iceland, there are scores of others that fish as well, and some, on occasion, fish better. Laxa a Asum is a good example. Rising in a pair of lakes, Laxarvatn and Svinavatn, Laxa a Asum courses just 8 miles or so before reaching the Greenland sea on the island's north coast. Though shorter

than most Icelandic rivers, this one generates a catch of about 1,400 fish in a three-month season. That's roughly 100 fish per mile, or about one fish per mile per day. Only two rods per day are available on the river. On average, that works out to six fish per angler. The Club Lax-A provides full-service guiding and accommodations on the Laxa a Asum and offers a variety of packages on more than 20 salmon and trout rivers throughout the country.

Also in the north of Iceland are the Midfjardara and its three tributaries, the Austura, Napsa, and Vestura. The Midfjardara is also very short, only about 9 miles but it sees good runs of salmon particularly in June when the fish are bigger. These fish move on up into the tributaries

*Left **Lakes, high in the mountains, provide action for trout.***
*Right **This salmon fell for a sea trout tube, fly fished with a five-weight rod.***
*Far right **A river of little falls and pocket water, the Laxa i Kjose carries excellent salmon.***

as the season progresses and smaller fish fill the lower river. Over the last ten years, this ten-rod river has been averaging almost two fish per day per angler, but recently runs have declined a bit.

East

On the east coast, completely across the island from Reykjavik, is the Breiddalsa River. With its tributary, the Tinnudalsa, the river flows for more than 25 miles through farmland before reaching the Atlantic. The Breiddalsa tumbles over lava ledges, and swirls down chutes into pools that carry some salmon. Six rods generally take about 100 salmon per year. Among its pools, several are designated for fly fishing only. Arctic char are found in the lower mileage of the river and its estuary. At the headwaters of the Breiddalsa and its tributary are stocks of native browns. Anglers stay in the Hotel Blafell in Breiodaksvik.

South

On the 43 miles of the east and west branches of the Ranga in the south of Iceland, smolt socking and enlightened river management have resulted in salmon runs improving from 32 (that's right!) to 2,960 in 1997. Here is a place where the catch averages better than two fish per rod per day. While most fish are in the 6½ to 9 lbs range, fish up to 20 lbs are frequently brought to net. The Ranga also has a reputation of fishing well for sea-run browns and Arctic char and riverine browns that occasionally top 9 lbs. While the river accommodates ten rods, anglers are spread among

pools, where solitude and splendid wilderness complement each other. See Angling Service Strengir for information about lodging and guiding on the Ranga.

Near the little town of Vikm the southernmost town on the main island are a trio of rivers that are worth a look. The Vatnsa is very short, only about 4 miles, and both salmon and sea-run browns are in the river at the same time. The salmon run to about 9 lbs, with some of 13 to 15 lbs taken annually. Sea-run browns average about 4½ lbs. Further to the east are the Eldvatn and the Grenilaekur, among Iceland's finest sea-trout rivers. While some salmon enter these rivers, the main action is on 4½ to 9 lbs sea trout that begin to run in July and peak in the midst of August. Fishing remains quite good into early fall and it coincides with the best of the island's hunting for four species of wild goose. Club Lax-A will arrange lodging, fishing, and hunting.

West

High on the northwest coast is the Laxa i Dolum, a fairly small river with a good run of salmon. In its 15-mile path from Lake Laxarvatn, the river runs through a broad farming area, and contrary to many of the rivers in Iceland, this one is relatively slower. Seven rods generally take 1,300 salmon per year – a rate of better than two per rod per day – and these fish average 7½ lbs with an occasional salmon running more than 15 lbs. July sees the first runs of salmon and these are the biggest fish of the season. Also in the northwest is the Faskrud, which enters BrieNafjorour at Hvammsfjordur after traversing a narrow valley. About 10 miles of the river hold fish, and the catch rate on this two- to three-rod river is about 240 salmon per season, or a little better than one per angler per day.

Among the better rivers in the west is the Grimsa, 18 miles of fly-fishing-only water with 60 named pools and a tradition of sport fishing for salmon that goes back to the 1860s. Limited to ten rods and open only in July, the Grimsa produces an average of two fish per angler per day. Double-digit fish are a distinct possibility on this river. Access is controlled by the Fishery Association of Grimsa, which maintains a full-service lodge on the river at Fossas.

Nearby, the Lodge at Anabrekka was established in 1870 where the river Langa flows into Borgardfjprdur about 84 miles north of Reykjavik. The Langa rises in Lake Langavatn and runs a fairly straight course for about 12 miles before it begins to meander as it slows in the plain above the sea. In the bends are pools that hold salmon. A five-rod river, anglers average 1.5

salmon per day throughout the season, and the fishing is generally best in July.

The Hvolsa and Stadarholsa are a pair of four-rod west coast rivers that are very small and produce about one salmon per angler per day. The best fishing is in August and numbers of anglers are also bringing shotguns for ptarmigan and goose hunting in late summer and early fall. A smolt-stocking program is underway on this river in an attempt to establish larger salmon runs. Angling Service Strengir operates a full-service lodge and provides guides.

Traveling to Iceland

Three airlines – Icelandic, Islandsflug and Nortlandair – provide a service to Reykjavik and around the island. Visitors who are not from Scandinavia or from Austria, Belgium, France, Germany, Italy, Liechtenstein, Luxembourg, the Netherlands, or Switzerland will require passports. Consult your travel agent, embassy, or department of state for current regulations.

The currency is the krona. Credit cards and travelers checks are widely accepted in Iceland, but be prepared to use cash in the hinterlands. Hotel and restaurant prices are 20 percent higher in Iceland than elsewhere in Europe. Many self-catering lodges do not provide transfers from the airport to the river you will fish, so it may be ncessary to rent a car. Iceland's highway system, essentially a ring around the island, is easily understood, but an international driver's license is required to operate a car.

TACKLE AND FLIES

To prevent the invasion of UDN (ulcerative dermal necrosis), Iceland has forbidden the use of fishing equipment from outside the country that has not been treated with a 2 percent solution of formaldehyde or similar disinfectant. Anglers may have a veterinarian in their home country apply the disinfectant and issue a certificate of disaffection. Or they may have their equipment disinfected at the airport. The latter course adds time and expense, but may be required if this chore is not tended to at home.

While ten- to 12-weight, two-handed or Spey rods of 13 feet plus will allow anglers to cover more water and to fish where backcasts are limited, they are not essential for fishing Icelandic rivers. The best bet is a 10-foot eight- to nine-weight system. Not only is this the land of glaciers and geysers, but it's also the land of perpetual wind. Often, overlining a rod – that is using a line that is one weight heavier than that for which the rod is usually weighted – will add the needed distance. Most anglers use weight-forward floating lines and sinking leader systems to get the fly down to the depth where fish are holding. But at times, salmon hold deep in the current. The only way to reach them is with a full sinking line. Reels should carry 100 feet of 20 lb. Dacron and leaders should be a bit on the stout side, 6½ to 9 lbs, because lava rocks in the beds of these rivers are very abrasive and, at times, razor sharp. While some anglers still favor reels with click-pawl drag systems, modern disc drags work so much better.

For sea trout, which are mainly fished with nymphs, wets and streamers, a six-weight system with sink-tip and sinking lines is the right medicine. Such will also work with Arctic char and wild brown trout, though a four-weight can offer more sport for the latter.

Good neoprene waders with caulked felt soles are essential on most of these rivers. Gore-tex or

similar breathable waterproof garments are equally essential. And while Iceland lacks mosquitoes, gnat-sized biting blackflies are a real nuisance. Bring insect repellant!

Salmon *Red Frances, Black Sheep, Black Frances, Green Butt, Hairy Mary, Black Tubes, Blue Charm, Laxa Blue, Collie Dog, Pingeyingur, Munroe Killer, Lady Ellen, sizes 10-14; also Bombers, Wulffs, Muddlers, 8-12.*

Sea trout **Dries** *CDC emergers, Black caddis, Disco Crickett, 10-14.* **Wets** *Teal and Black, Connamara Black and Peacock, Spider, Sweep, Black Zulu, Hairy Mary Gray and Peter Ross, 10-14.* **Streamers** *Woolly Bugger in black, brown and olive; Black Ghost, Mickey Finn, 10-14.* **Nymphs** *Bead head black stones, Pheasant Tails, Gold-ribbed Hare's ears.*

Below **Pick a fly that suits you ... and the fish.**
Right **In Galway, you will find salmon water right in town.**
Far right **The River Bundorragha (Delphi) carries fine runs of salmon and sea trout in a stunning unspoiled valley.**

Ireland

When one thinks about fishing in the British Isles, Scotland with its salmon and England and its chalk-stream trout spring immediately to mind. They are, to be sure, lovely fisheries. But not to be discounted in the least is their enchanting island neighbor to the west – Ireland. Green hills roll softly rising into mountains of sandstone and granite that become increasingly stubby and barren as they gain elevation. Winds blowing in off the Atlantic are squeezed by the mountains, wringing out fine and gentle rains which nurture more than 8,700 miles of swiftly flowing rivers and countless quiet streams.

Spates of spring and summer trigger runs of Atlantic salmon in the rivers. Here too are sea-run brown trout almost as bright and silver as stainless. The rivers conduct fish to their home loughs and to the little tributaries where they spawn. Some rivers and lakes hold nonmigrating populations of landlocked salmon and brown trout. Rainbows are stocked in some public fisheries, and a growing number of anglers are using their salmon rods to pitch big, brightly colored streamers at pike up to 15 lbs. But it's the wild fish that draw anglers from throughout Europe and increasingly the Americas. They come for the wild fish and for the freshest air in all of Europe.

This is a land of writers and poets, where discourse is a highly refined recreation lubricated, of course, with Guinness. And once away from Dublin with its sky-scraping high-rise office and apartment towers, the land quickly reverts to a more rural nature, a country where most scratch out a living, or try anyway, from the frail soil.

Tourism is a huge industry. Everything from stately castles like Ballynahinch to the dairyman's thatched cottage now hosts guests.

During the summer roads can be crowded with sightseers, but few are anglers and solitude and fish can be found on many streams. Salmon runs begin with the new year and continue into early fall. In most locales, early summer coincides with peak fishing. Warming weather and falling waters slow the fishing somewhat in the months of high summer. But quality angling spikes again briefly in September before the general closure at the end of that month.

Ireland has it share of private waters to which access for any but the select few is all but

impossible. And there are also numbers of streams which licensed anglers can fish for free. However, a good bit of the best water on the island is owned or leased by angling associations or commercial establishments, including scores of lodges and inns. Permits, reasonably inexpensive, are readily available in the little towns close to salmon and trout fisheries.

Many towns of even modest size support at least one shop that caters to anglers. And there's always a pub patronized by local anglers. Ireland can be a haven for anglers who are weary of the hurly-burly crowds of the American West and Alaska. The fish may not be as large or as plentiful as in New Zealand, Russia, or Alaska. But this is Ireland, and fly fishing has deep roots here.

Ireland is currently divided with a third of its population living in Northern Ireland and the balance in the Republic of Ireland. Climate is mild all the year round, thanks to the remnant of the Gulf Stream known as the North Atlantic Drift, but it is damp. As Fodor's says: "Nobody ever went to Ireland for a suntan." You can no more escape the drizzle of the Emerald Isle than you can avoid its history, not that you'd want to. Stone ruins of castles and forts seem to grace nearly every crossroad community. Some of the properties have been in the same families since before the last millennium. As you fish this land, find a pocket history and read it. Your fishing will be better for it.

Virtually every stream in Ireland holds sport fish of one sort or another. Salmon (Atlantic salmon and landlocked salmon) and trout (brown, sea trout, ferox trout, gillaroo trout, sonaghan

trout, rainbow trout, and very few char) are
considered game fish. Other freshwater fishes
include pike and coarse fish: perch, bream, rudd,
tench and dace. Saltwater fishing is available as
well for such species as codling, bass, dogfish,
whiting, flounder, pollack. Fly fishing is primarily
pursued by anglers seeking salmon and trout,
though pike and bream may also be taken with
the fly.

Cork

Located in the southwest, the County of Cork is
Ireland's largest and perhaps its most varied.
Behind its rocky headlands and golden beaches are
the sandstone hills and a number of outstanding
salmon and trout rivers. Recovering its fame these
days is the River Bandon, which rises in Nowen
Hill and winds 46 miles through bucolic valleys to
the English Channel at Kinsale. Salmon, sea trout,
and browns may be taken from February 15
through September 30. Some of the best salmon
pools lie between Inishannon and Togher Castle.
The lower river is excellent for spring salmon,
grilse and sea trout. The upper river with its riffles,

small rapids, runs and pools resembles trout water everywhere, which it is. David Lamb is the proprietor of the Kilcoleman Fishery at Enniskeane. He lets out a wonderful stone gatehouse and provides the services of a ghillie. Other productive waters in County Cork include River Ilen at Skibereen.

Derry

Three rivers on the western highlands of this Northern Ireland county are considered first-class salmon waters: the rivers Bann, Agivey, and Bush. The Bann is the outflow of Lough Neagh. At first blush, the Bann does not appear to be a high-quality salmon fishery because of its slow flow. But a number of weirs and lock dams create holding pools for fish. The most productive stretches are

Culiff Rock and Portna. Disabled anglers will find fishing stands at Craigavon. The Agivey is a tributary of the Bann, and this small salmon river, like the nearby Bush River, provides reasonable catches. However, while these three rivers are primarily fished with spinning tackle, fly anglers can find success.

Donegal

Sharing its eastern border with Derry, Donegal is Ireland's northwesternmost county. A rugged and rocky sea coast rises inland culminating at the 2,600-foot peak of Mt Errigal. This is the home of Donegal tweeds woven on handlooms in thatched cottages. The county includes nearly 50 trout and salmon streams, but three fisheries here are

notable. The River Drowes drains Lough Melvin and has good runs of salmon in March and grilse in June. There is also some brown-trout fishing here. The Foyle is a tidal fishery below Lifford with good sea-run trout and better salmon. It may pay to check out the Rosses, primarily a brown-trout fishery near the town of Dungloe.

Galway

The mouth of Galway Bay is protected by the Aran Islands and inland, behind Galway City, is a lush countryside of bogs and meadows that ultimately ascends to the mountains of the interior. Loughs and rivers abound. More than 130 are recognized as salmon and/or trout water. World renowned, is the Ballynahinch Fishery where salmon fishing excels in summer. Ernest Schwiebert called it "Perhaps the finest fly-fishing destination in Ireland." Though the watershed spans some 25 miles, the best angling is concentrated below Lough Ballynahinch. Anglers using two-handed Spey rods will have a much easier time with the trees and bushes lining the river than will anglers of single-handed rods. Ballynahinch Castle/Hotel near Recess controls access to seven beats on 3 miles of the river, which is known also as the Owenmore. The Upper Ballynahinch Fishery comprises angling on the Recess and Owentooney Rivers and several loughs including Orrid, Shanakaella, Derryneen, and Cappahosh. Sea trout, salmon, and some grilse become very aggressive with the rains of July and the action continues until salmon season closes at the end of September and trout winds up one month later.

A visitor to Galway should also check out two

more rivers, the Corrib and the Culfin. The Corrib carries salmon, sea-run trout, and browns. Friar's Cutt is brown and salmon water. The Galway Weir has good salmon and grilse from April into July and again in September, and New Beat requires wading if one is to reach the sea-run trout that hold therein. Less than a mile long, the slow-flowing Culfin is quite good for grilse in June and, along with sea-run trout in July.

Kerry

The little town of Waterville sits by Lough Currane about 110 miles south of Shannon on the western tip of County Kerry. Sea trout and salmon run up Ballinskelligs Bay to Lough Currane, and they provide some of the finest fly fishing on the island. This town is well known as an angling center, and such luminaries as Arnold Gingrich and Charles de Gaulle have cast their flies here.

The attraction is the fish: salmon in late March and April, sea trout in May to mid-June when the grilse reach their peak. Traveling anglers will hire a ghillie and a boatman and fish the reefs and shoals of the Lough. Afterwards, they'll have a pint in Fisherman's Bar in the Butler Arms, a local hostelry favored by anglers with great good reason.

Waterville is a stop on the famed Ring of Kerry, a winding scenic road that traces the perimeter of the Iveragh Peninsula, which contains the highest mountains in Ireland. Dingle Bay, named for the mountainous peninsula to the north, is fed by another wonderful river, the Maine, which in turn takes its waters from the Brown Flesk and the Little Maine. The Maine is a great river for salmon, sea-run trout, and brown trout with the end of the season September and October, respectively, providing the best angling. Also meeting saltwater at the head of Dingle Bay is River Laune, which carries the waters of the

Lakes of Killarney. Contrary to the fishing in the neighboring Maine, salmon fishing peaks here early in the season followed by grilse in June.

Leitrim

While the River Drowes is in County Donegal, Lough Melvin from which it flows is located in Leitrim, the county to the south. Covering 36 kmsq, this large lough is known for the quality of its trout and salmon. The season opens for salmon and sea trout on February 1 and two weeks later, browns become legal. All three close on September 30.

Mayo

While there are many rivers and loughs in the wilds of County Mayo, none is a better regarded fishery than Loughs Cullin and Conn, and the Moy

River carries the outflow from Lough Conn. An estimated 500,000 wild trout cruise the Conn. Here, too, salmon run from March to May and grilse from may till the end of July. At the charming village of Pontoon, Cullins waters flow into Lough Conn. The pool by the bridge yields scores of salmon each season. The Pontoon Bridge Hotel is a full-service angling resort with its own tackle shop. The hotel features a summer fly-fishing school with the curriculum tailored to meet students' needs. The school director is Alan Pearson, a world champion angler who was a member of the first English team to compete in the World Fly Fishing Championship. The hotel can arrange boatmen and ghillies and permits to fish the River Moy, one of the finest in all of Ireland. Spring salmon enter the river in April and that is when they are at their best. Grilse show up in May and provide peak action in June. Spring salmon average 6½ lbs and grilse just less than 4½ lbs.

Tyrone

This county in Northern Ireland may lack a sea coast, but its principle game-fishing rivers, the Derg, Foyle, and Mourne, are excellent salmon fisheries. The Derg rises in the lough of the same name in nearby Donegal. It is known as one of the better salmon rivers in Ireland, with most fish being taken in the weeks of late spring and early summer. Good stocks of sea-run and brown trout use this river as well. Just north of Newtonstewart, the Derg joins the Foyle. The Foyle is tidal to Lifford and angling for salmon is confined to the section from Lifford Bridge downstream. Opening on April 1 for salmon and sea trout, fishing on the Mourne begins later than on most other Irish rivers.

Traveling to Ireland

Check with the Irish Consul or tourist office closest to your home for current information about passport and any financial requirements for entry. Primary airports for international passengers are Shannon and Dublin. Regional airlines serve smaller cities. Train and bus service is limited. Renting a car is by far the best alternative. Driving is on the left.

The Irish pound (IR£) is standard currency. British pounds and American dollars are accepted as currency in some establishments, but it is better to convert pounds sterling or dollars into Irish pounds at a bank once you get to Ireland. Where credit cards are used, you may make purchases and allow the credit card company to compute the best rate of exchange. Convert Irish pounds to the currency of your home country before leaving the country.

Tourists may bring the equivalent of one carton of cigarettes or 50 cigars, but no oral smokeless tobacco, and one liter of distilled spirits, two of wine and 12 of beer. One is allowed the equivalent of 34 Irish pounds' worth of other goods per adult traveler. Fishing tackle generally poses no problem.

TACKLE AND FLIES

While salmon on larger waters may be more thoroughly fished with a 10 to 12 foot, two-handed or Spey rod of nine- to 12-weight, single handed rods of 6 to 8-foot in eight- or nine-weights work just fine. Reels – very smooth disk drag – should be spooled with a floating weight-forward line backed with 100 to 150 yards of braided Dacron. While the floating line (and a cache of sinking leaders) will handle most salmon chores, spare spools carrying sink-tip and sinking lines may come in handy. For trout, drop back to a 6-foot, five- or six-weight with the same lines available. Bring extra tippet material in 3X–5X. Ghillies find that flies rigged within a triple cast (two droppers behind a point fly) are particularly productive.

Waders are required frequently enough to make them worth bringing. The bottoms of the rivers can be slippery. Felt-soled wading shoes are very useful. And remember that rain is frequent. You'll thank your lucky stars for a good Gore-Tex jacket and hat.

Salmon *Traditional patterns* Blue Charm, Green Drake, Green Butt Bear Hair, Hairy Mary, Lady Caroline, Lee Blue, March Brown, Peter Ross, Silver Grey, Teal and Silver, shrimp patterns, Silver Doctor, Sooty Olive, Spent Gnat, Thunder and Lightning, Undertaker, 4-12; Bombers and Wulffs, 4-6; for grilse, sizes 8-14.

Trout *Dries* Connemara Black, Elk-hair Caddis and Black Caddis, 10-14; Olive Compara Dun, 14-20; Mayfly Dun, 10-16; Adams, 12-16; March Brown, 12-18; Lunn's Particular, 16-20; Blue-winged Olive, 14-20; Royal Wulff, 8-12; Green Drake, 10-14; Grasshoppers, 12-14; Ants 12-16.

Nymphs Gold-ribbed Hare's Ear, March Brown, Mayfly Emerger, Pheasant Tail, 8-12.
Streamers Woolly Bugger in black, brown, and olive, 8-12.

New Zealand

A member of the British Commonwealth, New Zealand is a string of mountainous islands – North, South, and Stewart – lying to the east of and separated from Australia by the Tasman Sea. Together North and South Island are roughly the same size as California in the US or the British Isles. Seasons are reversed from those in the northern hemisphere.

For many anglers who travel the world, New Zealand is Mecca. North and South Island hold scores of lakes and rivers where trout grow to legendary size. Scenery is spectacular – glacier sculpted mountains and high alpine meadows, lush forests of firs and ferns, bright rivers tumbling around boulders until they pause and pool up only to race headlong down the next chute. Not only is the fishing superb, but the country caters to tourists who fish. Licensed guides, inns dedicated to anglers, tackle shops, and transport to remote sections of the islands are all readily available and competitively priced.

New Zealand's trout waters have gained a bit of a reputation as somewhat crowded and overfished. Don't believe it. While pressure is heavy on streams close to metropolitan areas, the number of anglers declines as distance increases from paved roads. In Kiwi country, anglers of varying skill, physical condition, and pocket book can find the fishing holiday of a lifetime. And the nonfishing mate or spouse will discover an abundance of museums, historical and cultural sites, parks, and shopping.

These islands, part of the ancient continent of Gondwanaland, were split into Antarctica, Australia, and New Zealand by movement in the earth's plates about 70 million years ago. Isolated by geography and uninhabited by humans until people of Polynesian ancestry arrived about AD 700, New Zealand is a preserve of wild and exotic species – flightless birds populate dense woods where tree ferns grow 50 feet tall and where more than 60 species of orchids splash color through the forest. This land and its people are conscious of the uniqueness of their environment, and they work hard to preserve it.

The various districts of the country set seasons and limits for waters within their jurisdiction. Nonresident license fees are charged per district, but a special "tourist" license is available for those who plan to stay a month and fish in more than one district. If you book into a fishing lodge, your host will make all the required arrangements. If you're fishing freelance, a visit to a local tackle shop will help you determine what license you need and where to obtain it.

New Zealand has generous creel limits on many of its streams. And in some cases, it may make sense to remove juvenile fish from an overpopulated stream or lake. But in the main, "catch-and-release" fishing is increasingly important here as pressure on the waters depletes stocks of larger trout. Take the lead from your host or guide, and if you're fishing alone, let your conscience guide you.

North Island

On North Island, two active volcanoes – Mt Raupehu, (9,000 feet) and Mt Ngauruhoe, (7,500 feet) – and their dormant neighbor Mt Tongariro (6,500 feet) dominate the core of this the smaller of New Zealand's two major islands. The island is a bit warmer than its southern sister; when you fish here you have a distinct feeling of being in a subtropical paradise. Its rivers and lakes fish best in spring (October through November) and fall (February through March). The height of summer – December and January – may be too warm and bright for good midday angling, but the fishing then generally improves at nightfall.

Forests of tree fern and toi are as lovely as they are impenetrable, making access to wild rivers cutting down through deep gorges quite difficult. North Island has several marvelous national parks, forests, and preserves that nurture headwaters for many rivers with fishable trout populations. Trails provide some access to these waters, but in the main, fishing remote streams is not a matter for shanks's mare. Instead, helicopters are the favored way to reach the best isolated waters.

Floating in rafts is not. Unlike the great rivers of the American West where driftboating is *de rigeur*, North Island rivers are clearly green as bottle glass and trout are uncommonly wary. They'll spot an angler a hundred feet away and dash for cover. One cannot float over these fish and then expect them to take a fly. Nor, once you've found a pool that yields a trophy trout or two, can you expect to return and fish it again the next day. This is particularly true of the remotest waters, which seldom see anglers. Once disturbed by human presence, trout will take a day or two to resume their normal routine.

Skittish fish like these are often best approached from downstream. The best way to fish the rivers is to work up to the fish. Walk the banks or trails along the heights of deep gorges and spot

your trout. The rivers are clear enough to do that. Plan your stalk to casting position, for that's what it is. Approaching trout in North Island's streams is much like hunting for deer or stag. Patience pays and a quiet approach is a must. No doubt you'll need to wade to reach casting position, but do so carefully lest you scare the fish. The rewards are rainbows and browns of 4½ to 12 lbs. You'll find very good fish here, and they will be large. But don't expect massive numbers of trout.

Superlative fishing on North Island is concentrated in four areas: Lake Taupo/Tongariro River on the northern flanks of Mt Tongariro National Park in the center of the island; the northern volcanic highlands from the geothermal district of Rotorua southeast through Urewera National Park; Cape Egmont, which pokes into the Tasman Sea on the southwest corner of the island; and the low mountains running southwest from Palmerston North to Wellington, the capital city. These regions offer a wide range of angling opportunities. Some streams you can park your car beside, for others you'll need a helicopter, and there's everything in between.

As is the case almost everywhere, you'll find the best fishing in terms of size, number, and consistency if you hire a guide or book into one of the many fine fishing lodges in the mountains of North Island. Tops on everyone's list is Tony Hayes's Tongariro Lodge on Lake Taupo. Accommodations are first-rate, and his guides know both the lake and the myriad array of rivers and streams in the mountainous central section of the island. He operates fly-outs to isolated waters that rarely see anglers as well as excursions to sections of the Tongariro that are accessible by four-by-four and a brief walk.

Veteran Kiwi angler Tony Orman's *21 Great New Zealand Trout Waters* provides detailed information on several rivers and lakes and how to fish them. His picks for North Island are: Lake Aniwhenua, Lake Okataina, Awakino River,

Raukituri River, Tongariro River, Lake Otamangaku, Stony River, Tukituki River, Mangatanoka River, Hutt River, and Ruamahanga River.

South Island

Separated from North Island by Cook Strait, South Island is very different in character from North Island. The Southern Alps, peaking with 12,300-foot Mt Cook and capped by glaciers, run up the west coast of the island. This rugged terrain spawns hundreds of streams and scores of lakes, most of which contain brown and rainbow trout. The mountains create an environment which is not unlike that of the Pacific Northwest in the United States. To the west of the mountains is a land of heavy rainforest and headlands and to the south, the deep probing estuaries of Fijordland National Park. To the east is a magnificent string of glacial lakes and below them the rolling, almost semi-arid, plateaus host some of the most productive sheep stations in the world.

Because of the cooler climate and lack of rainfall, South Island's waters are less fertile when compared with streams on North Island. Big brown and rainbow trout live in the huge lakes on the eastern flanks of the mountains – Hawea, Wakatipu, Wanaka, Takapo, and Te Anau – and run the streams to spawn. Ernest Schwiebert suggests that a lack of food in the spawning streams makes these lake-run rainbows and browns more willing to nail a fly. However, he says, they are increasingly fished over and thus increasingly selective.

Along with the rivers and lakes that flow to the southeast from the serrated crest of the Southern Alps, a number of good streams can be found in the vacinity of Abel Tasman (the first European to reach the islands in 1642) National Park on the northwest tip of the island. While known for its brown trout, South Island also has significant runs of quinnat salmon. Try the

Right Water bottle glass makes big New Zealand trout wary as can be.

Ashburton, Rakaia, Rangitata, Waimakariri, and Waitaki Rivers. January through March are the best months.

In the heart of South Island's best trout country – the region on either side of Route 6 from where it crosses the Southern Alps at Haast Pass to its junction with Route #8 at Cromwell – is Cedar Lodge on the Makarora, which provides helicopter and fixed-wing fly-outs to rivers of Mt Aspiring National Park and huge private ranches as well. Rivers range from delicate cataracts with pools like jade beads on silken thread to mature rivers of braided channels and undercut banks. The owner of Cedar Lodge is Richard Fraser, and you should ask him about fishing the Hunter and delightful Dingle Burn.

For a change of pace, you might want to check on the spring creeks – clear water staking of brown trout to 4½ lbs plus – in the vacinity of Kumara. Excellent accommodations with cuisine and wines to match are provided by Lake Brunner Lodge. The owner guides anglers on the nearby Matiri, Blackwater, Gowan, Matakitaki, and Buller. Downstream from Lake Brunner, Orman recommends fishing the Arnold for browns.

In terms of public waters, Orman suggests: Aorere River, Motueka River, Karamea River, Pelorus River, Arnold River, Lake Alexandrina, Makarora River, Upper Clutha River, Lake Dunstan, and the Mataura River.

Traveling to New Zealand

Passports must be valid for at least three months beyond the date of intended departure. Visitors may be required to show sufficient funds to maintain themselves during their stay. No vaccinations are required.

TACKLE AND FLIES

While salmon on larger waters may be more thoroughly fished with a 10 to 12 foot, two-handed or Spey rod of nine- to 12-weight, single handed rods of 6 to 8 feet in eight- or nine-weights work just fine. Reels – very smooth disk drag – should be spooled with a floating weight-forward line backed with 100 to 150 yards of braided Dacron. While the floating line (and a cache of sinking leaders) will handle most salmon chores, spare spools carrying sink-tip and sinking lines may come in handy. For trout, drop back to a 6 foot, five- or six-weight with the same lines available. Bring extra tippet material in 3X–5X. Ghillies find that flies rigged within a triple cast (two droppers behind a point fly) are particularly productive.

Waders are required frequently enough to make them worth bringing. The bottoms of the rivers can be slippery. Felt-soled wading shoes are very useful. And remember that rain is frequent. You'll thank your lucky stars for a good Gore-Tex jacket and hat.

Salmon *Traditional patterns* Blue Charm, Green Drake, Green Butt Bear Hair, Hairy Mary, Lady Caroline, Lee Blue, March Brown, Peter Ross, Silver Grey, Teal and Silver, shrimp patterns, Silver Doctor, Sooty Olive, Spent Gnat, Thunder and Lightning, Undertaker, 4-12; Bombers and Wulffs, 4-6; for grilse, sizes 8-14.

Trout *Dries* Connemara Black, Elk-hair Caddis and Black Caddis, 10-14; Olive Compara Dun, 14-20; Mayfly Dun, 10-16; Adams, 12-16; March Brown, 12-18; Lunn's Particular, 16-20; Blue-winged Olive, 14-20; Royal Wulff, 8-12; Green Drake, 10-14; Grasshoppers, 12-14; Ants, 12-16. **Nymphs** Gold-ribbed Hare's Ear, March Brown, Mayfly Emerger, Pheasant Tail, 8-12.
Streamers Woolly Bugger in black, brown, and olive, 8-12.

One cannot bring foodstuffs, plants, or animal materials into the country. It is recommended that travelers dispose of these in bins provided for the purpose before approaching customs.

Other prohibited items include firearms (except with required permit), certain drugs (carry a prescription from your physician), and products made from specific game and nongame animals.

Check the New Zealand embassy or consulate for an up-to-date list. In addition to personal effects, each person can bring into New Zealand goods up to a combined value of without paying duty or tax. Passengers over 17 years of age may bring in up to 250 g of tobacco products and 4.5 liters of wine or beer or 1,125 ml of distilled spirits.

Norway

For more than 500 million years, a great slab of the earth's crust – the Eurasian Plate – has been pushing against the stationary Scandinavian Shield. The force has buckled up the land, forming a ridge of highlands that surface in Ireland and trend northeast through Scotland, ducking under the North Sea and rising again in the south of Norway. Stretching for nearly 1,000 miles from Lindesbes in the south to Varanger Halvøya in the north, these highlands form the spine of the Scandinavian Peninsula, that chain of mountains shared by Norway and Sweden.

Norway is a nation of rivers. Glaciers in the last 100 million years rounded and sculpted the mountains and hollowed out deep valleys as they pushed west to the sea. The glaciers are all but gone now, save the immense ice field at Jostedalsbreen, but the effects of the ice remain. Rivers plunge sharply down out of the mountains and then hustle through gentle u-shaped valleys, running over beds of rounded cobble laid down by the retreating ice. They flow into fjords, some more than 3,300 feet deep, rimmed with sheer cliff walls towering hundreds of meters above the water. Fjords trace sinuous courses to the Norwegian Sea in the south and the Arctic Ocean above the Lofoten Islands, two-thirds of the way up Norway's coast.

A third of Norway lies above the Arctic Circle. Were it not for the North Atlantic Drift, an extension of the Gulf Stream, the country would be a barren land of bitter cold. Not only does the warm current bathe Norway's shores with temperate water, but it brings the westerly winds and the rains that condense as ocean breezes climb

Left **Despite the ice of January, the fjord at Oslo fishes well for sea trout.**

Right **High mountain lakes in the Telemark region offer fine early season angling for browns.**

the mountains. In the south, summer temperatures average 59 to 68°F, and in the north it's about 7°F cooler, quite temperate for a country whose land pokes so deeply into the Arctic.

The winds and their rain are classic blessing and curse. Without them there would be no rich, lush forests and clear-water streams that have nourished Atlantic salmon and sea-run brown trout for millennia. But for a century and a half, these moderating winds have brought industrial smoke across the North Sea and deposited its chemicals as acid rain on Scandinavian soil. Pollution abatement programs in the UK are helping as are remediation efforts in Norway, and little by little the fisheries are responding.

And, as have most countries whose rivers feed the North Atlantic, Norway has seen decreasing runs of salmon. Further, and sadly, many of Norway's great salmon and sea-trout rivers carry stocks of fish infected with *Gyrodactylus salaris*, a salmon-killing parasite. Regional fisheries managers are attempting to remove fish carrying the parasite through the use of rotenone, a chemical that kills fish when applied but which reportedly has little residual impact. The best known of the infected rivers is the Lærdal. Other rivers, such as the Fålm, see closed seasons on salmon in order to protect spawning stock. And the opening of some rivers is being delayed by two weeks or more to give the first run of salmon, typically the biggest fish, a chance to spawn without pressure from anglers. These are major steps in efforts to preserve and enhance game fishing in Norway.

Lest one get the wrong impression, angling in this country of stunning landscape and warm friendly people remains excellent. More than 700

rivers host runs of salmon, sea trout and Arctic char. There are currently 40 infected with *Gyrodactylus salaris*, of which 13 have been treated and cleared for fishing, eight are still in treatment, and 19 are still infected. These are scheduled for treatment in the future. Countless headwater streams and lakes carry wild brown and brook trout. Larger rivers contain grayling. The bigger salmon, some up to 66 lbs, enter the rivers first and fishing for them is best from mid-June until mid-July. They are followed by runs of smaller fish but in greater numbers. Sea trout normally peak in August and the flaming char of the north fish best in July and August.

Generally speaking, salmon seasons run from May 1 to September 1 in the south. In the north, the season begins a month later, but ends on September 1 as well. Many rivers are subject to special seasons. Check the dates for the rivers you plan to fish. Licenses are required of all anglers

over age 16 years, and permits will be required to fish freshwater rivers. On many of the best salmon, sea-run brown trout, and char rivers special sections are reserved for fly fishers.

North

The Arctic Circle cuts through Norway near the vast Svartisen ice field, yet the country continues more than 300 miles further into its northernmost county Finnmark. Here flows the most famous salmon river in Norway and perhaps of all the world. It is the Altaelva, known simply at the Alta for the town with the airport at its mouth. Royalty and anglers of means have come from afar to fish the river since the 1840s, drawn by salmon of legendary size – up to 66 lbs – and sure of a tranquil and truly unspoiled river valley. The river rises in the treeless Arctic barrens of Finland, flows north across the vidda, a high tableland, before

Left **The Numensdalagen in southeast Norway, near Oslo, is one of the country's top salmon rivers as this 16-pounder (above) attests**

Opposite **Rivers like the Ljora east of Trysil, near the Norwegian border, hold excellent browns and grayling.**

dropping into a canyon. Here the river twists through chutes, runs, and pools floored with cobble and boulders. Salmon hold in the pools and take cover behind the boulders.

Along its banks, at infrequent intervals, are fishing camps where, in July and August, visiting anglers with ample wallets may test their tackle on really huge salmon. While the behemoths recorded from 1920 to 1950 may run no more, fish of 44 lbs and more are quite frequent and salmon of double digits that are memorable on other waters attract little more than a passing glance here. In the decade from 1983 to 1993, five of seven International

Game Fishing Association tippet-class records for Atlantic salmon were set on the Alta. Fishing is tightly controlled. Permits are extremely limited. The expense to fish this river is quite high. Is it worth it? Just ask those who make the pilgrimage to fish this river year after year after year. For more information about fishing the Alta, contact Frontiers in London or AKU Finnmark in Alta.

Among the other good salmon rivers of Finnmark is the Neiden, which, like the Alta, has its headwaters in Finland, and flows into an arm of Varangerfjorden southwest of Kirkenes. A section of 1,300 feet below the bridge at Neiden is

reserved for fly fishing. The bigger fish run up to 26 lbs early in the season, but drop to 6½ lbs or so as water levels fall. Across the fjord to the north, and halfway between Vadsø and Vardø, is the Komagelva, a short stream with char as well as salmon. At the head of Porsangen fjord is the Stabburselva, which comes in from the west just north of Lakselv, and the Borselva, which flows into the fjord at the base of the Sværholt-Havoya peninsula. Of the two, Stabburselva is the larger and hosts a better and bigger run of salmon, best fished from late June until mid-July. Grilse and char follow into August.

Central

As one progresses southwest down Norway's coast, the land mass narrows to little more than 6 miles at the head of Rambaken fjord. Continuing as high mountains topped by icecaps, the country begins to broaden around Trondheim. To the south of this modern city is the mouth of the Gaula. English anglers, who pioneered sport fishing for salmon in Norway, have been coming to this river since 1835. They would recognize it today. The larger salmon, those of 20 lbs, are not unusual, and typically enter the Gaula in mid-May and work their way up the river to the falls in Hålt Valley 60 miles from the mouth. The season on the river opens on June 1 and continues through August. The upper reaches, above the turbulent rapids at Gaulforsen, are best fished in July and August.

Early in the season, big bright orange and red patterns fished with sinking or sink-tip lines provide really good chances of hooking a double-digit salmon. A rule for this river is: the rougher the water, the larger the fly. Sea-run brown fishing begins in July and continues into September after salmon is done. Most sea trout here are small, yet they are tailor-made for light rods. Despite its proximity to a major city, and the fact that highways line its banks, this river fishes well throughout its length. Numerous lodges and inns are located along the river and there are ghillies with their boats. Harling or back-trolling is a favored technique on this river. The angler sits in the stern of a wooden rowboat and works the fly through salmon lies as the boatman rows upstream at a speed just less than the current.

The Gaula is the primary salmon river of the region, but in the next drainage to the southwest flows the Orkla, known for large numbers of salmon in the 20 lb class. Fishing on this river of white-water rapids and slick pools has been improving during the last decade. While the river retains much of its bucolic charm, the lower section is a favorite among local fly fishers from mid-June through the close of season in late August. Accommodation is readily found in the river's towns.

North of Trondheim at the head of Beistadfjorden is the small city of Steinkjer, which sits at the mouth of the Namsen. Harling is the method of choice on the big, lower waters, and above the falls as well. On tributary rivers – particularly the Sandddøta and the Bjøra – conventional fishing with one- or two-handed rods is all that's needed. Fish in the 30 lb class come regularly from the river below Fiskumfoss. The Overhalla Hotel in Ranensletta caters to anglers and offers fishing on 4 miles of the Namsen as well as beats on the Bjøra, Søråa, Storem, Bertnem, Veiem, and Vibstad.

West

If Norway were likened to a spoon, its northern reaches above Trondheim would be the handle and the wide, oval land mass to the south would be a bowl. In the western part of the bowl lies the county of Sogn og Fjordane. From the North Atlantic Sognefjorden projects well over 60 miles into the country and at its head it splits into three arms. The southernmost arm carries the waters of the Lærdalsevla, the splendid Lærdal so loved by European royalty and knowledgeable anglers the world over.

The reason: big fish, in this case salmon in excess of 55 lbs and scenery to match. Waterfalls pour from occasional hanging valleys along the Laerdal's course. Big salmon move into the lower

river in May and become legal quary in June, but it is not until August that they reach the upstream beats. Stocks of large salmon have declined here, as they have throughout the hemisphere, but the loss is offset by sea-run browns of 15 to 20 lbs. Like the Alta, this is a fairly exclusive fishery, with the best water spoken for well in advance. (Note: as this is being written late in 1997, the Lærdal is closed to all fishing. The ban was levied after the river was treated with rotenone to prevent the spread of *Gyrodactylus salaris*, a salmon-killing parasite. Fishing in the Lærdal will not be reopened for a number of years.)

Sea trout run in the Arunlandselva in the next drainage south over the mountains. They can be

quite large, up to 20 lbs, but in the 11 lb range are much more common. Anglers who come to this area should plan to visit the Norwegian Wild Salmon Center (Norsk Villakssenter) in Lærdal. The center provides opportunities to observe salmon in their native habitat as well as fly-tying demonstrations and numerous historic and scientific exhibits. The center is also a first-rate source of information about salmon fishing and related services and accommodation in Norway.

South

Just south of the border between Hordaland to the north and Rogaland to the south, the Suldalslågen

empties into Hylsfjorden at the little town of Sand. A compact river that flows about 14 miles from lake Suldalsvatnet, this is another of the historic big-salmon river first opened by English fly fishers. The river fishes best for salmon in August to mid-September; sea-trout fishing picks up then as well. With many runs littered with boulders, a number of white-water rapids, and scores of swift pools, this stream presents anglers with a number of fishing challenges. Sections are reserved for fly fishing. Accommodation and guiding services are available nearby.

As one rounds the southern tip of Norway, the mountains of central Norway dip until swallowed by the North Sea. At one time many of the rivers

Opposite **Norway's spine, rivers pool and trout abound.**

Right **A brace of salmon means a fine day's fishing.**

in this region contained great runs of salmon, but low pH from acid rain has changed the nature of the rivers. The Tovdalselva, for instance, is now better known for brown trout with brook trout in its headwaters. Some salmon and sea trout frequent the mileage between Birkeland and the sea. The Audna, which enters the North Sea near Vigeland, contains runs of 6½ lbs salmon and sea trout to 2 lbs. The Nidelva near Arendal also contains some salmon, as does the Otra at Kristiansand.

A better bet than salmon in this area is probably sea trout, which can be fished in many places at night, right from the beach. The Strand Hotel by the sea in Fevik has a long-standing tradition of serving fly-fishing guests, and the waters of the Nidelva are about 10 minutes away.

East

While the terrain west of the mountains falls rapidly to the sea, the land to the east of the crest descends gently as a tableau of rolling hills and river valleys that surround Oslo, the nation's capital. In this, the most heavily populated region of Norway, the fishing for anadromous salmonids is limited. However, the Numedalslagen which enters Oslo Fjorden at Larvik to the southwest of Oslo is known as one of Norway's top salmon rivers and good fishing can be had up to Hvittingfoss. Well north of Oslo rises the Glomma, Norway's longest river. Its headwaters near Roros and the mileage to Koppang offers very good trout and grayling. And just below the confluence of the Vorma in the area of Sorum, the river provides good grayling and a few large browns. These lower waters, about 25 miles

from Oslo are very popular and access is quite easy. And an evening's good fishing may be had for sea trout in Oslo Fjord. Among productive locales is Fornebu, near Oslo's airport, Konglungen and Kalvøya.

Traveling to Norway

Passports are required of all visitors to Norway, and those planning on staying longer than three months will need a visa. The capital, Oslo, is the point of entry for most international travelers who arrive by air via Scandinavian Airlines System

(SAS), Finnair, KLM, and British Airways. There's a ferry service from England docks at Bergen on the west coast. Visitors are allowed to bring into the country the equivalent of one carton of cigarettes and one liter of liquor.

Norwegian is, of course, the national language, but it has two dialects: bokmål and nynorsk. However, most Norwegians are multilingual and quite fluent in English, German, and other European languages.

An excellent network of rail and regional airlines connects many of the small towns close to good fishing, but not all of these towns have car

rental services. It may be wise to rent a car in a city and then drive to your destination. Anglers visiting rivers in the far north will have transportation provided as part of their package, but those fishing in the lower two-thirds of the country may find it advisable to rent a car.

Norway is an expensive destination. The currency, kroner and øre, is stable. Credit cards are accepted and ATMs are available in most larger cities, but they may not be accepted or present in small towns.

TACKLE AND FLIES

On big rivers in Norway, two-handed Spey rods of 12-foot and ten- to 12-weight are needed to fight large salmon in heavy water. Spey rods will increase the reach of most anglers allowing them access to salmon lies which cannot normally be approached by those using single-handed rods. A single-handed 10 foot rod for a nine- or ten-weight makes a good backup road. And a six- or seven-weight is ideal for all but the largest sea trout.

Here as well as elsewhere when big fish are involved the reel is absolutely key to playing and landing big fish. Drags should be flawlessly smooth, and the mechanism of the reel quite simple. Large arbor reels are very popular for salmon in Norway. Between 100 to 150 yards of 30 lb braided-Dacron should be spooled as backing. Weight forward floating, sinking, and intermediate lines should be brought along, as should an extra spool loaded with a shooting head and floating, intermediate and sinking tips. Abrasion is a problem in rocky Norwegian streams. Plan to fish 10 foot leaders of 6½ to 9 lbs test. Lower water conditions in late summer may require more delicate leaders, but generally speaking, these fish are not leader shy. Waders, felt or caulked soled boots, and walking staffs are very important here.

Salmon *Flies* Akroyd, Thunder and Lightning, General Practitioner, Silver Grey, Red Abby, the Rats (rusty and yellow); Green and Red Butts, Black Doctor, Jack Scott, and the Dunkeld, 4 to 10; Bombers and Wulffs 4-8; also tube flies: Sunray Shadow, Garry, Akroyd, Green Highlander, 4-6.

Trout and grayling *Flies* Adams, 10-14; Blue-winged Olive, 12-18; Caddis (black and elk hair), 8-14; Comparadun, 10-16; March Brown, 10-12; Midges 16-24; Telemarkskongen, Olsen, 8-12; Jungle Cock Silver, Zulu Silver, 8-10; Gold-ribbed Hare's Ear, Pheasant tail, 8-12; Woolly Bugger, 6-12.

Sea trout *Flies* Bunny Leech, Muddler Minnow, Ice Nobbler, Istobis, Minnow Muddler, Silver Fancy, Mallard & Claret, Connemara Black, 6-12.

Opposite **You will find browns in the lakes of the Hardangervidda, Norway's high central plateau.**
Below left **When nothing else works, try a Royal Wulff for wild browns.**
Below right **In the main, Norway is a country of big rivers with good salmon.**

The Pacific

The world's largest ocean is sprinkled with volcanic islands and coral atolls that rise above the seemingly endless Pacific. Around many of those located in the tropics, bonefish and trevally are common. Some of the islands, like Christmas,

Midway, and Fiji, have developed tourist infrastructures and fishing programs. Others like Bikini and Mili are rather new in the game and are either somewhat primitive or unspoiled depending on one's take. The key to whether an

island is "fishable" is not so much the size of its reef or flat, but whether or not it is economically feasible to fly a thousand miles to a speck in the ocean for a week's fishing. Where there is scheduled air service, and the country is promoting tourism, it can be done. But where there are no regular flights, it's tough to get there. (That may be why in some of those places, like Kanton Island, for instance, the fishing is marvelous.)

Christmas Island

As far as fly fishing is concerned, Christmas Island is the most famous. It was named by Captain James Cook, whose HMS *Resolution* spent the holiday there in 1777. Under British protection for the next 202 years, Christmas Island and the surrounding members of the Gilberts became part of the new Republic of Kiribati and donned the formal name of Kiritimati in 1979. Anglers still call it Christmas Island (don't confuse Kiritimati with the Christmas Island just south of the coast of Java in the Indian Ocean).

Located about 1,400 miles south of Hawaii, Christmas Island or Kiritimati is the largest atoll in the former Gilberts. It is shaped a bit like an open claw with the settlements of London and Paris adorning the tips of each pincer. Separating the two is tiny Cook Island and behind them is the open shallow lagoon of St Stanislas Bay. Twice daily, tides flush the flats in the bay. If the fishing isn't right on one tide, cross the bay and fish the other side. Bottoms are generally sandy and easily waded. Here the game is to cast to tailing bones of

Opposite **Trevally off Christmas Island can top 70 lbs.**

Right **Miles and miles of flats, populated with wary bonefish, surround many Pacific islands.**

2 to 6½ lbs. Anglers will frequently play a dozen fish a day, sometimes more. And once in a while a 11 to 13 lb fish will be brought to bag. Trevally, a species akin to jack crevalle, appear in three varieties – giant (up to 110 lbs), blue (15 lbs), and striped (22 lbs). Accommodation is available in the Captain Cook Hotel, a collection of six thatched-roofed bungalows and lodge of 24 rooms, some with air conditioning, with all the comforts of home.

Bikini

A maze of 26 islands in the Marshalls, 2,580 miles west of Hawaii, Bikini gained notoriety in 1946 as the site of a post-World War II nuclear test that involved 95 surplus warships. Testing continued into 1954 when a massive blast that vaporized three islands fired the imagination of a French designer to name his new two-piece bathing suit after the explosion. Radiation levels have abated and now the island is turning to diving and fishing to promote a tourist economy. The fishing is superb. Sand, coral, and marl flats within the atoll and around nearby islands teem with swallowtail, bluffing trevally, long-nosed emperor, snapper and bonefish. Heavy tides through narrow channels at times have bonefish holding behind heads of coral. Then you can fish them like trout. An advantage? Only until a lightning bone of over 6½ lbs turns and runs with the ripping tide. Mahi-mahi slap flies offshore as do the "bad boy" yellowfin and dogtooth tuna. Guests fly out from Honolulu to Majuro and thence to Bikini staying a full week to

Left **Flats boat, Pacific-style, eases an angler toward bonefish.**
Right **Bonefish range from 2 to 6 lbs with some over 11 lbs.**

catch the next return flight. When not fishing, guests lodge in lagoon-side guest cabins with air conditioning and private baths.

Mili

About 560 miles west of Bikini at the other end of the Marshalls is this atoll – 22 miles wide – anchored by Wau Island. Here is a location that is so far off the beaten path that downed aircraft from World War II have yet to be cleared from the jungle. Flats hold bluefin, big-eyed, yellow-spotted, and black trevally, goat fish, bonefish, grouper, gray and yellow snapper, coronation trout, squirrel fish, and red bass. Anglers sight-fish for bluefin trevally, snappers, or bones, finding them stationery in the current as on Bikini. The flats are easily waded or can be fished from poled skiff. Six guest cottages rim the ocean side of the island, each with private bath.

Midway

Roughly 1,300 miles west and north of Hawaii, Midway has been an important stop on the transpacific route since the early 1900s. Nearby, the US won an important strategic victory that changed the course of World War II six months following Pearl Harbor. For 50 years after the end of the war, the US government restricted access to Midway and the waters for 200 miles around it. Then, in 1996 the military transferred ownership of the island to the US Fish and Wildlife Service. Officers' quarters were renovated into a hotel, and a handful of guests – 30 per week – were allowed to visit the island. Among them are anglers who sample Midway's outstanding sport fishing available offshore (marlin, tuna, and some sailfish)

and in the shallows near the island. Though flats are not nearly as extensive as at Christmas Island or Bikini, those surrounding the shore hold bonefish and trevally. There are no really bad seasons to fish Midway – blue-water species are best in spring and summer but bonefish and trevally are good all year. Wind can be a problem. With no high ground, there's no lee side on this island.

Traveling to Pacific Islands

While it may sound like a cop-out, the best way to fish these places, like fishing in Mongolia, India, or Africa, is in the care of a competent agent and guide. Space is very limited on these islands and transportation – arranging plane schedules and transfers – is extremely tricky. The standard caveats about trip and health insurance apply here in spades. Entry to these locales generally requires passport and visa. The latter will be obtained for you by your agent.

Keep in mind that trips to these islands require at least three flights. Wisdom suggests carrying fishing gear, cameras, flies, and any medicine with you on each aircraft. A spare pair of shorts is easier to find than a 12-weight in the wilds of Mili.

TACKLE AND FLIES

Giant trevally can test even the stoutest fly tackle. Bring a 12-weight and reels spooled with floating, saltwater tapers as well as sinking tarpon tapers. An extremely reliable drag system is an absolute essential, as is 650 to 10,000 feet of 33 lb Dacron backing, for playing these big fish. For bones, you can drop down a line weight or two. Bring extra spools and extra lines with you. You won't be able to buy anything there.

Trevally *Clousers, 2-6; Crazy Charlies, Maribou Shrimp, Christmas Island Special, Mini Shrimp, 4-8; Deceivers, Tarpon Flies, Whistlers, Mackerel, Streakers, 1/0-3/0; Sailfish, 7/0; Poppers, 2/0-8/0.*

Russia

Below **On the Panoi, streamers are the ticket for salmon.**

Below right **Helicopters made for the Russian Army, airlift anglers to secluded water.**

Right **To be successful on rivers of the Kola Peninsula, you fish where you must and worry about fighting the salmon later.**

Russia is not so much a place as a state of mind. The appetite is whetted at the thought of all the wonderful and unspoiled wilderness fishing contained in the region from the Finnish border east to the Bering Strait. The country will ever be exotic: an amalgam of European and Asian cultures tensioned by decades of virulent political distrust yet united in human goodness and dignity. It is a land which requires infinite patience. Democracy is still new. Gone are the old authoritarian structures. And in their places are growing new private businesses and governmental bureaucracies to handle the needs of traveling

anglers. The broad expanse of Russia holds the last trove of mostly untapped angling in the world, and exploring a frontier is never easy.

First-class lodges exist in those locations – the Kola Peninsula in the west and Kamchatka in the east – where salmon and steelhead fisheries are known to be first-class. These operations tend to be allied with companies in the US, UK, or New Zealand that specialize in up-scale angling vacations. Yet a number of smaller operations also provide accommodations and guide services. These outfitters are less likely to speak fluent English, to offer helicopter travel to remote rivers if the water they normally fish is not producing, or to loan tackle. Communications will be difficult: fax and e-mail are not as ubiquitous as among the top-tier lodges, and delays will be frustrating. On the other hand, traveling anglers who want to experience the warm heart of Mother Russia may find just what they seek by booking with a small local operation.

Salmon – Atlantic on the west and kings, cohos, sockeye, and chum in the east – are the main attraction along with what may be the world's best wild steelhead fishing on Kamchatka. Trout are found as well. Brown trout inhabit most of the streams of the Kola Peninsula. Many of those rivers also host runs of sea trout, those big ocean-feeding stream-bred browns. Some also see Arctic char and grayling. Kamchatka rivers hold rainbows, Dolly Varden or bull trout, Arctic char and grayling. Taimen, the large salmon-like fish that belongs to a separate genus, is found in interior Russia, as are brown trout and grayling.

The Kola Peninsula

Like a fat thumb more than 220 miles long and 125 miles wide, the Koloskij Poluostrov juts eastward, the Barents Sea to the north from the White Sea to the south. Virtually all but a smidgen of the southeast tip of the peninsula lies above the Arctic Circle and many days are cold and gray. Yet summer days can climb to 75°F, shirtsleeve weather were it not for the mosquitoes. But mosquitoes there are, as one would expect on a long arctic plateau that contains more than 20,000 rivers and streams and five times as many lakes and ponds. Aside from the range of highlands that extends from the border with

Finland to the west and climbs to nearly 4,260 feet
just east of the Murmansk-Kanalaksa highway, the
peninsula is a gently sloping tableland that slopes
away to the seas on three sides.

Salmon rivers drain the plateau, cutting down
with considerable volume. The best salmon rivers
are big, up to 650 feet across, but as water levels
fall in July and August they can be waded. The
Panoi is the most famous of the rivers on the Kola,
and with good reason. Fish are not as large as
those of the Norway's Alta but very good fish are
more numerous. Hook-ups with six or eight
salmon per day is not an unusual occurrence,
though, like everywhere else, vagaries of water
level and clarity can put Panoi salmon off their
bite. Rising north of 1,250 foot g. Jumper Uajv,
the Panoi flows generally southeast for roughly
250 miles before entering the White Sea.
Headquarters for fishing this river is a modern
mini-tent city at Ryabaga run by the Panoi River
Company about 50 miles from the river's mouth.
Accommodation would be first-class even if it
weren't in the wilderness, and the food matches.
During the season – May through September –
guests ride helicopters to productive beats. The
home pool provides entertainment for those
inclined to work off dinner, and while salmon are
definitely the main event there, sea-run brown
trout are not to be discounted. Fishing on the
Panoi is reasonably consistent throughout the
season. August is occasionally plagued with low
water. Fall arrives early September, mosquitoes are
gone, and the rains bring fresh runs of salmon into
the river.

The Panoi divides the Kola Peninsula more or less in two. South of the river lies the Taiga, a region of forest and lakes and reasonably gentle rivers. The foremost of these is the Umba which enters the White Sea about 75 miles east of Kanalaksa. It was here that a pair of Americans, Gary Loomis of rod building fame and Bill Davies, opened up the fabulous Kola fisheries by creating the first Alaska-style lodge on the peninsula. Flyfish in Kola now runs the log lodge on the lower Kola and uses boats and helicopters to ferry anglers to productive beats. Fishing here can begin as early as May and continue well into the fall until shut down by weather. The best runs of salmon are those of late summer and early fall when fish tend to be bigger, averaging 9 to 18 lbs. Fish enter the river with ice-out in May, but good runs of salmon begin to appear in mid- to late June. The Varzuga, a broad and shallow river that's nearly as long as the Panoi, drains a watershed east of the Umba. The Varzuga and its tributaries, the Pana and Kitsa, offer better wading than the Panoi or the Umba, but fish tend to be slightly smaller. They are, however, plentiful. Four camps operate on the river, which fishes best in May and June.

North of the Panoi, the peninsula takes on the look of tundra. Gone are the spruce and birch of the south. In their place grows low, stunted scrub that gives way to barren rock and sand as one approaches the Barents Sea. This is a rugged land, swept by squalls, and the rivers match the landscape. The Kharlovka River, about halfway down the peninsula from Murmansk, has a

Left **Spey rods give anglers a decided advantage on the big rivers of Russia.**
Right **Cathy Beck admires a fine Russian salmon.**

reputation for good-sized salmon. During a week's stay, each angler will normally play at least one fish of 22 lbs. Melt swells the river into late June and long casts are required to reach the most productive salmon lies. As water levels fall in July and August, the game begins to equal out for users of single-handed tackle. Flyfish in Kola set up a permanent camp on the Kharlovka and concentrates its angling on the lower 5 miles of the river below the falls.

Roughly 12 miles west of the Kharlovka is the Rynda, a slightly more manageable river that produces, on occasion, behemoth salmon. The river record is a 50 lb fish. Spey rods are not required to work these waters. Salmon enter the system in June and that's when most of the bigger fish are tailed. Later fish are smaller but more numerous. Fishing begins to wind down in August. Flyfish in Kola operates a camp on the Rynda and also has operations on a third north-coast river, the Iokanga. Rising near the headwaters of the Panoi, the Iokanga's lower third provides its best angling. Here the river steepens as it flows to the sea. Long swift runs and pools. Anglers seeking trophy fish should aim for June.

Kamchatka

Like a necklace of volcanoes, the Aleutian Islands drape across the Northern Pacific leading toward Kamchatka, a geologically unstable peninsula which has been the site of numerous eruptions and earthquakes long before white settlers arrived in the 1700s. The cold Qya Siwo washes down out of the Bering Sea across the east coast of the peninsula, and to the west, it is bounded by the Okhotsk Sea. A chain of mountains, Sredinnyy Khrebet, forms the spine of the peninsula and a

second group, the Vostocnyy Khrebet, which includes the 15,500-foot volcano Kljucevskaja Sopka, merges with the first near the southern tip. The Kamchatka River rises near the junction of the two mountain ranges and flows north for about 155 miles before bending east and making an additional 62-mile run to the sea.

The Kamchatka and its tributaries are rich with rainbows, steelhead, char, taimen, salmon (coho, sockeye, chinook), grayling and lenok. The best fishing begins in July and continues into mid-October for the fall runs of steelhead. In addition to the Kamchatka, the Zhupanova River, about 50 miles north of Petropavlosk, boasts good runs of salmon, steelhead, and trout. Two outfitters from the US guide anglers on the Zhupanova. Tony Sarp of Katmai Wilderness Lodge in Alaska

operates Purga, a charming cedar building with completely civilized amenities (read that "private baths"), about 30 miles up from the mouth of the river. Ouzel, another Alaskan outfitter, offers float trips with mobile camps. Steelhead and rainbows are primary quarry and the summer and early fall runs are the best.

Kamchatka is indeed a marvelous fishing frontier. Many of its rivers have not been fully explored. The Wild Salmon Center of Edmonds, Washington, USA, in cooperation with biologists from Moscow State University, have been running field studies to establish benchmarks for the fishery before it becomes overly commercialized. Kamchatkan steelhead may be among the few strains in the world that are genetically pure. Each summer the Wild Salmon Center recruits anglers

to take part in scientific expeditions to gather data. Volunteers pay their own ways, and they have opportunities to fish rivers that may never have seen a fly.

Other Locations in Russia

Obviously there are more fly-fishing locations in Russia than the Kola Peninsula and Kamchatka. Feeder streams of Ozero Baykal (Lake Baikal) contain trout, grayling and omul, a salmonid that is distinct to this lake in southcentral Siberia. Baikal is five times the size of the US Great Lakes

combined. The Caucasus along the Georgian border have populations of trout. So must the Urals, stretching from Kazakhstan to the Arctic Ocean. There is much fly fishing for hearty anglers who possess the wherewithal to get about Russia and reserves of persevering patience as big as the Eurasian continent.

Traveling to Russia

Passports and tourist visas are required of all visitors who stay longer than 48 hours. While cashing travelers' checks is possible in major cities,

it is very difficult in outlying areas. Credit cards are more universally accepted, but only in larger cities.

For English-speaking travelers, language will not be a problem at lodges. But it will pose difficulties in rural areas. So too will communication: phone and fax service is frequently unreliable.

Travel light! Space on the helicopters used to ferry anglers to riverside lodges or camps from regional airports is very limited. Pack only what you need and do adhere to weight and size restrictions suggested by booking agents, outfitters or airline companies.

TACKLE AND FLIES

Spey rods of 10 to 12 feet in 11-weight make fishing the big-salmon rivers easier, particularly early in the season when snow melt floods riverbanks leaving limited room for back casts. However, one can make do with one-hand rods, particularly if shooting heads are used. Reels with 500 feet of 22 lb braided Dacron backing will give you a reasonable shot at holding on to a running salmon. Obviously a good drag is a must.

A seven- or eight-weight rod will be fine for trout, though a six will provide more sport.

If you opt for the heavier trout rod, you can press it into duty should your salmon rod fail.

If you're staying at a well-appointed fishing lodge, you can count on finding flies and miscellaneous terminal tackle. Otherwise, bring everything with you including spare reels and spools of line. These fish are not at all choosy, though trout and grayling on vodka-clear interior streams may well be leader shy.

Steelhead and salmon Any of the traditional patterns are good. Flyboxes should be stocked with a variety of ties including fuller versions of hair wings for high water and sparse ties for water that is low. Tube flies are particularly effective. While most fish are taken on wets, a box with bombers and Wulffs in various colors should be part of your kit. Sizes range from 1/0 on the Panoi to 6s on other rivers. Steelhead flies should be 4s to 8s.

Rainbows Bring mice that can be skittered on the surface and muddlers of various sizes. Don't overlook large **nymphs** – particularly stonefly imitations. **Streamers** – the beadheaded Woolly Buggers in various colors – also produce, as well as sculpin patterns.

Stream trout *Caddis (light to dark), Blue-winged Olives, and Adams, 8-16; and Prince and Hare's Ear nymphs both beadhead and plain in sizes 8-14.*

Opposite **Distance is important when casting to salmon in Russia.**
Below **It is Atlantic salmon like this that bring anglers from around the world to these waters.**

Scotland

The English gave us their dry flies fished with limber rods and gossamer leaders. The Scots gave us flies in muted colors of the mountains, and long rods swung with two hands to cover rivers of the ilk of the streaming Dee. And they gave us that persistent patience to cast and drift and cast again, those movements of repetitious monotony so essential to taking salmon in Scotland or anywhere else.

Scottish salmon are generally not as large as the bruisers of Siberia or Alaska. But whatever the fish may lack in size, the country more than makes up for with its Highland-bred traditions of independence. So fearful was the Roman commander of marauding Picts, the natives of Scotland who refused to be subjugated, that he built Hadrian's Wall – about 75 miles long – to protect his legions. Exploits of the freedom-loving fourteenth-century warrior Robert the Bruce thrive in the stories that Scots tell their daughters and sons. And while peat no longer warms most hearths in the stone cottages of this rural and rugged land, the hearts of its people glow with the poetry of Robert Burns, encouraged, perhaps by a dram of The Glenlivet or Glenfiddich – two of the finest pot-still whiskies ever rendered of waters fit for wild brown trout. But remember, too, that this is the country of John Knox and strict Protestant doctrine. Thus fishing on Sunday is very limited if available at all. Plan trips for midweek.

The country is usually divided into three regions: the northern Highlands and Islands, the Midland Valley, and the Southern Uplands. Each contains excellent fishing, largely for salmon and

Far left **The Deveron runs from Cabrach to Banff and is known for large browns of fresh and sea-run persuasion.**

Left **Waters of the Tummel feed the Tay and fish well for grayling, sea trout and salmon.**

trout, but also for sea-run browns, and in the far north, some char. The northern Highlands are rift down the middle by Glen Mor, which cradles Loch Lochy and Loch Ness. Above the valley lie the Northwest Highlands with scores of lochs and lochans (small lochs), some of which seldom see anglers. About 150 miles northeast of the mainland are the Shetland Islands; just off the north coast sit the Orkney Islands; and around to the west you'll find the Hebrides.

Southeast of the valley are the Grampian Mountains with 4,406-foot Ben Nevis, the highest peak in the United Kingdom. Rain and snow on the Grampians feed the Dee, the Spey, and the Tay, three of Scotland's storied salmon rivers. Below the Highlands is the Midland Valley with Edinburgh, Glasgow, and Dundee. This is the industrial core of the country and most people live there. But between the midlands and the border with England lie another set of rolling uplands drained to the east by the famous Tweed and to

the west by the Clyde, a river system that seems to be recovering.

For frugal anglers who are willing to fish other than famed stretches of blue-ribbon rivers, Scotland can provide a less expensive destination than other countries where salmon fishing flourishes. As is the case elsewhere in the UK, the best beats are privately owned. Some day and week tickets are available to traveling anglers, but they are most often only obtainable through the lodge where one stays or through an angling association or ghillie with whom one books a trip. To fish the best of the available beats, book at least 18 months in advance. And be prepared to accept a lesser beat on your first trip. Repeat customers have access to better beats as they open. Salmon and sea-run brown trout seasons vary with each stream. The best rule is to contact the lodging where you intend to stay or the association that is arranging your fishing for specific information about seasons.

The Islands

Starting with Arran in the mouth of the Firth of Clyde and swinging north and then east to the Shetlands, a string of islands lies off the coast of the mainland. Some are so small as to have no fishing, but others do. And they provide a fascinating alternative to more pressured waters on the mainland. On Arran, rivers see excellent numbers of sea-run browns as well as salmon. Arran rivers fish best after spates and from August into October. Across Kilbrannon Sound is Kintyre, a long peninsula that would be an island were it

not for the bit of land at Tarbert. Salmon and sea-run browns are excellent on the Carradale Water, a small spate river. To the north and east is Islay with a number of good rivers: Grey, Laggan, and Sorn. Tickets and accommodation are provided by the Port Askaig Hotel. Near the southern tip of Islay is the little town of Port Ellen, and the Machrie Hotel offers salmon and trout fishing on the River Machrie.

While the Isle of Mull has a few game-fish lochs and rivers, better angling is found on the Isle of Skye well up the coast and just inside the Hebrides. Waters on Skye are preserved for the most part. However, the Skeabost House Hotel at Skeabost Bridge offers beats on the Snizort River, supposedly the best salmon river on the island. Other salmon rivers include the Kilmuluag, Lealt, Ose, and Staffin. North Uist, in the Hebrides west of Skye, contains some 400 lochs and lochans, some of which may be yet to be fished. Guests at the Langass Lodge Hotel and Lochmaddy Hotel have access to a number of salmon rivers and lochs. The largest of the Hebrides, the island of Harris and Lewis, contains some salmon but better trout in lochs. Harris is the ancestral home of that lovely and durable woolen tweed.

The Orkney Islands and the Shetlands far beyond them are tops of submerged mountains formed some 500 million years ago, an extension of the highlands of Ireland and Scotland. On the Orkney, most angling is found in lochs for brown trout with Loch Harray having the best reputation. The Tingwall Valley holds the best brown-trout lochs on the Shetlands, but there are literally

Right **Try the browns and salmon on the Morar, south of Mallaig on the West Highland coast.**
Far right **On Loch Voe in the Shetlands, anglers seek brown trout.**

hundreds to choose from and many are underfished. Sea-run browns ply some of the rivers and enter some of the lochs, including Spiggie, which is reserved for fly fishing only.

The Northwest Highlands

Ancient metamorphic rocks underlie the wild northwestern mountains where crofters once strove to raise a living from shallow and all but sterile soils. Some of the best fishing in the Highlands is found in the old counties of Caithness and Sutherland. The Thurso, which enters the ocean downstream from the same-named town, is highly regarded for its spring run of salmon. The season is among the earliest in Scotland, opening in mid-January and running to the first week of October. Trout fishing is also quite good. The Ulbster Arms Hotel in Halkirk provides guests with opportunities to fish the river and a number of lochs.

To the west of Thurso at Melvich, the Halladale River drains the northern slope of the Helmsdale watershed. From early March fishing is excellent for salmon in the range of 6½ to 11 lbs. Grilse run in June and average about half the size of the salmon. Accommodation and permits are provided by Forsinard Hotel in Forsinard. The Helmsdale River, which empties into the North Sea, is also an excellent salmon fishery. Beats on the upper river are controlled by Roxton Bailey Robinson, a booking agent in Hungerford, England.

Further to the west, the outflow of Loch Naver passes through Altnaharra before reaching the coast near Tongue. Close by is a shorter river, the Borgie. While totally preserved, a few tickets for

good beats on these salmon and sea-run-brown rivers are available. Try the Altnaharra Hotel in the old county of Sutherland, which contains a fine tackle shop, provides instruction, and offers the services of ghillies. For the Borgie, check out the Borgie Lodge Hotel at Skerray.

Rounding Cape Wrath – salmon and sea-run browns to the west – brings one to the town of Scourie, which according to *Where to Fish* is an "Excellent centre for sea trout, brown trout and salmon fishing." Of 200 trout lochs, the Scourie Hotel has beats on more than half. Fishing peaks in late summer. As are most of the rivers in this area, the Inver is held by private hands, but a river that is nearly as good is the Kirkaig. Access is available through Inver Lodge Hotel at Lochinver, which also offers permits for brown trout on

several lochs in the area.

Among the waters fished by guests at Inver Lodge are the upper beats on the Oykel, another excellent salmon and sea-trout fishery. Waters from the west slope of Ben More (3,000 feet) feed the Inver, and those that fall on the east flow into the Oykel, which, not far below Lairg, enters Dornach Firth. Fish the upper waters in summer and the lower waters in spring and fall. To the south of the Oykel watershed is the Conon. This river opens in late January and fishes well for salmon and sea-run browns into the fall. The mouth of the Conon is about 12 miles northwest of Inverness, but the best accommodation for anglers are to be had at the Coul House Hotel in Contin.

Though there are hundreds of rivers and lochs in these lovely uplands that contain good stocks of

salmon, sea-run browns and wild brown trout, two more deserve special mention: Loch Eilt and the Ailort River. The loch produces some of the best angling for large sea-run browns in the country, and salmon teem in the river, which enters the Sound of Arisaig about 18 miles south of the Isle of Skye. Lochailort Inn provides accommodation and sells tickets.

Glen Mor and the Grampian Mountains

Straight as a die and as narrow as it is deep, Glen Mor runs from Fort William on Loch Linnhe to Inverness and divides the wild Northwestern Highlands from the Grampian Mountains to the southeast. The result of ancient and intense

faulting, Glen Mor contains Loch Lochy and its more famous neighbor Loch Ness. Over 820 feet deep, Loch Ness is a fine fishery with sea-run browns at Aldourie and Dochfour. Salmon seem to concentrate off Fort Augustus and at the mouths of rivers such as the Enrick, Foyers, and Moriston. Among other rivers feeding Loch Ness are the outflow of Loch Quoich and Loch Garry. The national brown-trout record came from Loch Quoich, and the Arctic char record from Loch Garry. Salmon in the system fish well after July 1 and into October. The Tomdou Hotel at Invergarry provides boats for loch and rivers, ghillies and boatmen, and tickets for guests.

Rising again southeast of Glen Mor, the highlands take the name of the Grampian Mountains and contain several smaller ranges including the Monadhliaths and the Cairngorms. Here originate three of the principal salmon rivers of Scotland, the Spey, the Dee, and the Tay. From its headwaters in the Corrieyairack Forest high in the Monadhliaths, the Spey follows a northeasterly course for 107 miles to its mouth on Moray Firth just east of Kingston. The river's tranquil valley

Far left An open and cheerful river, the South Esk is good for salmon and sea trout.

Left The outflow of Loch Awe is one of the finest western salmon rivers.

Right Grayling are the primary quarry on Loch Tummel.

drops little above Grantown-on-Spey and fishing is not so good. But below as the valley narrows, the river steps up the pace raced into beats and pools – Castle Grant, Ballindalloch, Carron and Arndilly – of legend. The Avon joins the Spey at Junction Pool adding clear cold waters from Glens Livet and Fiddich of whisky renown.

To fish the upper mileage, book into the Seafield Lodge Hotel, in Grantown-on-Spey, Morayshire. The Gordon Arms Hotel in Fochabers serves anglers who wish to fish lower reaches. While salmon in the Spey have been in decline, netting at the mouth of the river was stopped in 1993 and fall runs have been improving. And because this is one of the most famous salmon rivers in the world, bookings on the best beats are difficult to come by particularly in the height of the season in late spring and early summer. Plan to make reservations at least a year in advance. Even if you settle for less than optimum dates, you'll likely not be disappointed by your visit to these gentle and historic waters.

The River Dee is another wonderful river for fly fishing for salmon; it's where the Royal family has fished for generations. Rising on the southern flanks of Ben Macdhui (4,300 feet), it flows 96 miles east to the North Sea at Aberdeen. The river has seen reduced numbers of spring fish, but a moratorium on netting at the river's mouth and a voluntary delay in the opening of the season from February 1 to March 1 is showing some promise. The river also carries sea-run browns and riverine browns as well. Permits to fish the lower reaches of the Dee are available from Banchory Lodge Hotel, Banchory. The lodge also provides ghillies and instruction. Salmon fishing is reasonably good in

all reaches of the river and the little towns along the way – Aboyne, Ballater, and Braemar – offer a variety of accommodations and tackle shops. Tributaries offer fine angling for wild browns.

The third, but by no means the least, of the region's major salmon waters is the Tay. From the slopes of Ben Lui (1,450 feet) above Crianlarich, the Tay gathers its waters from River Fillan (excellent trout and salmon early in the season and in early fall) and other tributaries including the Dochart and Lochy (very good from July–September) before entering Loch Tay below Killin. The best months to fish the river above the loch are May through July and again in September. Tickets are available from Ben More Lodge Hotel at Crianlarich. Downstream, below the outflow of Loch Tay, is the town of Aberfeldy, a good headquarters for fishing the loch, the river, and the surrounding streams and lochs in the hills. The town boasts a tackle shop, ghillie service, and sources of instruction. Among the better places to put up is the Weems Hotel in Weems. The river

slows and meanders a bit in its lower reaches west of Dunkeld (for which a bright orange fly is named). To fish the famed pools on the big water of the Dee, check into Tayside Hotel and make use of its permits for private water and other services for visiting anglers.

Among other good Highland salmon and trout rivers are the Don, particularly from Kildrummy to Strathdon, in Aberdeenshire; the Findhorn's rocky pools in early and late summer near Moray; the Lochy above Fort William during the height of summer and early fall; and the Awe below Loch Awe, a very good though short river for salmon in mid- to late summer.

The Midland Valley

This lowland region with the cities of Glasgow and Edinburgh is the most populous region in Scotland, and it is also the country's industrial center. While the midland terrain couldn't be called a plain, it lacks the elevations and relief

that give birth to fast, cold water in which salmon thrive. Still, a number of the rivers of the area see limited runs of salmon and sea-run browns, and many are overcoming decades of pollution. The Clyde – nearly as long as the Spey – gains its waters from high in the uplands to the South. Once famed for its salmon, now fishing is better for brown trout and grayling. Some salmon are caught in its tributaries including the Gryffe and River Leven. Loch Leven, itself, is one of the richest trout fisheries in Scotland, widely known for rapidly growing Loch Leven trout.

At Ayr, a small river with the same name enters the Firth of Clyde. Browns abide in the upper reaches, and the river also carries some salmon and sea-run browns. Also in Ayrshire are the Irvine, Garnock, and Annick rivers, which offer angling for salmon and sea-run browns from midsummer through fall. Across the Firth of Forth from Edinburgh is the Eden. This is a trout river with runs of salmon and saltwater browns. It flows

into the North Sea at St Andrews and it is one of the very few Scottish rivers that can be fished on Sunday. Its upper reaches have a reputation for providing outstanding dry-fly angling for nice-sized browns.

Southern Uplands

The Tweed is the longest river in the region. From its headwaters in the Lanark Hills near Moffat to its mouth on the North Sea, the river is 96 miles long. Its incredible productivity and proximity to England – it forms much of the westernmost border – make this a very popular salmon river. Even so, the river is seldom booked to capacity so traveling anglers can usually find a beat, though the most productive ones on the lower river are hard to come by. The water is open for salmon and sea-run browns from February through November. While low summer flows require fine presentations of smaller flies on lighter leaders, there are still

salmon to be caught. The river fishes best in spring and again in the fall. Among the better beats are the scenic Bemersyde near St Boswells, Ravenswood across from Bremersyde, Boleside where River Ettrick enters the Tweed, and Fairnilee near Galashiels. Lodgings are numerous; there's something in every hamlet along the river's course. A good place to start is with Clovenfords Inn at Galashiels.

While the Tweed is certainly the main event in the Southern Highlands, it's not the only game in town. The Cree at Newton Steward in Wigtownshire has good salmon and sea-run browns early in the season. Accommodation can be found nearby at Bladnoch Inn in Wigtown. The Doon flows north from the Merrick mountain into the ocean at Ayr. Salmon and sea-run browns are good on the Doon after July 1. Also in Ayrshire is the Grivan, which begins to fish well for salmon in March and April. The Annan flows out of the Moffat Hills toward Solway Firth, and

Opposite far left **The famed Loch Leven is among Scotland's premier trout waters.**
Opposite left **Near Milton Dam on the Ericht, one finds brown trout and grayling.**
Below **Stretches of the Dee near Invercauld hold fine salmon.**

in late fall, the river sees good runs of salmon and anadromous brown trout. The Nith is the largest and best salmon river in the region of Dumfries and Galloway, though its trout are not large. The Warmanbie Hotel in Annan has beats on the Annan and Nith Rivers and access to Sunday fishing, a rarity in Scotland.

Traveling to Scotland

Along with England, Wales, and Northern Ireland, Scotland is part of the United Kingdom and the same travel regulations apply. Primary airports served from London Heathrow to Scotland are Edinburgh, Glasgow, and Inverness.

TACKLE AND FLIES

In reality, the size of the river, its flow, and time of year determine which tackle is most appropriate for any given salmon or sea-trout stream in Scotland. Scots ghillies prefer their two-handed rods long, 12 to 15 feet of ten- or 11-weight. They favor double-taper lines in floating, sink-tip, and intermediate sinking densities. Very fast-sinking lines are outlawed on some rivers because of misuse in foul-hooking fish. As far as backing is concerned, 330 feet of 17½ lb braided Dacron is about right. Reels must have good drags and large arbor reels offer a decided advantage.

Sea-run browns are as aggressive as the steelhead – saltwater rainbows – of North America's northern Pacific coast or Russia's Kamchatka. But they are much smaller fish. One of 6½ lbs is considered quite large. A seven- or eight-weight system, even a six-weight, seems about right. Floating and sink-tip lines are all that's

required. This set-up will work well when fishing lochs for browns. For the delicate Highland stream-bred browns, go light with a three- or four-weight.

Salmon *Jock Scott, Stoat's Tail, Thunder & Lightning, Munroe Killer, Hairy Mary, Willie Gunn, Blue Charm, Ally's Shrimp, Black Shrimp, Quin Shrimp, Red Shrimp, 4-12 in single and doubles, and tube ties.*

Sea trout *Teal Blue & Silver, Peter Ross, Black Butcher, Mallard, Claret, Invicta, 8-12.* **Dries** *Elk hair Caddis and Black Caddis, 10-14; Olive Compara Dun, 14; Mayfly Dun, 10-14; Adams, 12-16; March Brown 10-12; Lunn's Particular, 16-20; Blue-winged Olive, 14-20; Royal Wulff, 8-12; Stimulator, 10-12; Green Drake, 10-14; Muddlers, 8-12.* **Nymphs** *Gold-ribbed Hare's Ear, Pheasant Tail, Stonefly, 8-12.* **Streamers** *Woolly Bugger in black, brown, and olive, 8-12.*

South America

Stretching from the sunny Caribbean with its bonefish flats at Los Roques off the Venezuelan Coast to the barren grasslands of Tierra del Fuego – swept by the incessant winds of roaring forties, where sea trout grow like Atlantic salmon – South America offers anglers some of the most exotic fishing in the world. Climb aboard an old river boat and steam up the Amazon beneath the heavy forest canopy throbbing with cries of bird and monkey. Swing a leg over a horse and ride across the Pampas to a spring creek where brown trout are as colorful as if painted by Titian. Hie up into the Chilean Andes and fish below the glaciers.

While South America is only 150 miles longer than North America, it seems to extend so much further. Virtually two-thirds of the country lies in the tropics with the equator passing through the mouth of the Amazon. Precipitation varies from more than 20 inches per year to less than 2. Humidity is high and so are the temeratures: the highest recorded was 120°F in central Argentina. Along the western coast, like a crisp crust pinched up for a stubby piece of a giant pie, the Andes climb to nearly 23,000 feet and run the full length of the continent, covering nearly 5,000 miles along the extreme west coast. Born of the eastern rim of the Pacific Ring of Fire, active volcanoes and earthquakes are not uncommon at all in the Andes. With its endless rainforests, plains and mountains, the population density is quite low, averaging about 15 persons per square mile.

Twelve countries comprise South America. Founded by colonizing Europeans, particularly the Portugese and Spanish, but also English and Dutch, the cultures of these countries are an exotic blend of Amerindian or native peoples and expatriate continental European. Many of these families pioneered the vast ranch lands of the Argentinian Pampas and, south of the Rio Negro, spreads on the arid steppes of Patagonia. Patagonia includes all of South America below the Rio Negro and west to the Pacific. Its mountains are studded with high snow-capped peaks, and its valleys filled with some of the largest lakes in the world. The climate here is like that of Wyoming, becoming colder and wetter as elevation and latitude increase. Some of the best fishing in the world is found in the rivers of Patagonia, and some of the most unusual is to be had deep in the Amazon jungle. South America is a land of contrasts, to be sure, not the least of which are reversed seasons – summer in January – a real attraction for anglers in the Northern Hemisphere.

Tierra del Fuego

Tierra del Fuego lies at the end of the earth. Cool and damp on the best days, this "Land of Fire" is buffeted by the constant winds of the roaring forties. Separated from the mainland by the Strait

Opposite **Lush jungle lines the Rio Negro, a river known for peacock bass.**
Right **Large fish and abundant hatches lure anglers to the rivers of Patagonia.**

of Magellan, the western two-thirds of the island and adjacent archipelago are Chilean and the eastern third is Argentine. A low range of mountains – none higher than 980 feet – occupies the northern third of the island. But to the south, across an almost isthmus, relief becomes more rugged, and rivers more numerous. The big river here is the Rio Grande, and its headwaters rise from a number of lakes on Chile's side of the border. The lower section of the river, some 43 miles, flows through Argentina on its way to the Atlantic at the little town of Rio Grande.

Joe Brooks, fishing editor for *Outdoor Life* magazine in the 1950s, and later Ernest Schwiebert were among the first to champion travel to Tierra del Fuego. In the Rio Grande, Menendez, and MacLennan rivers, brown trout run to 28 lbs with 11 to 13 lbs being average. No one is quite sure how the browns found their way to these waters. Either Argentine or visiting English anglers stocked them in the 1930s, and the fish have adapted wonderfully. Not only are the offshore waters of the Atlantic alive with baitfish, but the rivers are equally nutirent-laden. None of these three rivers is large, so the fish are wont to be finicky. Down and across is the prescribed casting pattern, but often the wind has other ideas. When hooked, these fat browns take to the air as if they were steelhead, which they resemble in more than passing fashion. Lightning runs are the rule, and they do not tire easily. With bottoms of cobble, the rivers are generally easily waded and at times the rivers can be floated. Several lodges have beats on the river. The most famous is the

legendary Estancia Maria Beheti, an English cottage with more than 30 miles of Rio Grande. Brooks and Schwiebert made this their headquarters and their catches are recorded in the estancia's fishing logs. Adjacent is the Kau Tappen with about 15 miles of fly-fishing water.

In addition to waters in the central region around the Rio Grande is the 60-mile Lago Fagnano ù Comi, a sinuous lake in the shadow of Tierra del Fuego's highest peaks. Not only is fishing in the outflow of the lake very good, but browns and rainbows can be caught in a number of tributaries that feed the lake. Anglers stay in Campo Fagnano fly shop. And 50 miles north of the Strait of Magellan on the Rio Gallegos is Truchaike, a magnificent sheep ranch with nearly 25 miles on the river. Sea-run browns enter the estuary near the port town of Gallegos and mingle with nonmigratory stocks in late summer and fall. Chances of catching browns of 9 to 15 lbs are good here, and the estancia also contains a number of spring creeks where brook trout of a pound or two have taken up residence.

Argentina

The province of Neuquen on the Chilean border contains much of the best trout fishing in Patagonia. Scores of large lakes, some natural and others created as power-generating impoundments, lie in alpine-like valleys. They are fed by hundreds of swift, cold rivers pregnant with snow melt in summer. The mountains catch the rain, and eastward beneath their heights extends a rolling, semi-arid steppe drained by rivers of great clarity and of world renown for their brown and rainbow trout. Perhaps the most famous of these waters is the storied Boca Chimehuin, the outflow of Lago Huechulafquen near Junin de los Andes. Capped with snow, the volcano Lanin presides over the lake as it takes on the color of each day's sky. The mouth of the Chimehuin lies at the eastern end of

Left **Sinking tip lines are a must for fishing some of South America's larger rivers.**

the lake. When the wind blows from the west, it pushes the lake into regiments of waves that charge the shallows at the outflow. But big brown trout up to 13 lbs inhabit the mouth of the river. The season opens in mid-November, but it's normally into December before snow melt has flushed through the system. Then the fishing can be fabulous. Some of the best comes in late March and early April as falling temperatures trigger the spawn. The little Quilquihue which joins the Chimehuin is known for its spring runs of rainbows as well as for its browns. When fishing the Chimehuin, anglers frequently book into Hosteria Chimehuin, a lodge that has served fly fishers for years.

North of the Chimehuin is the River Malleo with its chalk-stream headwaters. The Malleo, a tranquil stream that chatters along a riffled, winding path, contains numerous long slow pools where dry fly fishing can be excellent. Downstream from Tres Picos, the river begins to brawl around outcrops of rock and through a gorge at Santa Julia. Fish here, according to Schwiebert, are less selective than their upstream kin. San Huberto Lodge controls access to 18 miles of the best water on the river. At its mouth, the Malleo meets the Alumine, the northernmost of this triumvirate of trophy trout waters. Together with the Chimehuin, they all carry brown-trout water except in the spring when spawning rainbows migrate up from the broad reaches of the River Collon Curç, below. In turn, the Collon Curç enters the Limay and both are excellent rivers to drift and fish. Another tributary, the Traful, flows from the lake of the same name and enters the Limay at the town of Confluencia. Like the others, this river sports big browns and rainbows. With 10 miles on the Traful, La Riviere estancia has

been described by *Forbes* magazine as "the finest fishing lodge in the world, period!"

While Bebe Anchorena, a legend among Argentine fly fishers, landed a 17-lb-plus brown on a tiny caddis from these waters, most angling calls for wet flies or streamers fished through deep pools or worked hard, under the brush against the bank. Countless charming inns are found in towns like San Martin de los Andes and Bariloche. Also there are plenty of English-speaking guides, some of whom grew up on nearby estancias and others who've come from Buenos Aires and throughout the world for the fishing.

Though the brunt of fly fishing in the Patagonian Andes is focused on the mountains and tablelands of the Neuquen province, trout are by no means restricted to this region. They flourish all along the Andes. For example, Esquel, some 125 miles south of San Martin de los Andes, is Parque Nacional Los Alerces, which includes four major lakes and a number of rivers and spring creeks in the steppe. The pressure on these waters may be less than those of the larger area further north. Yet accommodation in Quime Quepan, a charming lake-front chateau in the park, is every bit as good, and guides are available.

Chile

Across the mountains from Esquel lies the drainage of the Futaleufu, a wonderful river that puts one in mind of the Yellowstone in the US although without all of the tourists. From January through mid-April, fishing with dry flies, nymphs, and streamers is superb. Browns in the 6½ to 11 lb range are reasonably common, as are rainbows of similar size. One can wade or float or access remote stretches by horseback. Jim and Sonia Repine operate Futaleufu Lodge, highly rated by some of the gurus of American fly fishing. Here you'll find excellent English-speaking guides along with exquisite cuisine.

More than 125 miles to the south of Futaleufu lies the Coihaique region, the heart of fly fishing in Patagonian Chile. Deeply incised by probing fjords, the Chilean coast is narrow and climbs rapidly in elevation. In only a few locations does one find the high prairie-like steppes of Argentina. But one such location is the valley of the River Cisnes east of Parque Nacional Queulat. The Cisnes and its numerous tributaries have a reputation as a dry-fly fishery, weather permitting. Wading is the normal manner of fishing this river, but its lower sections are floatable and in some places fishing from float tubes can be effective. Browns take center stage here, so much so that the main lodge on the river is called Posada de los Farios (lodge of the brown trout). The lodge is on the river and there's fishing on the doorstep. Another lodge, El Saltamontes (The Grasshopper), carries the name of a favorite food of big brown trout. This lodge specializes in dry-fly fishing and myriad spring creeks are but a few minutes away from this first-rate estancion. The waters here are very reminiscent of southwestern Montana in the US. The season runs from January through March.

Falkland Islands (Islas Malvinas)

With more than 200 islands, the Falklands attracted little attention until the Argentine military attempted to claim them by force in 1982. In so doing they projected this windswept speck of rock and grass some 370 miles northeast of Cape Horn into worldwide prominence. The rivers – the Chartres, Malo, San Carlos, and Warrah – are not long or deep. But they host two good runs of sea trout. The first come in spring (October and November) and the second in fall. Average weight is in the main about 4½ to 9 lbs, but 20 lb fish are possible. Not only are the rivers very good with virtually no fishing pressure, but tidal bays and estuaries offer outstanding fishing, much like that of the Danish coast. This is pretty much a do-it-yourself fishery; fly fishers among the resident population of 2,300 are few. The people here are warm and friendly and numerous small inns have been established since the conflict.

The Amazon

A number of floating lodges – river boats each with a handful of comfortable staterooms – ply the Amazon carrying anglers deep into jungle waters where peacock pavùn, bass from 4½ to 15 lbs will trash almost every popper tossed their way. In addition flyrodders catch red, white, and black piranha, pacu, wolf fish, and tarpon-like aruana. Fishing is generally from skiff piloted by an experienced guide. The end of the day's fishing finds anglers reboarding the ship. Several boats carry anglers in this fashion, among them the *Amazon Goddess* and *Amazon Queen* represented by Quest!, and the *Delfin* represented by Fishabout. The season runs from July through April and the boats run different sections of river depending on water level. Luis Brown, one of the pioneers of fishing for peacock bass in the Amazon basin, operates mobile river camps for fly fishers. Anglers fish from jon-boats equipped with casting platforms that nose into secluded lagoons and tributaries from the main waters of the Rio Plate (July thorugh November) or Rio Negor (December through April). Brown's river camps are on the luxurious side – tents with cooling fans and private baths and daily laundry service.

Traveling to South America

South America's several countries each has distinct travel policies. For the best information, contact the consulate office of the country you wish to visit.

Visitors from the USA and UK are only required to present a valid passport. Most countries permit tourists to bring two liters of distilled spirits and 50 cigars and 400 cigarettes without paying duty. Prices, of course, vary by country. You can expect to pay about as much for a first class meal in a top-of-the-line restaurant as you would at home.

Before you leave, check with your insurance carriers both health and auto if you plan to drive. Consider supplemental coverages if they're recommended by your insurer. Trip insurance is a particularly good idea for tourists visiting South American countries.

TACKLE AND FLIES

Almost perpetual wind, wide water, and gutsy fish of good weight demand a rod with power and backbone for fishing the sea-run leviathans of Tierra del Fuego. Most anglers use 9 to 10 foot eight-weights, though increasingly two-handed Spey rods are being found on the river. All three classes of line – floating, sink-tip, and sinking – have their places on these waters. You'll use floating lines most often, but when midday sun drives fish toward the bottom, the sinking line may be needed to dredge up a strike. Fish on the Falklands run smaller and you can get away with a lighter – say, six-weight – rod.

For Patagonian trout in Chile or the Argentine, two rods are recommended. A three- or four-weight 9 foot rod for fishing streams in the meadows provides ample delicacy of presentation with the length to handle good-sized fish. The second rod should be the ubiquitous six-weight. Floating, weight-forward lines will handle all chores, though sinking leader systems and a sink-tip line may come in handy.

In the Amazon basin peacock pavùn can grow to 28 lbs or more. An eight-weight rod is the minimum required, and some anglers go heavier. Wind is seldom a problem, but throwing big poppers is. A weight-forward floating lines is the name of the game here. Reels designed for

saltwater have a definite place here.

Sea-run browns *Woolly Buggers in black both bead or cone head and plain; Black Clouser Minnows, Montana nymphs, sculpins – size 4-8 – and Matukas in 6-8.* **Dark dries**: *Black Gnat, Blue Dun, 12-14; black Stonefly 6 or 8.*

Trout in Patagonia *Adams, Blue-Winged Olive, Elk Hair Caddis, Hoppers, Humpy, Royal Wulff, sizes 8-16; wet or dry: Muddler Minnows (black as well as tan), 4-10; and nymphs including Hare's Ear, Pheasant Tail, Stonefly, 10-14* **Top-water flies for Peacock** *poppers, Dahlberg's Divers in red/white, yellow/white, blue/white, size 1/0-4.*

Sweden

The Kjølen Mountains that run the length of Scandinavia descend into a rolling tableland that slopes eastward to the Gulf of Bothnia. Rather than the deep fjords of Norway, here glacial hollows are filled with wide lakes: Vänern, Vättern, Hjälmaren, and Mälaren in the south, and Storsjön, Uddjaure, and Tornetrask in the north. From these and hundreds of other lakes, rivers flow to the sea. They lack the velocity of the turbulent, dashing rivers of Norway, and they do not have the runs of salmon, though there are some anadromous salmon here. Their landlocked kin are to be found in the lakes where they can be fished with flies soon after the ice melts. Brown trout, both those that remain in fresh water and those that breed there but forage in the sea, are very popular quarry, as are Arctic char and grayling, the so-called sailfish of the north. A few locations have been stocked with rainbows. Brown trout, grayling, and char can be fished with flies in salt water near river mouths. And in the south, a land of thick forests and slow, blackwater rivers, northern pike and zander (walleye to North Americans) trade in those brackish waters between fresh water and sea.

Sweden faces the same problems as plague salmon fisheries in the North Atlantic: excessive commercial harvests at sea, disease, and acid rain. Seasons on some streams are limited and others face closure as authorities seek ways to at least maintain, if not enhance the quality of cold-water fishing. Throughout the country much is being done to reintroduce salmon in rivers where they once ran. Agreements with countries neighboring the Baltic are reducing the commercial harvests. Efforts are meeting with some success. Salmon have been taken in downtown Stockholm, the country's capital. Far to the north runs are increasing in the Torne and Kalix.

The South

The most populous part of Sweden, this is also the region of the country's greatest lakes. Separated from Copenhagen by a narrow channel known as Øresund, the inshore waters contain both sea-run brown trout and, where there's ample fresh water, pike. Both can be caught on flies. Pike are found in the shallows and readily take big, bright streamers like Dalhbergs. Some of these fish go 30 to 40 lbs, and the salt tends to invigorate their fight.

On the west coast south of Halmstad, the Lagan flows into Kattegat, the large bay that separates Sweden from Denmark. Rising in the uplands near Sunnerbo, the lower mileage of this river supports runs of sea trout and Atlantic salmon. Sea trout averaging 2 lb fish best in the spring and early summer; salmon in the 10 lb class hit their peak in August. Permits and references for accommodation are available through the Laholm Turistbryå. A bit up the coast to the west at Flakenberg is the Ätran River, which also has sea trout and a small run of salmon.

Inland and to the north, the Klarälven flows into Lake Vänern, the largest lake in Europe. Rising in a chain of small lakes near the Norwegian border about 93 miles to the north, the Klarälven is an outstanding fishery for trout in its upper waters and, where it enters Vänern, for landlocked salmon and big brown trout to 20 lbs. Fishing in the river is good throughout the summer. About 12 miles upstream from Karlstad at the river's mouth is a set of falls where angling for landlocked salmon is limited to fly fishing only. Klarälvens Sportfiske, has private beats near the falls and can provide lodging as well.

The east coast area around Kivik is noted for its sea-run brown trout. Accommodation and information are available through Simrishamns Turistbryå. The Mörrum, the river that drains Lake Äsnen, flows about 30 miles south to the Baltic east of Karlshamn. Once among Sweden's finest salmon rivers, now the Mörrum is known primarily for its sea-run browns. Holdover browns are fished as early as April as they make their way back to the sea. Browns, fresh from the sea, come into the

Left **Rivers of Sweden lack the turbulence of those in neighboring Norway.**

Below **In the south, waters are large and carry stocks of sea trout and salmon.**

river in June. They increase in size until fall when really big (up to 28 lbs) sea trout begin to show up. Some salmon do use the Mörrum. The largest begin running in May and June and streams of grilse follow as the season progresses. A river with a heavy flow, even in August, the Mörrum's boulder-strewn runs are open to both fly and spin fishers. Guides and information are available from Sportfiskecenterum.

Though salmon have been taken in Stockholm, the islands to the east of the city on the Baltic Coast constitute a better fishery. Here anglers catch sea trout and pike on flies.

The North

The best fly fishing in Sweden is found in the counties north of Gävle on the Gulf of Bothnia. Species include Atlantic salmon, landlocked salmon, sea and riverine brown trout, and Arctic char and grayling in both salt and fresh water. Waters of note for salmon and sea-run browns include the Ljusnan south of Söderhamn and the Ljungan which meets salt water below Sundsvall. Rising in the shadows of Sweden's rugged mountains – 5,900-foot Helgasfjället and 4,900-foot Lunndörrsfällen – the Ljungan is highly regarded for char and grayling in its upper reaches and grayling and trout lower down near Ange. Bookings in a number of hotels, inns, and lodges can be obtained through the Ange Tourism office.

Another good river in this area is the Indalsälven, well known for its sea trout and grayling with occasional salmon at Timra. Also reaching the Gulf at Timra is the tiny Mjällån River, which flows through Viskjö. Strict size limits are enforced on the Mjällån's sea trout, grayling, brown trout, and occasional salmon. The best runs of sea trout occur in May and June, with grayling and trout remaining fairly constant throughout the summer. Fishing on the Mjällån can be organized by Blixt Sport in Umeå.

Fishing for salmon up to 40 lbs, and sea trout are also limited on sections of the Ångermanälven at Sollefteå. The Ångermanälven is a large river. It heads in the high mountains just east of the Norwegian border and flows through a long chain of lakes in southern Lappland before reaching the Gulf of Bothnia above Harnösand. The upper reaches of the river and its tributaries are good for

Far left **Some of the finest sea trout fishing in the world is found in the crossing tidal currents off Ystad on Sweden's southern tip.**
Right **Inland rivers offer dry fly action for browns and grayling and char.**

trout and char in late summer. Larger salmon enter the lower reaches of the river in early summer and fish best in June and July. Sea trout are available throughout the summer. The Sollefteå Tourist Office offers guide services and hotel bookings.

Above the university town of Umeå is the Vindel River, which, in the vicinity of Sorsele, fishes well for sea trout during the height of summer and grayling into the fall. About 30 miles below Sorsele, the Vindel enters an impressive set of ten rapids that occasionally holds salmon. Among its tributaries, the Lais is of particular note for sea trout and grayling. And 18 miles north of Skellefteå flows the Byskeälven, a river where 90 percent of salmon are caught on flies from mid-June into July. Top Ten Fishing Sweden provides self-catering cottages on the Byske and also on the Kalixälven which flows into the top of the Gulf of Bothnia at the town of Kalix. The Kalixälven and the Torneälven about 30 miles to the east are seeing increasing runs of bigger salmon thanks to reduced commercial harvesting of wild stocks in the Baltic. According to Sportfiskarna, the Swedish federation of anglers, the Byske, Kalix, and Torne are probably the best salmon rivers in the country. Seasons are set annually and generally run from mid-June to mid-August.

Traveling to Sweden

Passports are required of all visitors, but visas are not needed unless one is staying longer than three months. Travelers from the US may bring the equivalent of one liter of liquor and a carton of cigarettes into the country. The amount of currency one can bring into the country is not limited, but most establishments accept credit cards. And they are generally well accepted throughout the country. Prices will seem expensive.

Sweden is a healthy, outdoor-sports-oriented country, and the whole country seems to go on vacation in July. Reservations at the best inns and hotels in areas where the fishing is great will be difficult to come by, unless made well in advance. Even then the fishing will be crowded. In most cases, the angling is better in June and August. Try to avoid July if you can.

Highways in this country are well maintained and traffic regulations are rigorously enforced. Car rentals are available at most airports with connecting flights from Stockholm. But be aware that gasoline prices are very high.

Sweden's weather is generally temperate in the summer. Less precipitation falls in Sweden than in Norway and summers tend to be just a bit warmer. Even so, showers crop up at will and rain gear should never be far from hand.

TACKLE AND FLIES

While two-handed rods are *de rigueur* on many salmon rivers in Scandinavia, most anglers find that single-handed 10-foot rods of eight- to ten-weight serve quite well for salmon in Sweden. Shooting heads (floating and sink-tip) are used with increasing frequency, though weight-forward systems will answer the need in all but the most difficult cases. About 100 yards of braided Dacron is ample backing on reels with good drag systems. As is the case elsewhere, reels with large arbors are finding favor among anglers out for large game fish. In addition to a system for salmon (which can be used with fine wire tippets for saltwater pike as well), bring along a six-weight system for sea trout and a three-weight for grayling and small-stream angling for brown trout.

Trout *Dries Tailor Sedge, Vulgate, Compare Dun, Caddis, Par-glen, Dumpy Butt, 12-14.* **Nymphs** *Tailor Caddis, Vulgate Nymph, Caddis, 10-14.* **Streamers** *Fox hair, Blindsill, Whitlock sculpin, Woolly Bugger, 6-10*

Salmon *Stoat's Tail tube fly, Davy Wotton, Muddlers, General Practitioner, Esmond Drury, Tosh, Jock Scott, 4-10.*

United States of America *Alaska*

Alaska. The name alone conjures up images of clean, free-flowing rivers that teem with five species of Pacific salmon, rainbows, Dolly Varden, and steelhead. Hulking brown bears swipe salmon, garish in their spawning colors, from the rushing waters. Overhead, bald eagles circle as an otter slides down the river bank. Alaska is by far the largest of the United States covering 361,700 square miles. Including thousands of islands, the state has more than 32,300 miles of shoreline. It is a land of fire and water. Katmai National Park includes the Valley of Ten Thousand Smokes, a reminder of the volcanic forces that built the mountains, among them the 21,300-foot Mt McKinley, the tallest peak in North America. Alaskan mountains contain more active glaciers and ice fields than anywhere else in the inhabited world. The state's three million lakes are drained by more than 3,000 rivers, many of which are accessible to sport anglers.

The climate of Alaska varies. The North Pacific Current swirls counterclockwise circulating warm waters from the Pacific Ocean along the southern coast of Alaska moderating temperatures and providing moisture that charges the rivers. During the primary fishing season from June into September daytime highs average 59°F and lows, in the neighborhood of 41°F. Abundant mosquitoes and blackflies, as well as the cool temperatures suggest long-sleeved shirts and trousers. Raincoats and hats are a part of everyone's summer wardrobe. Summer storms seem to brew up in nothing flat, but after dumping their rain, they dissipate just as quickly. Boots with rubber bottoms and leather uppers are a good idea here.

Sport fishing is concentrated in three areas: the Southeastern Panhandle, the Interior surrounding Anchorage (the state's largest city), and the southwest, which includes the famed region encompassing Bristol Bay and Lake Iliamna. Part of the charm of Alaska is its out-and-out wilderness, and the way most tourists get around is by aircraft and ferry.

Lodges catering to anglers are numerous and range in sophistication from riverside tent camps to rough-hewn inns of log and stone where accommodation and cuisine are completely first-class. An extensive system of state and privately operated campgrounds serve tourists who want to rough it. Much of the water is public, but little of it can be reached without the aid of a bush plane and a guide.

Opposite **Alaska's Copper River rainbows, thick as your thigh, draw anglers from all over the world.**
Right **Sockeye salmon run in the little rivers of Kodiak Island.**

Southeastern Panhandle

Glaciers cap the high mountains of the Brabazon, Fairweather and Coast ranges on this narrow strip of US territory that lies between Canada's British Columbia and the Pacific Ocean. The mainland, here, is deeply incised by fjord-like arms of the sea, and large islands – Prince of Wales, Revillagigedo, Kuperanof, Chichagof, and the Admiralties – are separated from the continent by straits through which tides race at speeds of nearly 10 knots.

The daily ebb and flow of the tides bring fresh charges of the five species of Pacific salmon. Each species has at least two names: chinook or king, silver or coho, red or sockeye, pink or humpy, chum or dog. The season begins with the first runs of steelhead in late April and May. Angling shifts into high gear with the arrival of chinooks in May. Silvers come next in late June and in July these bright fish are joined by reds, pinks, and chum. Overall the salmon angling is best in mid-August.

For the dedicated fly fisher, southeastern panhandle is a bit off the beaten path, so strong is the lure of the salmon and trout fisheries of Bristol Bay/Lake Iliamna in the southwest. And much of the fishing at resorts in the panhandle involves trolling, sometimes with bait, for salmon migrating through on surging tides. There are no large rivers on the islands or the little strip of mainland. But there are streams, marvelous clear streams, where first steelhead and then rainbows and cutthroats run. These rivers are seldom more than 100 feet wide and not very deep. Wading is reasonably easy. Among the best bets are the rivers of Prince of

Wales Island, especially the Karta, which steelhead use both spring and fall. Among the better places to stay on Prince of Wales is rustic Boardwalk Wilderness Lodge, built of hand-peeled spruce log. Its balconies overlook Thorne Bay, and every morning its boats carry anglers to the mouths of the island's streams. Across on the mainland, check out Misty Fjords Lodge on Mink Bay. Rivers produce fine cutthroat fishing in June and July and some salmon.

Bristol Bay/Lake Iliamna and the Southwest

This is the Alaska of which everyone dreams. The

reason? Bristol Bay, that cusp of ocean which swings in against the mainland just north of the Alaska Peninsula. The bay nourishes millions of salmon which in summer, move up scores of rivers to spawn. Rainbows, too, winter in the brackish waters of river mouths before swimming upriver for their spring spawn and to forage. Lake Iliamna, nearly 160 miles long and over 980 feet deep, is remarkably fertile. Fish run up the Kvichak River from Bristol Bay, rest in Iliamna, and then head into the rivers that feed the lake.

The Kvichak/Iliamna system is not the only superlative fishery in the Bristol Bay area. Entering the Bering Sea to the north is the Kuskokwim and its tributary the Aniak, the Kanetok, and the

Goodnews. Togiak Bay is fed by the river of the same name. The zigzagging Wood Lakes system contains five major lakes and such wonderful connecting rivers as the Agulowak, Wind, and Peace Rivers. To the east is the Nushagak. South of the Iliamna are the Alagnak and Nonvianuk, and further south the Naknek, which all drain the stunning Katmai National Preserve and Katmai National Park. Katmai is known as much for its rainbows and salmon as it is for its large population of Alaskan Brown bears.

With a few exceptions, these rivers are reasonably similar. Those draining lakes flow through low, boggy glacial plains before merging with their saline bays. Riverbeds are normally small cobble, and river structure is more a function of gravel bars and cut banks on the outside of bends. Outboards or jet boats ferry anglers from hot spot to hot spot, and those who travel longer distances do so by float plane or helicopter. Rivers that feed the lakes have more drop and thus maintain more of a pocket-water quality. Not to be overlooked is fishing in the lakes themselves.

Fishing begins with spring-spawning rainbows that are moving out of the rivers to feed in the fertile oceans and bays. They are voracious, feeding on salmon smolts that are journeying downstream at the same time. Among the rainbows are thousands that have not spawned but which are moving into the rivers to gorge on young salmon. Kings are the first of the salmon to move into the river systems. They begin arriving in June and continue into August. Sockeye along with pinks and chum salmon fill the streams in July, before giving way to acrobatic silvers. On some streams anglers can double up in late August and early September on silver salmon and rainbows, now grown fat on salmon caviar.

The waters of Kodiak and Afognak Islands, separated from Katmai to the north by Shelikof Straits, exhibit the same general features as those on the mainland. And fishing tends to follow

Opposite **At times, anglers share Alaskan rivers with grizzly bears, which, of course, have the right-of-way.**

Above **Green yarn patterns work well for sockeyes.**

Right **Sometimes it is tough to find a rainbow trout in the midst of a run of red salmon.**

similar patterns – kings in June, sockeye and pinks in July, and in October on the Karluck fabulous runs of steelhead. Kodiak and Afognak streams and lakes see much less pressure than do those across the strait.

Lodges are more than plentiful in the Bristol Bay/Iliamna region and on Kodiak and Afognak Islands. Dick Matthews's Enchanted Lake Lodge in the Katmai area, Mike Cusack's King Salmon Lodge on the Naknek, and Ted Gerken's Iliaska Lodge at Iliamna are all good bets. On Afognak, try Afognak Wilderness Lodge at Seal Bay and on Kodiak, Saltery Lake Lodge offers splendid access to both river and stream fishing. Kodiak boasts a road system that allows anglers to drive to a dozen good rivers where salmon and Dolly Varden run.

Right *The largest of Alaskan salmon is the king which can weigh more than 50 lbs.*

Opposite right *Dolly Varden, a char, provides great sport on three-weight rods.*

The Interior

The native people of central Alaska, the Athabascans, had a word for the soaring peak that dominated their landscape. They called it Denali, "the high one." And indeed, Denali or Mt McKinley as American explorers named it, towers over the southern central interior of Alaska. It glows with the sun and can be seen from Anchorage, about 125 miles to the south. Denali and the other peaks of the Alaska Range form a semicircle enclosing the lower Talkeetna Mountains and the drainage of the Sustina River. In the lowlands beneath the western flank of the mountains flows one of the most productive rivers in Alaska, the Talachulitna, known fondly among anglers as the "Tal." Only 62 miles northwest of Anchorage, the river sees kings up to 57 lbs in late June and early July. By the end of the month pinks, sockeye, chums and silvers have entered the system. Light-tackle angling for rainbow – fat with salmon spawn – and silvers occupies August and into September. The river is easily waded, and a number of lodges work its waters. Among them are Talstar Lodge, which runs a very good school for women fly fishers in June, and Talaheim Lodge, which uses helicopters to carry anglers to waters that no one else can reach.

South of Anchorage, across Turnagain Arm of Cook Inlet, is the glacial-capped Kenai Peninsula. The Sterling Highway allows motorists to reach a number of good waters, particularly the Kenai and Kasilof Rivers and Deep Creek at Ninilchik. King salmon reach this area in late May, somewhat earlier than elsewhere in the state. June brings sockeye; July, pinks; and August and September, silvers. The Kenai is a tourist destination and its roads draw numbers of motorists. Why not? They pass through the magnificent Kenai National Refuge where you are likely to see moose, caribou, and bears without leaving your car. Ferry service departs Seward and Homer for Kodiak Island and Valdez to the east. Hotels, motels, and resorts are more than abundant. However, Osprey Alaska in Cooper Landing on the Kenai River has a reputation for serving fly fishers.

Traveling to the USA

Travelers may need a visitor's visa. Refer to page 145 for further information.

TACKLE AND FLIES

Anglers come to Alaska to fish for big fish and lots of them. Kings can run to 44 lbs and more, but normally salmon are in the 6½ to 9 lb range. Trout are usually much smaller; a nice fish weighs 5½ lbs or so. Big rods are not really necessary: a good seven- or eight-weight will serve quite nicely. That is, of course, unless you want to catch a massive king on a fly. Then a ten- or 12-weight is needed to fill the bill. Floating weight-forward lines with 150 yards of backing will get the job done. Many salmon and steelhead anglers are beginning to use reels with large arbors for a faster retrieve. That makes more sense than multiplying reels that depend on gearing to speed up spool rotation. Things have a way of breaking in remote lands, so simpler is generally better. Reels should have good disk drags that are smooth under pressure. Given a

choice between a reel with a fast retrieve rate and one with an excellent drag, go for the drag.

Alaskan fish are not particularly finicky or leader-shy. You won't need gossamer tippets or micro flies. Some times it's helpful to be able to get down to fish, and a leader system of various sinking weights will be very useful. Tippets of 2X to 5X should cover all situations. A leader with a total length of 6½ to 10 feet will generally suffice.

Most fishing is done by wading, and water is generally cool if not cold. Three-mil neoprene waders will keep most folks warm enough. But remember, Alaska can have its 80°F days, and if you're wearing neoprenes you'll work up a sweat. A better choice is a pair of heavy stocking foot waders made of one of the breathable fabrics. You can add as many layers underneath as you need to stay warm and you'll never work up a sweat. Felt-soled wading shoes are all that you'll need.

Many of Alaska's best waters flow through low, marshy bottomlands where insects can drive one nuts. Some anglers resort to headnets. Others rely on good insect repellents. Bring with you a supply of the brand that you know works for you.

Trout, grayling and char feed on eggs from spawn in salmon and their smolts and fry. Salmon and steelhead are not feeding, per se, yet, but rather acting out of instincts imprinted, it is supposed, when they were hungry fingerlings. Thus the most productive patters will be egg patterns, streamers and nymphs. Most lodges and guides maintain a stock of flies that have been proven to work on the waters they fish. But it's a good idea to stock up on some basic patterns in different colors. Remember that eggs and decaying flesh constitute a major portion of the diet. Include white, cream, yellow, organ, pink and red in your selections. Buy or tie twice as many as you think you'll need. It's a shame to run out of your favorite when you're 100 miles from nowhere. And if you have some left over, you can use them on your next trip.

Trout, Grayling, Char *Egg patterns* Glo-bug, Pinkies, 6-8; Babine Special, Two-egg Sperm Fly, 2-8; Fat Freddies, 3/0-2. **Streamers** Alevin, 6-10; Alaskan Smolt, 2-6; Black-nosed Dace, 2-8; Coronation, 2-8; Woolly Buggers and Bunny Flies (white and ginger), 2-6; Egg Sucking Leech, 2-6; Muddler Minnows, 2-8; Woolhead Sculpins, 2-6; Mickey Finn, 2-8; Matuka Streamer, 2-8, Alaska Mary Ann, 2-6. **Nymphs** Bitch Creek, 2-8; Gold Ribbed Hare's Ear, 8-16; Pheasant Tail, 12-14; Woolly Worm, 2-10; Flashabou Nymph, 8-16. **Dries** Adams, 10-16; Back Gnat, 12-18; Blue-Winged Olive, 14-18; Humpy, 10-16; Little Yellow Stone, 12-16, Mouse, 2; Wulff, (royal, gray and white) 6-14.

Salmon/Steelhead Boss, 1/0-6, Krystal Bullet, 4; Alaskabou, Flash Fly, 3/0-4; Maraflash and Sparkle Shrimp, 1/0-4.

United States of America *east*

When hearty Pilgrims from Holland and the British Isles landed on the shores of North America, they found a land of endless forests of spruce and pine. Rivers were thick with spawning Atlantic salmon. Their landlocked cousins abounded in long, cold lakes carved in the rolling plains by glaciers. Boggy streams and kettle ponds, the color of dark morning tea, held brightly speckled brook trout.

We know what happened. Rivers that carried the salmon were dammed in the 1800s to provide power for mills. The vast forests were cut, feeding timber to the factories that milled the lumber that built the houses in cities and towns. Every scrap of arable land was cleared for farming. And the fish were netted and caught without regard. By the early 1900s, the land was played out, rivers flowed thick with sediment and industrial waste, and the fish were gone away.

The recovery of these waters has been nothing short of miraculous. Atlantic salmon, the most prized of the salmonids, are again found in such rivers as the Connecticut and Merrimack, though not in fishable populations. Brook trout have returned to much of their native range, and introductions of brown and rainbow trout – while a questionable practice today – have created viable fisheries in many rivers such as the Housatonic where none existed before. Smallmouth bass, a most spirited fighter, provides lively sport in waters too warm for trout. And runs of bluefish and striped bass, up to 37 lbs, bow the fly rods of anglers who fish beaches near estuaries and the waters of inland bays.

Quaint coastal towns, once ports for tall-masted clipper ships, offer traveling anglers accommodation and refreshment in homes that date from the 1700s. So too do inland crossroad communities, where you'll find charming bed-and-breakfasts in houses of colonial style. Grand mansions of the Victorian era, built as vacation homes for wealthy industrialists and now running as lodges or inns, dot the shores of many lakes. And here and there are old sporting lodges of peeled log and stone, where the first fly fishers in America compared their notes and sired the fly patterns we use today.

Tourism and fishing are big business in the East. L.L. Bean, which gained fame by supplying sportsmen and -women for treks deep in New England's forests, hangs its shingle in Freeport, Maine, and it is open 24 hours a day. Orvis, founded in 1853 and known for both its bamboo and graphite rods, is headquartered in the old resort town of Manchester, Vermont. There you'll find the American Fly Fishing Museum and the Equinox, a grand and historic four-star hotel.

Americans have taken to fly fishing like bees to pollen, and you are apt to find swarms of anglers on the most accessible stretches of public water. One answer is to check with a local tackle shop –

Left **Freestone rivers predominate in the northeastern United States.**

Opposite **Falls on the famed Beaverkill where American dry fly fishing was born.**

there is at least one in every town near good trout water – and hire a guide who has the right of entry to private sections of the river.

Another option is to equip yourself with one of the many good regional fishing guidebooks and a set of maps, and to strike off on your own (asking permission, of course, of the owners of the private land you wish to cross). Or book a stay in one of a number of lodges that specialize in fishing. Tariffs for lodges vary from a few hundred dollars to a couple thousand per week and usually provide fishing on private stretches of very good water. In most, but not all cases, you get what you pay for.

Each state sets its own seasons (some of which differ from river to river), regulations, and license fees. Some states charge an additional fee for a "trout" license or permit. Fee fisheries, that is rivers to which access is granted with the purchase of a daily ticket as is the case on most good waters in Europe, are few but increasing in number. Virtually all states have set aside waters that are restricted to fly fishing only and many of those mandate catch-and-release angling.

Maine

This, the easternmost state in the US, has the fewest people per square mile and the greatest number of fishable lakes and waters in the region. The craggy coastline provides some opportunity, especially around Portland, Bath, and Boothbay Harbor, to fly-fish for saltwater striped bass. Fishing is best from the summer months into early fall when the bass begin to migrate south along the Atlantic coast. As one would expect, marinas are abundant and charter boats fairly easy to find.

But you may have to look for a bit to find a captain who understands fly fishing. L.L. Bean can offer recommendations.

Landlocked salmon – a *Salmo salar* subspecies trapped in freshwater during periods of continental glaciation – open the inland fishing season in early May when winter ice leaves the state's lakes. Lake trout begin to strike then too. Some of the best action is found on Grand Lake, a long watercourse that shares the US border with New Brunswick, Canada, about 30 miles south of Houlton. On other lakes such as West Grand Lake near the pristine village of Grand Lake Stream, on Moosehead Lake north of Greenville, and in the Rangely Lakes area near the New Hampshire border, you'll troll big salmon flies – Grey Ghosts, 93s and Black Dace – and salmon of 3 to 6½ lbs will smack them. Best be there early in the season. As the water warms, these salmon move deeper and eventually beyond the reach of conventional fly tackle. In the swift outlets of some lakes, particularly Grand Lake Stream, the west branch of the Penobscot, and the Moose River, landlocked salmon can be caught on a fly all summer long and into the deep fall.

Atlantic salmon are also making a comeback in Maine, though fishing for them is much better in New Brunswick to the east. The Machias River has a small run of Atlantic salmon as well.

Brook trout, too, grow big in the isolated lakes and streams of Maine. "Speckled trout," as they're called locally, sometimes top 2 lbs in larger lakes and in ponds that are seldom fished. Among the best brook trout waters in Maine are Lake Millinocket at Libby Camps (not the Millinocket Lake near the town of the same name), the Rangely Lakes area, and numerous ponds in the

streams that connect them. After ice-out in May, these lakes fish well for landlocked salmon and lake trout. As the season progresses, brook trout and browns can be caught on traditional fly patterns. And even in the heat of August, a nymph dredged through a spring hole will produce a nice trout. Perhaps the loveliest time to fish these waters is in the waning days of September, when maples turn yellow and red and birch flutter gold in the sun. Fish for brookies and browns then, brilliant in their spawning colors. Treat them well and there will be more fish come spring.

Among the most storied streams in New England is the Battenkill at Manchester, Vermont. This river sees much pressure – it flows, literally, through Orvis's back yard – but it is still a good bet for 10 inches brookies and browns taken on small – 14-18 – mayfly and caddis imitations. From the town of Arlington south and west to the New York state line, the river slows and widens. Bigger brown trout of 12 to 16 inches predominate, nice fish for a three-weight system. Manchester is loaded with colonial bed-and-breakfasts and first-rate historic inns. And the fine restaurants in this town will not leave an educated palate unsatisfied.

New York

If a traveling angler must make no more than one stop in the eastern United States, he or she might want to consider the Beaverkill/Upper Delaware River region on the western flanks of the Catskill Mountains about three hours north of New York City. This is where dry-fly fishing in America was born of patterns developed on England's chalk streams. History is a palpable presence on the Beaverkill. The spirits of Theodore Gordon, who pioneered American dry-fly fishing, and Lee Wulff, that innovative angler who fathered the fishing vest and explored so many of the North American sport fisheries that we enjoy today, haunt these streams.

vicinity of Portage about 18 miles due west of Presque Isle. Ever voracious, brookies will strike most well-presented streamers, nymphs or dries, and they are not finicky about size. Bigger fish are often trolled in late May but the fishing does not peak until June and July.

The biggest surprise in Maine waters is the resurgence of the smallmouth bass. These scrappy fighters will smash a streamer in spring or fall and, in the summertime, slam surface poppers and frog imitations with utter abandon. And once hooked, smallmouth battle with all the heart of a welterweight boxer. A fight with a smallmouth of even 1 lb isn't over until it's brought to net. A warm-water fish,

smallmouth are found in most of the lakes and rivers in the state. Among the most productive are the Kennebec and Penobscot rivers and Lake Sebago.

New Hampshire/Vermont

These two states sit like fraternal twins, divided by the Connecticut River. The upper reaches of this river, above Colebrook, New Hampshire, is one of the better year-round fisheries for brown trout, some as large as 6½ lbs. At Stewartstown, the river jogs east ascending into the Connecticut Lakes area. There you'll find Lake Francis, the four Connecticut Lakes, numerous ponds and the

dating from the 1850s. Now managed as a trophy trout (browns to 35 inches!) fishery, anglers pay a fee for four hours on a private beat. Strictly first come, first served, this state park treats each guest as if he or she were a member of the club.

Pennsylvania

Just as American dry-fly angling was pioneered on the storied Beaverkill, it was refined by Vincent Marinaro whose landmark A *Modern Dry-Fly Code* is the bible (now out of print) for spring creek anglers in the US. Marinaro and his henchman, Charlie Fox, did their work on the Letort, as fine a limestone creek and as frustrating as you'll find anywhere in the world. The browns that grow to 23 inches beneath the flowing cresses of this utterly clear stream don't get that big through foolishness. Stealth, precise casting of small flies with fine leaders, and close imitation of naturals is essential for an angler to be successful. Yet during a hatch of sulfurs or tricos on a warm summer's evening, one may be fortunate.

This is a year-round fishery, and the hamlet of Boiling Springs, nearby is the site of a fine tackle store as well as a number of inns and bed-and-breakfasts that cater to anglers.

Traveling to the USA

Travelers may need a visitor's visa. Refer to page 145 for further information.

Most of the Beaverkill is private, but a stay in Larry Rockefeller's Beaverkill Valley Inn, or a sojourn at Joan Wulff's fly-fishing school, among the best in the United States, will give you access to the browns (up to 17 inches) in a mile of its hallowed waters. About 30 miles west is the confluence of the east and west branches of the Delaware River. Constantly cooled by flows from two reservoirs, these waters consistently produce rainbows of 20 inches and more. Fishing peaks in mid- to late summer. Several lodges host anglers

who fish the upper Delaware, but the ultimate and least commercial of them is Starlight Lodge, a huge log bed-and-breakfast that's off the river. Serious anglers who tie their own flies will feel right at home here.

If your travel brings you into New York City, plan to spend a day fishing Connetquot State Park Preserve near the town of Islip on central Long Island. This spring-fed creek was once the exclusive property of the Southside Sportsman's Club, a gentleman's hunting and fishing club

Tackle and flies for fishing in the eastern US is specie-dependent. For trout and smallmouth bass, generally speaking, a six-weight system with a 10 foot rod and a disk drag reel loaded with a weight-forward floating line will meet most angling requirements. But for streams like the Beaverkill, Battenkill, and Letort, a three-weight system, again with weight-forward floating line, may allow a more delicate presentation. Casts are not long, but they should be accurate.

For trolled salmon, an eight- or nine-weight system is required. Again, the reel should have a smooth disk drag and at least 100 yards of backing. You can use this system for saltwater striped bass, but most anglers prefer longer 10-foot rods in ten-

weights with shooting heads – short, heavy sections of fly line tied to a lightweight running line. With a shooting head, one can generally cast 25 percent farther than with a standard weight-forward line. And the added energy will turn over big poppers and streamers that striped bass so love.

Wading is the technique employed for fishing most of the waters in the eastern US. Water temperatures may be cold so three-mil neoprenes may feel good. Or don long underwear under your trousers and use a breathable wader with a Gore-Tex membrane. Felt-soled wading boots are important. Anglers who fish fall runs of saltwater striped bass will appreciate chest-high neoprenes.

Trout *Dries* Blue-Winged Olives, 14-20; Midges, 20-26; Sulfurs, 14-18; Isonychia, 10-16; Light Cahill, 12-18; Trico, 20-24; Caddis, 12-16; Ants 14-18; Hoppers, 8-12; Henderickson, 12-16; Royal Coachman; 12-16; Adams, 10-16; Pale Morning Dun, 12-18. **Wets** Scuds, 12-18; Hare's Ear, 10-16; Pheasant Tail, 10-16; Prince; 10-16; Woolly Bugger, 10-14; Mickey Finn, 6-10; Hornberg, 6-8.

Salmon *Grey Ghost, Ninety-three; Black-nosed Dace; Royal Coachman Bucktail, all 4-8.*

Smallmouth *Crayfish, Hellgrammite, Woolly Bugger, Clouser Minnow, Dahlberg's Diver, all 2-4; Poppers, 2-6.*

Striped Bass *Skipping Bug, 2/0-2; Clouser Minnow, 2/0-4; Deceivers, 2/0-2; Spearing, 1/0.*

United States of America *south*

From the string of coral islands that probes the subtropics to the barren heights of the oldest mountains in North America, the southern United States is a region of considerable contrast. Running from Maryland southwestward into Alabama, the Appalachian Mountains form the region's backbone. Mountain streams run cold and provide good habitat for rainbow and brown trout and for little native brook trout as gloriously colored as wild flowers. Lower, on the piedmont, massive impoundments harbor largemouth bass and those rivers that flow swiftly carry smallmouth bass. Below the lowest falls on the river, the coastal plain is pocked with tangled black-water swamps until it gives way to beaches pounded by surf that holds striped bass, and further south, tarpon, snook, redfish, and bonefish.

In the mountains a light jacket may feel good even at the height of August's summer heat, and in the depths of winter on the Florida Keys, there are still days of sweltering humidity. During prime fishing seasons of spring and fall, mornings may be frosty on the uplands with afternoons more than shirtsleeve warm. In summer coastal areas are pounded by afternoon thunderstorms and the mountains receive about 1 inch of rain every three days. Fall and winter are typically drier than spring and summer.

Settled by pioneers from the British Isles, the South was, and is still, primarily an agricultural region. While cities – Washington DC, Charlotte, Atlanta, Miami, New Orleans, and Dallas/Fort Worth – are as urban as any in the world, their suburbs soon diminish and become countryside.

Tourist amenities are concentrated along the Atlantic and Gulf coasts and in mountain valleys. Aside from those resort areas, accommodation and restaurants are apt to be modest, but it's generally possible to find a place that is clean and quiet and where food is simple and good. Where there is quality sport fishing near coastal and mountain resort towns, you will find guides and tackle stores that cater to anglers. On major lakes managed by the Corps of Engineers or the Tennessee Valley Authority are a number of marinas where guides with boats can be hired. Fishing is very good throughout the region, but it might only be termed world-class in a few locales. Seasons are generally open all year, although specific waters may be closed in an attempt to manage the fishery.

North Carolina

On the western border of the state rise the highest mountains of the Appalachians, and some of the tallest peaks are contained in the Great Smoky Mountain National Park. This is the most heavily visited of more than 300 national parks in the United States. Yet it is largely inaccessible by road, and it offers anglers opportunities to fish for brown and rainbow trout up to about 15 inches. Though the lands of the park are shared by the states of Tennessee and North Carolina, the better angling is on the eastern or North Carolina side of the park.

Of particular interest are five freestone streams: Eagle, Hazel, Forney, Noland, and Deep Creeks. Of the quintet, only Deep Creek can be reached by paved road. The others require a boat trip across Fontana Lake or a hike up and over the lower ridges of the Smokies. Open to angling throughout the year (as of this writing), park

Left **Mountain streams of the Southern Appalachians are known for fine brookies, browns and rainbows.**
Right **Rivers of the foothills abound with feisty smallmouth bass.**

streams fish best in spring and fall. Stocking of trout was abandoned in the mid-1970s. The result has been the development of a fairly aggressive brown-trout fishery that grades into rainbows as the velocity of the streams increases with elevation. In the headwaters of these creeks are protected populations of a unique strain of brook trout found only in the Southern Appalachians.

When Fontana Lake was created in the 1940s, its rising waters forced the abandonment of many small mountain hamlets along the creeks. The largest was on Hazel Creek where today remnants of the town can still be seen. A railroad right-of-

way parallels the creek providing easy walking for anglers. You reach the road by boat from Fontana Marina. The course of Deep Creek is also shadowed by a road for just over a mile. Then, as is the case with Eagle, Forney and Noland, anglers follow well-marked trails.

Numerous primitive campsites are available in the watersheds of these creeks, and all that's required is proper equipment, food, and registration with the National Park Service. Bryson City, North Carolina, is the closest town to Deep Creek, and there you will find an array of motels and bed-and-breakfasts. Fontana Village

Resort occupies an entire community that was built to house workers who built the dam. Their houses have been turned into guest cottages and motels and cabins with kitchens have been added during the past few decades.

Is the fishing in the Great Smoky Mountains on par, say, with that in Yellowstone National Park in the State of Wyoming? Definitely not. Yet in June, when boughs heavy with the pink-tinged blossoms of mountain laurel bend and touch streams flowing slick and black, where deer come to drink, and where a 12 inch brown rises and sips your little Adams, there are much worse places to be.

Georgia

The oh-so-gently rolling forests of south Georgia are cut by sluggish rivers that hold little fascination for anglers. But on vast private plantations, some assembled prior to the American Civil War, numerous ponds and small lakes boast significant populations of largemouth bass. They range from 3 to 15 lbs and readily take poppers and hairbody bugs presented with fly tackle.

Numerous tiny creeks in the mountains of northern Georgia around the town of Helen offer anglers sport with wild rainbows and browns, the Chatahoochee River from the base of Buford Dam all the way to downtown Atlanta provides a quality, tailwater fly fishery. While some of the fish are stocked, the section just north of Atlanta's city limits has a reasonable population of good-sized browns. And the city includes a wide variety of tackle stores as well as, of course, accommodation.

Florida

Florida is one state with two distinct cultures. There's old Florida, the land of cattle ranches, citrus groves, and massive vegetable farms. This is largemouth bass country, and it's renowned

throughout the world. Then there's the Florida of the subtropics, that string of reef-like islands and their bonefish flats that separate the Atlantic Ocean from the Gulf of Mexico.

Bass fishing is big business in Florida and its headquarters is at Roland Martin's Lakeside Marina in Clewiston on Lake Okeechobee. This, broad, shallow lake covers more than 730 square miles, and contains outstanding habitat – grassy beds, flooded stumps, natural channels, submerged reefs, and hectares of reeds and lily pads – for largemouth bass. Some will argue that there are better bass lakes, but none is so consistent throughout the year as Lake Okeechobee. Even in the heat of high summer when temperatures on the lake can reach 60°F, fishing early and late in the day can bring explosive action from bass in the 3 to 6½ lbs range. Fish run larger in spring and fall. Poppers and hairbody frog imitations are the most effective fly patterns for bass anglers, most of whom use eight-weight, weight-forward systems. The fly fisher who seeks pure sport will bring a light three- or four-weight and toss small poppers and big nymphs for slab-sized bream.

Roland Martin is one of America's premier bass anglers, and his operation in Clewiston includes motel and condominium accommodation, a restaurant, and marina where guests can hire guides, rent boats, and buy some tackle. Fly fishers are advised to bring their own gear. This is the land of the bait-casting rod and spinner bait.

Lake Okeechobee is the headwaters of the Everglades, a 68-mile-wide, 6-inch-deep freshwater river that flows into Florida Bay. The Everglades provides good wilderness fishing for largemouth and far to the south, in the vicinity of Flamingo where the water becomes saline, for snook, redfish, and tarpon. The angler who seeks those species will be well served by a visit to the Florida Keys.

Stretching from Miami on the north to Key West, the southernmost point in the United States, the Florida Keys offer excellent angling for

a variety of species. On the flat marl shoals to the east of these small islands, bonefish school and feed on shrimp and crab. On the edges of the flats and over sunken hulks in the channel, you'll find an occasional permit as well. Bonefishing is at its height from September to November and again from February through April. While schools of bonefish are larger in the Bahamas across the Gulf Stream to the east, the size of bonefish in the keys is typically larger – 4 to 9 lbs. Anglers fish from flats boats, low shallow-draft outboards that are poled across the clay shoals which bonefish search for food. It is generally not possible to wade here because of the soft bottom. The best bonefishing in the Keys is centered on the area between Islamorada to the north and Marathon to the south. Further down the Keys tarpon grow more plentiful. These big fish with their large silvery scales range from 35 to 125 lbs. The prime months for these are April and May.

The biggest problems with fishing in Florida's keys are three: wind, tourists, and which species to pursue. Wind blows almost incessantly from gentle zephyrs that barely flutter a flag to the hurricanes of late summer and fall. You can count on a steady breeze that intensifies toward midday and dies in early evening. Cheap airfares into Miami and good highways make the Keys an all-season tourist destination. Who can escape the allure of regal palms, soaring birds, and shallow seas that turn from azure to topaz with the tide? Finally, there's the question of which fish – bonefish, tarpon, permit, snook or redfish? The answer to that one is easy. Spend a week and fish for them all.

Traveling to the USA

Travelers may need a visitor's visa. Refer to page 145 for further information.

TACKLE AND FLIES

For fishing in the Appalachians including the mountains of Virginia, North Carolina, Tennessee and Virginia, a three-weight rod of 6 to 9 feet is ideal. Waters are apt to be low and clear when the fishing is best and presentations should be reasonably delicate. Weight-forward and double-taper lines work quite well. Casts need not be long. Fine leaders (5X and smaller) of 10 to 11 feet are almost essential. Felt-soled wading shoes are very important as are lightweight chest-high waders. The water is often deeper than it looks.

For largemouth, an eight-weight system is ample. Leaders need to be strong enough (3½ lbs)

to pull bass out of the thick cover they favor.

A bass rod will be adequate for most light saltwater use, but an 11 foot, nine-weight rod will work better. Often you'll be forced to cast into the wind. A nine- or ten-weight rod loaded with a saltwater taper line will provide the power you need. If you're headed out for tarpon, plan on a 12-weight system. A 100-lb fish requires lots of backbone.

Trout *Dries Male Adams, 12-16; Elk Wing Caddis, 12-18; Blue-Wing Olive, 12-18; Blue Quill, 16; Royal Wulff, 10-16; March Brown, 12-16; Light Cahill, 12-16; Yellow Palmer, 12-16; Gnats, 20-24; Adams, 20-24; Black Ants, 12-16; Hoppers, 10-14.* **Nymphs** *Hare's Ear, Tellico, Pheasant Tail,*

Brown/Dark Stonefly, Zug Bug, all 12-18. **Streamers** *Woolly Bugger, 10-16; Muddler Minnow, 6-8; Black-Nose Dace, 6-12; Little Rainbow, 6-12.*

Bass *Dahlberg's Diver in purple, frog, and black, 2; Frog, 2-6; Hare Water Pup, 1/0; Chug Bugs, 2-6; Wiggle One, 2-6.*

Bonefish *Crazy Charlie, 4-6; Del's Merkin, 2/0-6; Crab, 1/0-2.*

Tarpon *Deceivers, 2/0-2; Huff's Tarpon Fly, 4/0-2/0.*

Snook *Deceivers, 2/0-2; Skipping Bug, 2/0-2; Clouser Minnows, 2/0-6.*

United States of America *west*

From the storied golden triangle where Idaho, Montana, and Wyoming meet to the famed tailwaters of Arizona, New Mexico, and Utah, the western third of the United States offers some of the finest angling for trout and salmon in the world. Pushed up by volcanism and the collision of continental plates, the rugged Rocky Mountain chain marks the eastern rim of the region. The Coast and Cascade ranges, running north from Los Angles, into Canada at Vancouver, define the area's western boundary. Vast high plains lie in between. In the hot and arid south, they are desert, studded with tufts of creosote bush and sage. To the north where snow covers the ground for much of the winter, grasses and stands of lodgepole pine prevail. With the exceptions of the rainforests of the Pacific Northwest, the western slopes of the Sierra Nevada and the heavily timbered highlands of Yellowstone and surrounding mountains, the West is quite dry.

Yet heavy mountain snows, born of moisture-laden Pacific winds, feed hundreds of streams and rivers. Big rivers brawl around boulders and plunge through deep gorges racing through long green

Opposite **The Green River below Flaming Gorge Dam, in Utah, is perhaps the best tailwater fishery in the West.**

Left **Browns and rainbows average 15 to 16 inches on rivers in the West.**

Below **With its geysers and bubbling fumaroles, Yellowstone National Park is one of the most exciting fisheries in the world.**

pools accessible only by daring raft travel. Rivulets as clear as ether seep from the bases of rocky slopes and coalesce into spring creeks that wind through high mountain valleys. Lakes and ponds dot the countryside and estuaries probe the headlands along the Pacific. There is water here to suit the taste and skill of any angler, and they abound with native cutthroat trout, rainbows, steelhead, Dolly Varden (bull trout), stocked brook and brown trout, and a very few grayling.

Because the waters of the West are charged by melting snows, the best fishing is governed by the time during which run-off occurs. Generally speaking, run-off begins in mid- to late May and continues through mid-July. This varies, of course, with each watershed and with the depth of the winter snowpack. Lake fishing is not as greatly impacted by the spring melt as is fishing in rivers

and streams. Tailwaters, the outlets below major flood-control or hydroelectric projects, may or may not be impacted by run-off depending on the water management plan for the region. The months of spring are typically wetter than those of summer, and fall is the driest season. Agricultural interests divert waters from many western rivers during dry periods in late summer and early fall. This results in lower stream flows which endanger trout populations and negatively impact fishing.

Trout thrive in cold Western waters and they grow larger, typically, than in the East or South. Not only is the West home to many of the best trout streams in the United States, but here, too, lives the myth of the cowboy complete with dude ranches, rodeos, and roundups. Even in the sparsest of towns, tourism is big business. Millions of Americans flock to the West each year in autos

and motorhomes. They head for towns like Jackson, Wyoming, and Las Vegas, Nevada, and places off the beaten path. More and more tourists come to fish, and secluded water, in the height of the season between July and the first week of September, is hard to find.

But it does exist. Much of the land in the West is owned by the federal government and thus open to public fishing. Several National Parks and National Recreation Areas provide anglers with quality waters in natural settings. Lands owned by the National Forest Service or Bureau of Land Management also include miles and miles of public fishing, but some of the waters on these lands may be private because the acreage is leased to commercial concerns. Anglers willing to walk a mile or two can find excellent fishing and solitude as well. Those with larger pocketbooks can avail

themselves of literally thousands of fishing guides and lodges, many of which fish private water.

Anglers must purchase nonresident licenses for each state in which they plan to fish. Typically, nonresidents may choose between buying a license for a few days or the entire annual season. In addition, some states may require special permits to fish for specific species. Also, many National Forests, Parks, and Recreation Areas charge entrance fees and some National Parks, such as Yellowstone, require anglers to purchase a fishing permit.

Each state sets limits for the waters within its boundaries. Some rivers, especially those that are managed as "Trophy Trout" or "Fly Fishing Only," may limit anglers to keeping only one or two fish which must be in excess of a specified length, say 20 inches. Other waters are posted as "No Kill" or "Catch and Release." On these, you can catch all the fish you wish, but you must let them go unharmed. The voluntary catch-and-release ethic thrives among anglers who fish the splendid waters

of the West, and it is one of the reasons why these rivers consistently produce very good fish.

Major airports are generally no more than half a day's drive from good fishing. Rental cars are readily available as is a wide range of accommodation, dining, and shopping. And in the regions where fishing is just barely better than good, you'll find stores with reasonable supplies of sophisticated tackle for the fly-fisher.

Southern Rockies

Arizona and New Mexico, and north of them, Utah and Colorado, comprise the southern tier of the Rocky Mountain States. Though nearly as dry as a desert, Arizona and its neighbor to the east, New Mexico, boast a pair of year-round fisheries where angling for rainbow trout is superb. In northern Arizona, Glen Canyon Dam impounds Lake Powell, and below the dam, the Colorado River flows icy cold and clear as Waterford crystal. Immediately below the dam, the river enters a

deep canyon of red sandstone. It traces a sinuous 16-mile course over thick beds of aquatic grasses, home to freshwater shrimp and insect larva on which rainbows of up to 23 inches feed.

For a few miles south of Lee's Ferry, the river flows across the valley floor before plunging into the 5,000-foot-deep Grand Canyon. Raft trips down through the Grand Canyon depart from Lee's Ferry, and so do anglers who ride jet boats up the river to fish below the dam. Rainbows in the river spawn from November into March, and fishing egg patterns can be awesome then. Midge imitations are effective in spring after the spawn, and nymphs, fished in the riffles, work well through the hot days of summer. It is possible to wade the river in the vicinity of Lee's Ferry, but it will be crowded. The best bet is hiring a guide to fish the water from Glen Canyon south. Lee's Ferry boasts two motels, the better of which is Lee's Ferry Lodge next door to Lee's Ferry Anglers, a complete fly shop and guiding service.

A day's drive east across the barren rocky

*Opposite and right **Flowing along the Yellowstone River is Armstrong Spring Creek, known for its marvelous hatches.***

plateau will put you in northern New Mexico, at Navajo Dam on the San Juan River. Before the dam was built in the 1960s the only trout in the San Juan were found in its headwaters in the southern Rockies. Today, the San Juan is one of the premier year-round tailwater fisheries in the United States. Water exits the dam at a consistent 42°F, and, through the 3½-mile fly-fishing-only section below the dam, remains in the mid-50s even in hottest days of summer. Rainbows up to 20 inches cluster closer to the dam and further downstream, browns up to 30 inches dominate. The fly-fishing-only section has ample public access, but it will be crowded. You'll find more room if you hire a guide and float the river from the dam toward town.

These fish are wary; they see a lot of flies. But competition for food is also keen among the trout, and careful anglers can be quite successful no matter which season they fish. Good patterns – midges, San Juan Worms and brassies – tend to be small: 18-24. The river is susceptible to high water during spring run-off from May to mid-June. But then the river broadens using myriad channels through willow flats. You can sight-fish to rainbows lying in these little streams. Stealth, here, spells success. The town of Navajo Dam contains two motels, two restaurants, and three fly shops that offer guiding and floats on the river.

With more than 6,800 miles of trout streams, Colorado has better than its fair share of great fishing. Most of it is concentrated in the high flat plateaus and rugged hills west of the Rocky Mountains. Much of the water is in private hands, but when you consider the abundance of trout mileage, relatively little is accessible only by paying a fee. While some of the rivers in Colorado are open for year-round angling, winters are snowy,

long, and hard. Best fishing is in spring before run-off begins in May and after it ends in June. Fall, when aspens turn golden and their leaves quake in the autumn sun, is a marvelous time to fish for native cutthroat trout and browns, rainbows, and brookies. Among the better rivers are the Blue, Dolores, Gunnison, Elk, North and South Platte, and White. Lakes and ponds also provide some trout fishing, but rivers are better. Most of the rivers are freestone. And most can be waded. Colorado boasts scores of ranches and lodges that offer guided fishing on private and public water.

In Utah, the best fly fishing by far is found on the wild and scenic Green River below Flaming Gorge Dam at the town of Dutch John. The fishery is very similar to that at Lee's Ferry. The river flows through a deep cleft in the mountains, and floating is the best way to find good fish: rainbows, cutthroats, and browns. Walk-in access is limited to a few boat launch ramps on public lands on the north side. However, working the edges of this constantly cool clear river can pay dividends. Trout lying in pools where trails follow the river are fairly used to seeing people. Patience and a careful presentation will often yield good fish, despite foot traffic nearby. The Green fishes best from April through October, and even when it is swelled with run-off, anglers take good trout in the 12 to 20 inch range. Dutch John lacks much in services and motels, but the needs of visiting anglers are more than met by Flaming Gorge Lodge. Here you'll find a restaurant and accommodations and a store which sells licenses, flies, and tackle.

Northern Rockies

At the turn of the last century, the focus of fly fishing in the United States was in the Catskill Mountains north of New York City. But in the 1970s that began to shift westward to where Idaho, Montana, and Wyoming meet near Yellowstone National Park. Robert Redford's movie, *A River Runs Through It*, whetted the American appetite for fly fishing and popularized fishing in the west. It has been, and is, a curse and a blessing. Fishing pressure is very heavy on public waters and more and more are being restricted to private access. To find solitude requires a trek of a few miles away from a road. Yet the popularity of fly fishing has spawned scores of first-class fly shops, guides, and resorts that cater to anglers. These are a boon to the traveling fly fisher. In addition, many of the improvements in tackle, patterns, and gear were pioneered to meet the special needs of these waters.

Winter in these three states is as bitter and long as spring; summer and fall are lovely. The Bighorn and Beaverhead Rivers in Montana can be fished in winter, but basically the best angling is found before meltwaters flood streams in May, after run-off recedes in mid-June or early July, and from September 1 to mid-October. Fall fishing has several advantages. Crowds are normally gone, brown and brook trout are approaching the spawn, and the countryside is utterly beautiful. Yellow leaves of birch, aspen, and cottonwood flutter in the wind against the loden forest of lodgepole pine and spruce. Early snows mantle mountain peaks in white and drive deer and elk and grizzly bear down to their winter ranges.

A recent survey by Trout Unlimited identified Henry's Fork in Idaho as among the most popular trout streams in the United States. The accolade is justly deserved. Most of the river flows through public land and is readily accessible to anglers who wade, though many fish the river from drift boats. Floaters generally launch below the dam at Island Park and drift down through a shallow canyon of pocket water. At Last Chance, the river slows and takes on the character of a spring creek. Below Osborne bridge, Henry's Fork picks up speed, heading for Mesa Falls. All three sections are good, fishing well from after run-off into October. The hamlet of Last Chance includes a very good fly shop, and a few miles south on Route 20, you'll find Henry's Fork Lodge, an eclectic world-class resort dedicated to fly fishing.

The lodge is about an hour south of Yellowstone National Park, which contains some of the best trout streams in the United States: the Yellowstone, Gibbon, Madison, and Firehole; Slough Creek and the Lamar; and the headwaters of the Snake. Each has slightly different character: from the exotic Firehole with its geysers and smoking mud pots and the gentle ribbon of the upper pasture section of the Gibbon, to the broad cobble bottom of the Madison and the crashing descent of the Yellowstone as it fights its way out of the canyon. Cutthroat are the trout native to the park, but all other species – rainbows, browns, lake trout, and brookies – have been introduced. And, while fishing the park's streams, you'll want to keep an eye out for bison and grizzly bears. Elk

roam the lower elevations in fall.

High water plagues the park until late June. Streams on the western side where mountains are lower reach fishable levels first. July and August are the months of heaviest fishing pressure (and the greatest traffic congestion). But in September until the park closes with the first snows in October, fishing can be stunning. AmFac Resorts operates six hotels in Yellowstone and the towns closest to the park's gates – Cody and Jackson in Wyoming and West Yellowstone and Gardiner in Montana – all support good tackle dealers.

The rivers that rise in Yellowstone also fish well outside the park, though private land may limit access. In addition, southwestern Montana fairly brims with trout rivers: the Bighorn, Big

Opposite **The Railroad Ranch section of Henry's Fork in Idaho requires a deft touch with light leaders for huge rainbows.**
Above **Time melts from your shoulders when you drift-fish Idaho's Snake in September.**

Hole, Beaverhead, Bitteroot, Missouri, Ruby, and Wise. The state of Idaho is equally rich in first rate fly-fishing rivers – Salmon, Selway, Silver, Snake, and Lochsa are among the finest waters. In southern Wyoming, there's the North Platte and Clark's Fork of the Yellowstone flows east from the Beartooth Range near Yellowstone before turning north into Montana. Guest ranches, bed-and-breakfasts, motels, and resorts abound as do guides and fly shops.

Pacific Coastal States

Humid winds blowing in from the Pacific rise as they meet the Coast and Cascade Mountain Ranges. Condensing moisture falls as rain – in some cases more than ¼ inch per day – providing rivers with abundant fresh charges of water. Cutthroat trout and salmon run up the rivers of the Coast Range to spawn. Many of the same rivers have populations of native cutthroat trout which, in some streams, run to the sea to feed. Though there are many fine rivers in California, Oregon, and Washington, the greatest fly fishing is angling for steelhead on Washington's Olympic Peninsula and on Oregon's North Umpqua River. Steelhead and salmon run in California's coastal rivers from the mouth of the Sacramento at San Francisco (a great striped bass fishery as well) to the Oregon Border.

But the best fly fishing in California is not for steelhead but for browns and rainbows in the high mountains and broad valley forests east of Interstate 5 and north of Redding. Waters offer wide variety from pocket water and broad runs of the Upper Sacramento, to the swirling pools of the upper McCloud, to Hat Creek, the most famous of California's trout streams. Hat Creek begins as a freestone stream on the slopes of Mt Lassen, but it slows and becomes a classic meadow stream of many meanders as it flows across the fertile Hat Creek Valley floor.

Joined by the Rising River just above Cassel, Hat Creek takes on all the characteristics of a spring creek. Below Cassel and above Lake Britton is a section of trophy water that the authors of *California Blue Ribbon Trout Streams* describe as both a fisherman's dream and a fisherman's nightmare. The water is very clear, calling for tiny flies and small tippets, and is known for multiple hatches occurring at the same time. Browns and rainbows of 2 to 6½ lbs feed warily on the smallest patterns except during the golden stonefly hatch in late May/early June. Fishing is good through the hot summer months and peaks with hatches of the October caddis.

A full day's drive north will carry you to Roseburg, Oregon, the turn-off to reach the North Umpqua River. The American author Zane Grey made his millions writing Westerns, but his passion was angling. He traveled the globe seeking world-record big-game saltwater species. From his early years on the upper Delaware River in Pennsylvania, fast waters claimed his summer ardor, and of the rivers he loved best was the one he came to at the end of his life, the North Fork of the Umpqua with its wonderful populations of steelhead. It was here that he suffered the stroke that ultimately took his life. Today the river is changed from the 1930s when he fished it. Logging caused flooding and siltation, but now restrictions limit the adverse effects of lumbering operations and the river is again fishing well. The river takes its name from the word for "thundering waters" in the language of the Yoncalla Indians, and indeed the roar of rapids fills the narrow valley. About 30 miles of the river is reserved for fly fishing only. Anglers wade with caulked, felt-soled shoes and wading staffs. Rocks are big and slippery and the current is swift. The best months are July through October and the best time of day to fish is early morning from dawn until the sun tops the Cascades to the east. Fish of 6½ to 9 lbs are possible though many will be smaller. As the season progresses, the water drops and clears and successful patterns become smaller. Plan to stay on the river at Steamboat Inn, a charming and secluded lodge built by the steelhead angler and conservationist Jim Van Loan. Scrumptious meals are prepared by his wife Sharon and her partner Pat Lee. The inn maintains a very good stock of steelhead patterns and tackle.

The Coast Range terminates in the Olympic Mountains on the peninsula by the same name in western Washington state. Rains that nourish thick spruce and fir forests, punctuated by white birches and patches of devil's club, also fill the wonderful steelhead rivers of the Bogachiel, Sol Duc, and Queets. Of these, the Sol Duc stands out. Three distinct runs of steelhead keep the river supplied with these bright silver fighters all year long. Sockeye move up the river in June, and July brings silver salmon. Chinook use the river in both fall and spring. And sea-run cutthroat follow the salmon up the river to feed on their spawn. While the tiny towns of Beaver and Forks provide motels and restaurants, anglers might consider Brightwater House, a very comfortable bed-and-breakfast with more than half a mile of private river access. Guides are available and tackle can be bought in Port Angeles.

Traveling to the USA

Travelers to the United States may need to obtain a visitor's visa from the United States consulate in a major city or the US embassy in their home countries. Under a pilot program, the US Department of State is waiving visitor visa requirement for citizens of the following countries: Andorra, Argentina, Australia, Austria, Belgium, Brunei, Denmark, Finland, France, Germany, Iceland, Ireland, Italy, Japan, Liechtenstein, Luxembourg, Monaco, the Netherlands, New Zealand, Norway, San Marino, Slovenia, Spain, Sweden, Switzerland, and the UK.

Driving in the USA is on the right-hand side of the road. Because of distances from airports to fishing locations, a rental car is often needed. An international driver's permit is required and may be obtained from the US embassy in your country.

Credit cards and travelers checks are widely accepted, however many fishing lodges and guides require cash. If you are planning to stay at a lodge, make arrangements for payment before you arrive. Otherwise, secure cash from a bank in a city near the locale where you plan to fish.

The waters of the West are so varied – spring creeks in the volcanic valleys of California, big rivers like the Colorado, steelhead streams like the Sol Duc and North Fork of the Umpqua – that traveling anglers must match rod length and weight to the water and species they intend to fish. A five- or six-weight rod of 9 feet or so is generally about right for most trout fishing. Three- and four-weights are ideal for spring creeks and can be used on calm days to take really big fish when they require tiny flies and light leaders. Steelhead demand at least a seven-weight system, but an eight-weight may do a better job of presenting large flies under windy conditions. Even if plans call for fishing only one stream during the trip, bring two rods. Accidents happen and plans change. Floating weight-forward lines are used by most anglers. But well-equipped traveling anglers will have sink-tip and maybe a full sinking lines in their kits.

Emergence charts, showing a schedule of hatching insects and the flies that imitate them, are available for most major Western waters. Local fly shops frequently feature ties that match hatches on nearby rivers or streams. It's best to buy flies there (when you get your license).

Dry-fly fishing is a highly refined art on Western waters, and most anglers prefer dries over wets. On the other hand, nymphs and streamers may take larger fish. An angler should be supplied with both.

Trout *Dries Adams, Blue Winged Olives, Pale Morning Duns, Caddis 14-20; Midges, 20-24; Humpies, 12-18; Golden Stoneflies, 6-8; Hoppers, 6-10; Ants, 14-18.*
Nymphs and Streamers *Stoneflies, 10-12; San Juan Worms, 8-14; Scuds, 12-16; Hare's Ears, 10-16; Pheasant Tails, 12-16; Prince, 8-14; Woolly Buggers, 8-14; Muddler Minnows, 4-12; Brassie, 14-20.*

Steelhead *Egg Sucking Leach, Blue Bruce, Umpqua Special, Black Prince, all 2-6; Purple Peril, 2-8.*

Wales

Two-thirds of Wales is of wonderful highlands
anchored by Snowdon (3,500 feet) and Carnedd
Llewelyn (3,560 feet) near Caernarfon in the
northwesternmost corner of the country, and the
summits of the Brecon Beacons that rise north of
Cardiff in the south. Mountains run through the
center and eastern section of the country, drained
by the headwaters of the Severn, the Wye, and the
Welsh river Dee.

Wales is a small compact country. Though its
8,000 square miles were united with England in
the sixteenth century, the mountainous barrier
between the countries allowed Wales to preserve
its distinctive culture and language of musical lilt.
The official language is English. But 20 percent of
the population speaks Welsh, and most of those
who hold to the native language live in the
western coastal counties.

Swift, cool rivers wend their ways down
through rustic farm valleys, passing quaint villages
on their way to their meetings with salt along the
coast of rock bluff and fine sand beach. Salmon,
sea-run brown trout, and brown trout thrive in
these rivers and the upland streams that feed
them. For purposes of flood control, hydroelectric
power, and recreation many of the headwaters
have been impounded. In many of these reservoirs,
as well as in natural llyns (lochs) and lakes, native
brown trout and migrating salmon and sea-run
browns fish quite well. Often major reservoirs and
rivers receive heavy stocking of browns, sea trout,
salmon or rainbows to offset deterioration of the
watersheds from agricultural, and in the lowlands,
industrial pollution. The deterioration of many

Left **Wales is a wild land, with wonderfully magical trout waters to match.**

Above **Llyn Llydaw is one of dozens of lakes in Snowdonia National Park and it holds fine trout.**

fine Welsh rivers in the middle part of this century left Wales with only a modest reputation as a destination for fly fishers. Why fish in Wales when you have English trout and Scottish salmon? The answer is that you will find excellent grayling and the best sea-trout in the United Kingdom.

Wales is a bit off the beaten path. One is unlikely to find here the crowds that are always attracted to better-known venues. Yet while crowds are few along the rivers and streams of Wales, the percentage of free water is no greater in Wales than in England or Scotland. The Welsh are intent on the resurrection of the rivers of the country, and it shows. In many rivers, long devoid of salmon, these great fish are starting to reappear. Sea trout, "sewin" in local parlance, are returning

too and they provide most of the best game fishing in the country. In the upper reaches, brown-trout fishing can be, in some cases, very good. The pastoral nature of Wales attracts tourists, and many farmers, who tend the sheep and cattle for which Welsh highlands are famous, also operate guest cottages. Small towns boast quaint inns. And if there's good water nearby, you'll find a fly shop close at hand.

As in England, anglers must possess a valid fishing license issued by the state as well as a permit or ticket issued by the proprietor of each particular fishery. Regulations including creel limits and season dates are set by the National Rivers Authority, which can also provide specific information about individual rivers, streams, and lakes. Seasons on each stream are set by the authority.

The North

Resembling the beak on a prehistoric bird, the Caernarfon peninsula juts into the ocean separating Cardigan Bay to the south from the Irish Sea and the island of Anglesey to the north. Snowdon and its sibling peak, Carnedd Llewelyn, rise in the midst of the region, but the land subsides further to the east. From a pair of tarns on the flanks of Snowdon begins a charming, though short, river – the Seiont – with good runs of salmon and brown trout of sea-run and riverine persuasions. The river flows through three lakes in its headwaters and then begins a series of runs, flats and pools until it becomes tidal at Caernarfon. Seiont Manor Hotel at Llanrug has beats for its guests.

Rising in the uplands south of Betws-y-Coed, the Conwy flows north through a lovely valley. Salmon fishing is best in May and June. In the following month, grilse enter the system. Action on sea-run browns begins in June and continues through September. The lower reaches are not particularly good fly fishing, but near Dolgarrog, a series of pools provide brackish water angling for salmon and sea-run browns. The upper stretches of the river are good for salmon and sea-run browns, and tributaries such as the Roe and Penmacho offer good brown trout. The National Trust has fly-fishing-only mileage on the upper Conwy and lets self-catering cottages. The Dolwyddelan also fishes well for salmon and sea-run browns.

Among the most famous rivers in Wales is the Clwyd, highly regarded for its sea-run brown trout in late June and for its salmon in spring and fall. The lower reaches of the river lack holding waters but improves above St Asaph where the river begins a series of pools and runs. Good water continues upstream through Denbigh and past Ruthin. Daily tickets on the best stretches are limited. Foxon's, a tackle dealer who caters to game-fish anglers, in St Asaph and the Black Lion Hotel in Llanfair can provide tickets on the Clwyd and nearby Elwy.

English Border

Britain is blessed with two Rivers Dee. The more famous is the salmon river in Scotland, and the other, for a few miles, serves as the border between England and Wales before entering a wide estuary to the east of Liverpool. Like its Scots cousin, the Welsh Dee sees a good run of heavy salmon. From the headwaters above Bala to where the river breaks out of the uplands west of Llangollen marks the best all-round section of the river. Visiting anglers can book into the Hand Hotel on Bridge Street in Langollen and fish the hotel's water. Near the headwaters, the Pale Hall Country House at Llandderfel offers very good salmon and trout and excellent grayling.

To the south of the Dee flows the Severn. While not a major game-angling river in England, its upper reaches in Wales do hold some salmon and sea-run brown trout as well as wild mountain browns. Two tributaries to the Severn, the Montgomery and the Knighton, offer good angling. The Montgomery is known for trout, salmon, and grayling, and the Knighton for trout only. Rising to the south, but nearby, are the headwaters of the Wye, one of England's best known salmon rivers. Above Hay-on-Wye, the river becomes better fly-fishing water. Though not

Left **Isolated coves offer some angling for sea trout.**

as fine a fishery as in the past, salmon fishing is best here from April through June and again in October. Pools at Rhayader Bridge occasionally produce some very big trout including a Wye record of about 9 lbs. Tributaries also provide good sport. Try Llanbadarn Fynydd and stay in the Lake Country House Hotel.

The South

Rising in the open and grassy highlands of Brecon Beacons National Park (location of Pen-y-Fan, the highest mountain in South Wales), the Usk is a free-stone trout river with occasional salmon. Limestone beds in the lower reaches contribute to the general fertility of the river. Near the headwaters at Crickhowell is Gliffaes Country House Hotel, a fine place to stay while fishing for browns of the Upper Usk. Tributaries of the river, particularly the Honddu, Grwyne, and Yscir, also provide good trout.

To the west is another river with its source in Brecon Beacons, the Taff, which flows into the mouth of the Severn estuary at Cardiff. Once heavily polluted, the Taff seems to be making a miraculous recovery. Fishing for salmon and sea-run browns is good up to Pontypridd, and above, the water hosts brown trout.

A third salmon and sea-run brown river, the Llwchwr, rises in the Taicarn Mountains and reaches salt water at Llanelli. It's known for its runs of sewin, but salmon also seem to be improving. Above Llangennech, the river becomes principally a brown-trout stream with occasional runs of salmon and sewin. Further west is the Towy, which enters the Bristol Channel below Carmarthen. Salmon of 9 lbs are often taken as are sea-run browns of up to 6½ lbs in the lower

reaches and the best time to fish for salmon is May through July; the sea-run browns arrive a month earlier. The river upstream carries good stocks of salmon, sewin, and trout, but much of the water is reserved. The Black Lion Inn at Llansawel controls a 2½-mile stretch of the river and has access on the Cennen, Cothi (an excellent river), and Teifi nearby. The Cothi Bridge Hotel at Nantgaredig offers beats on the Cothi and other preserved rivers.

West Coast

Pembroke Coast National Park, Britain's only national seashore park, rounds the southern peninsula of Wales from Amroth in the south to Cardigan in the north. This delightful blend of splendid sandy beaches and rocky headlands continues up the west coast to Aberdaron. Little fishing villages – more than a baker's dozen of them – dot the coast, and many are the mouths of good salmon and sewin rivers. From the south, at Fishguard there's the Gwaun; at Aberaeron, the

Aeron, and at Aberdyfi, the Dyfi, or Dovey as it's sometimes called. Aberystwyth lies in the center of this region, and it is the most popular seaside resort town in Wales. Here you'll find the Ystwyth, a fine little river for fishing for sewin at night. The west coast of Wales is a marvelous locale for combining a family seaside vacation with serious angling for salmon, sea-run brown trout, and riverine browns.

At Cardigan, the Teifi reaches the sea. From its headwaters in Llyn Teifi, the river has a fine reputation. On the lower mileage, salmon fish well

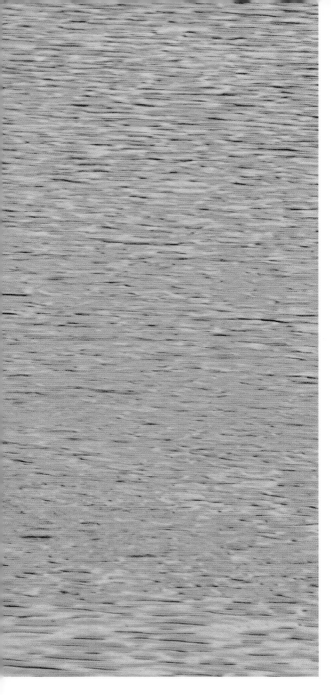

Left **A salmon swirls in the setting sun; what a way to end the day.**

levels the further upriver one goes, but fly fishing for brown trout improves. Guest houses and small hotels abound in the small towns along the Teifi.

As the coast climbs northward, it becomes more rugged and deeply incised by river estuaries. Just up the shore from Tywyn, the Dysynni enters the bay. An exciting river for most of its length, the Dysynni gathers its waters from Cader Idris, feeds Talyllyn Lake, cuts through the uplands before slowing at Peniarth. Fishing for salmon and sewin extends above Talyllyn Lake and into the tributaries. Brown trout is also good here. The lower sections fish best toward the beginning and ends of the season, and the Tynycornel Hotel in Talyllyn provides permits for fishing the upper river and the lake.

The Mawddach at Barmouth is another good western river, so good that it's mostly preserved. Salmon and sewin use the river from June through season's end. The George III Hotel issues permits for 11 miles of the Mawddach, and the nearby Wnion and Llyn Cynach Lake.

Draining the southern flanks of Snowdon is the Glaslyn, which enters Tremadog Bay at Porthmadog. This river is well known for its runs of sewin from May into October. Salmon is improving. Particularly good fishing can be had above the Pass of Aberglaslyn.

Traveling to Wales

As are Scotland and England, Wales is part of the UK and the same travel policies apply. Tourist information offices are found in most cities. International visitors will find excellent information at British consulate offices located in major cities worldwide.

TACKLE AND FLIES

Tackle and flies are much the same as would be used in Scotland: rods, nine- or ten-weight for salmon, six to eight for sewin (sea-run browns), three to six for trout. Weight-forward floating lines with sinking leader systems will do for most fishing. But a full sinking line may have some utility in deep lakes and estuaries.

Salmon *Silver Stuart, Stoat's Tail, Thunder & Lightning, Munroe Killer, Hairy Mary, Executioner, Willie Gunn, Blue Charm, Ally's Shrimp, Black Shrimp, Quin Shrimp, Red Shrimp, 4-12 in single and doubles, and tube ties.*

Sea trout *Teal Blue & Silver, Peter Ross, Black Butcher, Mallard, Claret, Invicta, 8-12.*

Trout *Dries Elk hair Caddis and Black Caddis, 10-14; Olive Compara Dun, 14; Mayfly Dun, 10-14; Adams, 12-16; March Brown 10-12; Lunn's Particular, 16-20; Blue-winged Olive, 14-20; Royal Wulff, 8-12; Stimulator, 10-12; Green Drake, 10-14; Muddlers 8-12.* *Nymphs Gold-ribbed Hare's Ear; Pheasant Tail, Stonefly; 8-12.* **Streamers** *Woolly Bugger in black, brown, and olive, 8-12.*

in April and May and continue throughout the summer. Yet, the better fishing is in September. The Castell Malgwyn Hotel, near Cenarth, controls nearly 2½ miles of good fishing on this portion of the Teifi. Upstream near Cenarth, the river flows over a set of spectacular falls. Fishing in this area is quite good, and the West Wales School of Fly Fishing provides instruction and referrals to accommodation for anglers. The Teifi remains a very good fishery all the way upstream to its headwaters above Tregaron. Salmon and sewin angling becomes increasingly dependent on water

Travel and fishing resources

Before dialling any of the phone and fax numbers listed here, it will be necessary to insert the international country dialling codes, followed by the numbers listed.

Africa

Kenya Tourist Office, 25 Brook's Mews, London W1Y 1LF, UK,. Ph: 171 355 3144; Fax: 171 495 8656

Charles Norman Safaris, Box 1567, Roosevelt Park 2129, Johannesburg, South Africa. Ph: 11 888 7386; Fax: 11 888 3168; email: fishafrica@intekom.co.za

South African Tourism Board, 442 Rigel Avenue South, Erasmusrand 0181, Private Bag X164, Pretoria 0001, South Africa. Ph: 12 347 0600; Fax: 12 455 4889

Trout Adventures Africa, 10 Dean St, 8001 Cape Town, South Africa Ph: 2126 1057; Fax: 21 24 7526

Zimbabwe Tourist Office, 429 The Strand, London WC2R 0SA, UK. Ph: 171 836 7755

Accommodation

Benguela Lodge, PO Box 87416, Houghton 2041, South Africa. Ph: 11 483 2734; Fax: 11 728 3767

Guma Lagoon Camp, Private Bag 013, Maun, Botswana. Ph: 674022; Fax: 674021

Hemingway's, Watamu, Nr Malindi, Kenya. Ph: 122 32276; Fax: 122 32256

Impalila Island Lodge, PO Box 70378, Bryanston 2021, South Africa. Ph and Fax: 11 706 7207

Mt Anderson Ranch, PO Box 2575, Randburg 2125, South Africa. Ph: 11 789 2677; Fax: 11 886 4382; http://www.malamala.com; email: jhb@malamala.com

Asia

Tourism Authority of Bhutan, Ministry of Trade, Power and Tourism, Thimphu, Bhutan. Ph: 2 23252; Fax: 2 23695

Tourism Bhawan, Department of Tourism, 1 Parliament St, New Delhi 110001, India. Ph: 11 301 3403; http://www.tourindia.com

Japan National Tourist Organization, 10-1 Yurakucho 2-chomo Chiyoda-ku, Tokyo 100, Japan. Ph: 3 3201 3331

Sri Lanka Tourist Board, 79 Stuarts Place, Colombo 3, Sri Lanka. Ph: 1 437058; Fax: 1 437953. UK Office: 13 Hyde Park Gardens, London W2 2LU, UK. Ph: 171 262 5009/1841; Fax: 171 262 7970

Australia

Angling Adventures, 84a Ryrie St, Geelong, Victoria 3220, Australia. Ph: 3 52 211722

Australian Tourist Commission, 2797 W. Franklin Parkway, Valencia, CA 91355, USA. Ph: 805-775-2000; Fax: 800-775-2000

USA Office: Level 4/80 William Street, Woolloomooloo, Sydney, New South Wales 2011, Australia. Ph: 2 9360 1111; Fax: 2 9331 2538; email: trades@atc.gov.au

Tasmania Travel & Australia Reservations, Executive Travel Planning Group, 4428 E. Willow Ave, Phoenix, AZ 85032, USA. Ph: 602 953 1827; Fax: 602 953 7279; http://www.australian.com

Tasmanian Fly Fishing School & Guiding Service, 116–118 Emu Bay Rd, Deloraine, Tasmania 7304, Australia. Ph: 6362 3441; Fax: 6362 3441; email: tasflyfish@vision.net.au

Trout Fishing Safaris of Tasmania, 2/45 Landsdowne Crescent, West Hobart, Tasmania 7000, Australia. Ph: 32 34 7286

Accommodation

David and Judy Church's B&B, 33 Pohlman St, Latham, Western Australia 2615. Ph: 2 6255 1246; Fax: 2 6255 2640; email: davec@pcug.org.au

Barra Base Lodge, Port Hurd, Bathhurst Island, Darwin, Northern Territory 0800. Ph: 80 978 3987; Fax: 80 978 3987

Jessie River Camp, c/o Angling Adventure, Shop 55, Market Square, Geelong, Victoria 3220. Ph: 52 21 1722; Fax: 52 21 8571

Alligator Camp, Alligator Airways Pty Ltd, Kununurra Airport, Kununurra, Western Australia 6743. Ph: 8 9168 1333; Fax: 8 9168 2704

Compleat Angler Lodge, Haddens Bay, Great Lake, Tasmania 7030. Ph: 59 8179; Fax: 59 8147; email: wildfish@netspace.net.a

London Lakes Lodge, c/o PO Brontë Park, Brontë Park, Tasmania 7140. Ph (USA): 800 528 6129, (Australia) 89 1159; Fax: 89 1122

Canada *east*

Travel Manitoba, 700-155 Carlton St. Winnipeg, MN, R3C 3H8, Canada. Ph: 204 945 3796; Fax: 800 665 0040; http://www.gov.mb.ca/Travel-Manitoba

Department of Natural Resources & Energy, Fish & Wildlife, PO Box 6000, Fredericton, NB, E3B 5HI, Canada. Ph: 506 453 2440

Department of Tourism & Culture, PO Box 8700, St John's, NF, A1B 4J6, Canada. Ph: 709 729 3810; Fax: 800 563 6353; http://www.gov.nf.ca

SEPAQ-Amtocpsto. 801 Chemin St. Louis, Bureau 125, Quebec, QC, G1S 1C1, Canada. Ph: 800 463 0863; Fax: 418 682 9944.

Tourism Nova Scotia, PO Box 519, Halifax, NS, B3J 2M7, Canada. Ph: 902 424 5000; Fax: 800 565 0000; http://www.gov.ns.ca

Travel Links Ontario, Queens Park, ON, M7A 2R9 Canada. Ph: 416 314 0944; Fax: 800 668 2746; http://www.travelinx.com

Tourism Quebec, PO Box 125, Victoria Square, Suite 260, Montreal, QC, H4Z 1C3, Canada. Ph: 514 873 2015; Fax: 800 363 7777; http://www.gouv.qc.ca

Accommodation

Gangler's Lodges, 1568 E. Wedgewood Lane, Hernando, FL 34442, USA. Ph: 352 637 2244

Healey's Lodge, General Delivery, God's Lake Narrows, MB, R0B 0M0. Ph: 800 353 9993

Nueltin Fly-in Lodges, Box 500, Alonsa, MB, R0M 0A0. Ph: 800 361 7177

Lake Obabika Lodge, PO Box 10, River Valley, ON, P0H 2C0. Ph: 705 858 1056

Lake of the Woods Houseboats, PO Box 1795A, Sioux Narrows, ON, P0X 1N0. Ph: 807 226 5462

Mattice Lake Outfitters, PO Box 157, Armstrong, ON, P0T 1A0. Ph: 807 583 2483

Air Melancon, 2 Chemin Tour du lac, Ste. Anne-du-lac, QC, J0W 1V0. Ph: 819 586 2220

George River Lodge, PO Box 88, St-Augistin, QC, G3A 1V9. Ph: 418 877 4650

Oasis du Gouin, 17 Champlain St, Repentigny, QC, J6A 5L5. Ph: 819 974 8825

Miramichi Inn, RR2, Red Bank, NB, E0C 1W0. Ph: 506 836 7452

Pond's, 91 Porter Cove Road, PO Box 73m Ludlow, NB, E0C 1N0. Ph: 506 369 2612

Chickadee Lodge, Prince William, NB, E0H 1S0. Ph: 506 363 2759

Cooper's Minipi Camps, PO Box 340, Station B, Happy Valley, Labrador, A0P 1E0. Ph: 709 896 2891

Riverkeep Lodge, PO Box V, Ashland, ME 04732-0561, USA. Ph: 207 435 8274

Big Intervale Salmon Camp, RR1, Margaree Valley, NS, B0E 2C0. Ph: 902 248 2275

Canada *west*

Cabela's Outdoor Adventures, 812 13th Ave, Sidney, NE 69160, USA. Ph: 800 346 8747; http://www.cabelas.com

Travel Alberta, PO Box 2500, Edmonton, AB, T5J 2Z4, Canada. Ph: 800 661 8888; Fax: 403 427 4321; http://www.discoveralberta.com/atp/

Tourism British Columbia, 1166 Albania St, Suite 601, Vancouver, BC, V6E 3Z3, Canada. Ph: 800 663 6000; Fax: 604 605 8400; http://www.travel.bc.ca

Northwest Territories Tourism, Box 1320, Yellowknife, NT, X1A 2L9, Canada. Ph: 800 661 0788; Fax: 403 873 7200; http://www.edt.gov.nt.ca/guide/index.html

Tourism Saskatchewan, 500–1900 Albert St, Regina, SK, S4P 4L9, Canada. Ph: 800 667 7191; Fax: 306 7872300; http://www.sasktourism.sk.ca

Tourism Yukon, PO Box 2703, Whitehorse, YT, Y1A 2C6, Canada. Ph: 403 6675340; http://www.touryukon.com

Accommodation

Frontiers Farwest, PO Box 250, Telkwa, BC, V0J 2X0. Ph: 250 846 539

MacKenzie Trail Lodge, 27134 NW Reeder Rd, Portland, OR 97231, USA. Ph: 888 808 7688

Kootenay Park Lodge, PO Box 1390, Banff, AB, T0L 0C0. Ph: 403 762 9196

Buffalo Mountain Lodge, PO Box 1326, Banff, AB, T0L 0C0. Ph: 403 762 2400

Jasper Park Lodge, PO Box 40, Jasper, AB, T0E 1E0. Ph: 403 852 3301

Pine Bungalow Cabins, PO Box 7, Jasper, AB, T0E 1E0. Ph: 403 852 3491

Plummer's Lodges, 950 Bradford St, Winnipeg, MT, R3H 0N5. Ph: 800 665 0240

Camp Grayling, 111 Gathercole Crescent, SK, S7K 7J3. Ph: 306 439 2655

Hatchet Lake Lodge, PO Box 262, Elk River, MN 55330, USA. Ph: 800 661 9183

Tincup Wilderness Lodge, 3641 Park Dr., RR4, Victoria, BC, V9C 3W3. Ph: 250 391 0400

Caribbean Basin

Canada-Cuba Sports and Cultural Festivals, 7171 Torbram Road, Ste. 51 Mississauga, ON, L4T 3W4, Canada. Ph: 905 678 0426

Bob Marriott's Flyfishing Store, 2700 W. Orangethorpe Road, Fullerton, CA 92833, USA. Ph: 800 535 6633; http://www.bobmarriotts.com

Shooting and Angling Destinations, 3220 Audley, Houston, TX 77098, USA. Ph: 800 292 2213; email: jbooth@detailco.com

Ministry of Tourism, PO Box N3701, Nassau, Bahamas. Ph: 322 7500; Fax: 800 422 4262; http://www.bahamas.net

Belize Tourist Board, 83 N. Front St, Belize City, Belize. Ph: 2 7213; Fax 800 624 0686. http://www.belize.com

Cayman Islands Department of Tourism, PO Box 67, George Town, Grand Cayman, Cayman Islands. Ph: 949 0623

Costa Rica Tourist Board, PO Box 777–1000, San Juan, Costa Rica. Ph: 223 1733

Instituto Guatemalteco de Turismo, 78 Avemida 1–17, Zona 4, Cintro Civico, Quatemala City, Guatemala, CA. Ph: 331 1333; Fax: 331 4416; http://www.travel-guate.net

Honduras Institute of Tourism, PO Box 140458, Coral Gables, FL 33114-0458, USA. Ph: 800 410 9608; http://www.hondurasinfo.hn

Mexico Tourism Office, Suite 1401, 405 Park Ave, New York, NY 10022, USA. Ph: 212 421 6655; Fax: 800 446 3942; http://www.mexico/travel.com

IPAT, Box 4421, Panama 5, Republic of Panama. Ph: 226 7000; http://www.pa/noticias/laprinse.index.html

Corp de Turismo deVenezuela, Av Bolivar, Parque Central, Torre Oeste Piso, 37 El Conde, Caracas 1010, Venezuela. Ph: 2 5741968; http://www.venezuela.com

Accommodation

Andros Island Bonefish Club, Cargill Creek, Andros Island, Bahamas. Ph: 368 5167

Deep Water Cay Club, Deep Water Cay, Exuma, Bahamas. Ph: 359 4831

North Riding Point Club, PO Box F. 43665, Freeport, Grand Bahama Islands, Bahamas. Ph: 352 3211

Peace & Plenty Bonefish Lodge, PO Box 29173, George Town, Exuma, Bahamas. Ph: 345 5555

Walker's Cay Hotel and Marina, Abaco, Bahamas. Ph: 353 1252

Belize River Lodge, PO Box 459 Belize City, Belize. Ph: 25 2002

Turneffe Island Lodge, PO Box 2974, Gainesville, GA 30503, USA. Ph: 800 874 0118; Fax: 21 2011

Rio Colorado Lodge, PO Box 5094, 1000 San Jose, Costa Rica. Ph: 710 6879

Casa Mar Lodge, 2634 West Orangethorpe Ave, Suite #6 Fullerton, CA 928833, US. Ph: 714 578 1881; Fax: 714 525 5783

Silver King Lodge, PO Box 02516, Suite 1597, Miami, FL 33102, USA. Ph: 381 1403

El Octal, PO Box 1, Playas del Coco, Guanacaste, Costa Rica. Ph: 670 0321

Zapata Fishing Safaris, c/o Pan Angling Travel Service, 180 North Michigan Ave., Chicago, IL 60601, USA. Ph: 800 5334353

Garden of the Queens, c/o Roxton Bailey Robinson, 25 High Street, Hungerford RG17 0NF, UK.

Ph: 1488 683222

Fins 'n' Feathers Inn, c/o Artmarina, 1390 S. Dixie Highway, Miami, FL 33146, USA. Ph: 305 663 3553

Posada Del Sol, 1201 W. US Hwy 1, North Miami Beach, FL 33408, USA. Ph: 800 642 3483

Ascencion Bay Bonefish Club, c/o Joe Fish, SA. DE C.V., Call Robe No. 34 Y 36 SM. 23, Cancun, Quintana Or, Mexico. Ph: 77500/98 84 61 05

Baja on the Fly, PO Box 81961, San Diego, CA 92138, USA. Ph: 800 919 2252

Tropic Star Lodge, 635 N. Rio Grande Ave., Orlando, FL 32805, USA. Ph: 407 423 9931

Macabi Lodge, Chapi Sportfish, Calle Geminis, Edificio Mayurupi, Apartamento 4-A, Santa Paula El Cafetal, Estado Miranda, Caracas 1061, Venezuela. Ph: 2 987 0032

Continental Europe

Austrian National Tourist Office, 500 5th Ave. South, New York, NY 10110, USA. Ph: 212 944 6880; Fax: 212 730 4568; and at 30 St George St, London, W1R 0AL, UK. Ph: 171 629 0461

French Government Tourist Office, 610 5th Ave., New York, NY 10020. Ph: 212 315 0888; Fax: 212 2470 6468; and at 178 Piccadilly, London, W1V OAL, UK. Ph: 891 244123

German National Tourist Office, 122 E. 42nd St, New York, NY 10168. Ph: 212 661 7200; Fax: 212 661 7174; and at Nightingale House, 65 Curzon St, London, W1Y 7PE, UK. Ph: 891 600100

Italian Government Tourist Office, 630 5th Ave., New York, NY 10111. Ph: 212 245 4822; Fax: 212 586 9249 and at 1 Princess St, London, W1R8AY, UK. Tel. 171 408 1254

Portuguese National Tourist , 590 5th Ave., 4th Floor, New York, NY 10036. Ph: 212 354 4403; Fax: 212 764 6137; and at 25A Sackville St, London, W1X 1DE, UK. Ph: 171 494 1441

Spanish National Tourist Office, 666 5th Ave., 35th Floor, New York, NY 10103. Ph: 212 265 8822; Fax: 212 265 8864; and at 58 St James's St, London, SW1A 1LD, UK. Ph: 891 669920.

Fisheries Research Institute, Zavod za ribistivo, Zupanciceva 9, SI-1000 Ljubljana, Slovenia. Ph: 61 126 20 19; http://www.2/arnes.si/~kjzavodrib6/

Accommodation

Waldhotel Marienbrocke, A-4819 in der Au, Gmoden, Austria. Ph: 76 12 40 11

Le Clos des Quatre Saisons, 2 rue de la Paix, 29450, Sizun, France. Ph: 98 68 80 19

Château Hôtel de Brelidy, 22140, Brelidy, France. Ph: 96 95 69 38

Hôtel Bichta-Eder, Quartier Cherche-Bruit, 64310, Saint-PÄe-sur-Nivelle, France. Ph: 59 54 21 14

Au Relais Aspois at Gurmenìon, 64400, Orlon-Sainte-Mari, France. Ph: 59 39 09 50

Hôtel du Vieux Pont, rue du Pont de la Legende, 64390, Sauveterre de Bearn, France. Ph: 59 38 95 11

Denmark and Greenland

Danish Tourist Board, Vesterbrogade 6D, DK 1620, Køpenhavn V, Denmark. Ph: 33 11 14 15

Danish Angling Society, Danmarks Sportsfiskerforbund, Worsaasgade 1, 7100 Veal, Denmark. Ph: 75 82 06 99

Greenland Tourism, A/S Pilestræde, 52 PO Box 1139, DK 1010, Køpenhavn K, Denmark. Ph: 33 13 69 75

England

The Rod Box, London Road, King's Worthy, Winchester, Hampshire S023 7QN, UK. Ph: 1962 883600

The Land Steward, Duchy of Cornwall Office, Liskeard, Cornwall, PL14 4EE, UK. Ph: 1579 343149

Specialist Angling Supplies, 1 Athelstan Road, Dorchester, DT1, 1NR, UK. Ph: 1305 266500

Environmental Agencies

Southern Region Guildbourne House, Chatsworth Road, Worthing, West Sussex, BN11 1LD, UK.

Ph: 1903 820692

Southwestern Region Manley House, Kestrel Way, Exeter, Devon, EX2 7LQ, UK. Ph: 1392 444000
Northwestern Region – Richard Fairclough House, Knutsford Road, Warrington, WA4 1HG, UK. Ph: (0) 1925 65399
Northeast Region Rivers House, 21 Park Square South, Leeds, LS1 2QG, UK. Ph: 113 2440191
Anglian Region – Kingfisher House, Goldhay Way, Orton Goldhay, Peterborough, PE2 5ZR, UK. Ph: 1733 371811
Midland Region Sapphire East, 550 Streetsbrook Road, Solihull, B91 1QT, UK. Ph: 121 711 2324; Fax: 121 711 5824
Thames Region The Environment Agency, Kings Meadow House, Kings Meadow Road, Reading, RG1 8DQ, UK. Ph: 1733 535000

Accommodation

Endsleigh House, Milton Abbot, Near Tavistock, Devon, PL19 0PQ. Ph: 1822 870248

Arundell Arms, Lifton, Devon, PL16 0AA. Ph: 1566 784666

Devil's Stone Inn, Shebbear, Devon, EX21 5RU. Ph: 1409 281210

Half Moon Inn, Sheepwash, Beaworthy, North Devon EX21 5AN. Ph: 1409 231376; Fax: 1409 231673

The Forest Inn, Hexworthy, Cornwall, PL20 6SD. Ph: 1364 63211

Rising Sun and Fox and Hounds Hotel, Eggesford, Chumleigh, Devon EX18 7SZ. Ph: 1769 580345; Fax: 1769 580262

Red Lion Hotel, Bredwardine, Hereford, HR3 6BU. Ph: 1981 500303

The Anglers Arms Hotel, Weldon Bridge, Morpeth, Northumberland, NE65 8AL. Ph: 1665 570655

Bracken Bank Lodge, Lazonby, Cumbria, CA10 1AX. Ph: 1768 898241

Sandford Arms, Sandford, Cumbria, CA16 6NR. Ph: 1768 351121

Royal Oak Hotel, Settle Market Place, Settle, North Yorkshire, BD24 9ED. Ph: 1729 822561

Finland

Finnish Tourist Board, 3rd Floor, 30–35 Pall Mall, London, SW1Y 5LP, UK. Ph: 171 839 4048

Viitasaaren Kunsta, PO Box 60, FIN-44501 VIITASAARI. Ph: 46 579 341

Finnair, 14 Clifford St, London W2, UK. Ph: 171 408 1222

Tervon Lohimaa/Jouni Rautiainen, Ayskoski, 72210 Tervo, Finland. Ph: 17 387 2450

Accommodation

Rukapalvelu Oy Safaritalo, FIN-93825 RUKATUNTURI. Ph: 89 8681 526

Tyninyrakari OY, Rautatienkatu 2, FIN-481000 KOTKA. Ph: 5 260 0288

Iceland

Angling Service Strengir, Fannafold 187, 112 Reykjavik, Iceland. Ph: 567 5204

Fishery Association of Grimsa, Skalpastadir IS-311, Borgarness, Iceland. Ph: 435 1401

Vagnhofda (Islandic Fishing Institute) #7, 112 Reykjavik, Iceland. Ph: 567 6400; Fax: 567 6420

Iceland Tourist Bureau, Skogarhlio 18, Reykjavik, Iceland. Ph: 562 3300

Accommodation

Club Lax-A, PO Box 336, 123 Reykjavik; Ph 565 5410

Hotel Blafell, Breiodaksvik, Ph: 475 6770

Ireland

EPS Angling Holidays, Fitzgerald House, Grand Parade, Co. Cork, Ireland. Ph: 21 275564

Nephin Beg Angling, Curragh, Castlebar, Co. Mayo, West Ireland. Ph: 94 22035

Fishery boards

Central Balnagowan House, Mobhi Boreen, Clasnevin, Dublin 9, Ireland. Ph: 353 1 8379206

Eastern Regional Balnagowan House, Mobbi Boreen, Clasnevin, Dublin 9, Ireland. Ph: 353 1-8379209
Southern Regional Anglesea Street, Clonmel, Co. Tipperary, Ireland. Ph: 353 52 23624
North Western Regional: Ardnaree House, Abbey Street, Ballina, Co. Mayo, Ireland. Ph: 353 96-22788
Northern Regional Station Road, Ballyshannon, Co. Donegal, Ireland. Ph: 353 72 51435
Western Regional The Weir Lodge, Earl's Island, Co. Galway, Ireland. Ph: 353 91 563118
Shannon Regional: Thomand Weir, Limerick, Ireland. Ph: 353 61 455171
South Western Regional 1 Nevilles Terrace, Masseytown, Macroom, Co. Cork, Ireland. Ph: 353 26 41221

Accommodation

Kilcoleman Fishery, Enniskeane, Co. Cork. Ph: 23 47279

Abbey Hotel, The Diamond, Donegal Town, Co. Donegal. Ph: 73 21014

Ballynahinch Castle Hotel, Ballynahinch, Recess, Co. Galway. Ph: 95 31006

Delphi Lodge, Leeane, Co. Galway. Ph: 95 42211

Butler Arms, Waterville, Co. Kerry. Ph: 66 74144

Commercial & Tourist Hotel, Ballinamore, Co. Leitrim. Ph: 7844675

Pontoon Bridge Hotel, Pontoon, Co. Mayo. Ph: 94 56120/56688

Moy House Bed & Breakfast, Foxford Road, Ballina, Co. Mayo. Ph: 96 21781

Belleek Castle, Ballina, Co. Mayo. Ph: 96 22400

New Zealand

New Zealand Tourism Board, PO Box 10017, Wellington, New Zealand. Ph: 7 348 4133; Fax: 7 499 9996; http://www.nztb.govt.nz

Accommodation

Tongaririo Lodge, Box 278, Trangi, North Island. Ph: 74 67946

Ocean View Lodge, 65 Ocean View Terrace, Sumner, Christchurch 8. Ph: 3 326 7527; Fax: 3 326 5611

Leader Lodge, Talbot Street, No. 1RD, Gore, Southland, NZ 9700. Ph: 3 208 1852; Fax: 3 208 1223

Maple Creek Lodge, Littles Road, RD 1, Queenstown, Otago. Ph: 3 442 7061; Fax: 3 442 9088; http://www.sp.net.nz.htm

Te Wanaka Lodge, 23 Brownston St, Wanaka. Ph: 3 443 9224; Fax: 3 443 9246

Cedar Lodge, Box 33, Cromwell, South Island. Ph: 294 50194

Lake Brunner Lodge, Route 1, Kumara Road 7871, Mitchells, South Island. Ph: 27 80163

Norway

AKU Finnmark, AS Kongleveien 11 N-9500 Alta, Norway. Ph: 78 43 48 40

Lågendalen Informasjon Brufoss, N-3275 Svarstad, Norway. Ph: 33 12 91 50

Theodore Dhalenson, PO Box S-103, 90 Stockholm, Sweden. Ph: 86 65 90 33

Veideren, Midt-Norsk Reiseliv, AS PB 65 N-7001 Trondheim, Norway. Ph: 47 73 92 93

The Norwegian Fly Shop. http://www.flyshop.no/

The Norwegian Directorate for Wildlife and Freshwater Fish, Elgesetergt, 10, 7000 Trondheim, Norway. Ph: 73 96 83 75

Norwegian Wild Salmon Center, PO Box 6, N-5890 Lærdal, Norway. Ph: 57 66 67 71

Norwegian Tourist Board, PO Box 2893, Solli N-0230, Oslo, Norway. Ph: 22 92 52 70

Accommodation

Overhalla Hotel, N-7863 Overahlla. Ph: 74 28 15 00

Strand Hotel, PO Box 16, N-4870 Fevik. Ph: 37 04 73 22

The Pacific

Midway Sport Fishing, Inc., PO Box 217, Newnan, GA 30264, USA. Ph: 770 254 8326; Fax: 770 254 8329

Harris Holidays, 67 Orsett Road, Grays, Essex, RM17 5HJ, UK. Tel. 1375 396688, Fax: 1375 394488; E-mail: diving@harris-travel.com; http://www.harris-travel.com/bikini.htm

Kili/Bikini/Ejit Local Government Council, PO Box 1096, Majuro, Marshall Islands. Ph: 692 625 3177; Fax: 692 625 3330; email: bikini@ntamar.com

Russian Federation

Flyfish in KolaSandkilsvègen 3, S-184 42 ükersberga, Sweden. Ph: 8540 68910; http://www.outdoor.se/flyfishkola

Kamchatka Angling Adventures, 2825 90th St, SE Everett, WA 98208, USA. Ph: 206 337 0326; http://www.katmai.com

Ouzel Expeditions, PO Box 935, Girdwood, AK 99587, USA. Ph: 907 783 2216

Intourist Travel Ltd, Intourist House, 219 Marsh Wall, London, E14 9EJ, UK. Ph: 171 538 8600

Scotland

Salmon & Trout Association, Fishmongers Hall, London EC4R 9EL, UK. Ph: 171 283 5838

Scottish Tourist Board, 23 Ravelston Terrace, Edinburgh, EH4 3EU, UK. Ph: 131 332 2433

Accommodation

Port Askaig Hotel, Port Askaig, Isle of Islay, PA46 7RD. Ph: 1496 840245

Machrie Hotel, Port Ellen, Isle of Islay, Argyll, PA42 7AN. Ph: 1496 302310

Skeabost House Hotel, Isle of Skye, IV51 9NP. Ph: 147 532202

Langass Lodge Hotel, Loch Eport, North Uist, HS6 5HA. Ph: 1876 580285

Lochmaddy Hotel,. Lochmaddy, North Uist, HS6 5AAPh: 1876 500331

Herrislea House Hotel, Veensgarth, Tingwall, Shetland Islands, ZE2 9SB. Ph: 1595 840208

Hildasay Guest House, Upper Scalloway, Scalloway, Shetland Islands, ZE1 0UP. Ph: 1595 880822

Ulbster Arms Hotel, Halkirk, Caithness, KW14 6XY. Ph: 1847 831206

Forsinard Hotel, Forsinard, Caithness KW13 6YT. Ph: 164 17221

Altnaharra Hotel, By Lairg, Sutherland, IV27 4UE. Ph: 154 411222

Borgie Lodge Hotel, Skerray, Tongue, KW14 7TH. Ph: 164 521332

Scourie Hotel, Scourie, By Lairg, Sutherland, IV27 4SX. Ph: 1971 502396

Inver Lodge Hotel, Lochinver, IV27 4LU. Ph: 1571 844496

Coul House Hotel, Contin, By Strathpeffer, IV14, 9EY. Ph: 1997 421487

Lochailort Inn, Lochailot, Invernesshire PH38 4LZ. Ph: 1687 470208

Tomdou Hotel, Invergarry, Invernessshire PH35 4HS. Ph: 1809 511244

Seafield Lodge Hotel, Grantown-on-Spey, Morayshire PH26 3JN. Ph: 1479 872152

Gordon Arms Hotel, High St, Forchabers, Morayshire, IV32 7DH, UK. Ph: 1342 820508

Banchory Lodge Hotel, Banchory, Aberdeenshire AB31 3HS. Ph: 133 082 2625

Ben More Lodge Hotel, Crainlarich, Perthshire FK20 8SQ. Ph: 1838 30021

Weems Hotel Weem, by Aberfeldy, Perthshire PH15 2LD. Ph: 1887 820381

Tayside Hotel, Stanley, nr Perth, Perthshire PH1 4NL. Ph: 1738 828249; Fax: 2738 827216

Clovenfords Inn, 1 Vine Street, Clovenfords, nr Galashiels TD1 3LU. Ph: 1896 850203

Bladnoch Inn, Wigtown, Wigtownshire, DG8 9AB. Ph: 1998 402200

Warmanbie Hotel, Annan, Dumfriesshire, DG12 5LL. Ph: 1461 204015

South America

Quest! Global Angling Adventures, 3595 Canton Hwy, Suite C-11, Marietta, GA 30066, USA. Ph: 888 891 3474 or 770 517 8886; Fax: 770 977 3095

Argentina Government Tourist Office, 12 W. 56th St, New York, NY 10019, USA. Ph: 212 603 0443

Brazil Reservation System, 1050 Edison St Suite C-2, Santa Yenez, CA, USA. Ph: 805 688 2441; Fax: 805 688 1021

Falkland Island Tourism, 56 John Street, Stanley, Falkland Islands. Ph: 22622

Accommodation

Estancia Truchaike, Esmeralda 719 – 2do. piso Dto. B; (1007) Buenos Aires – Argentina. Ph/Fax: 54 4394 3486/3513; e-mail; pmar@cano.com.ar

San Huberto Lodge, Sarmineto 311, San Martin de los Andes 8370, Argentina. Ph: 54 972 28437; Fax: 54 972 27572

Hosteria Chimehuin, Coronel Suarez y 25 de Mayo, Junin de Los Andes – Provincia del Neuquén, Argentina. Ph: 54 972 91132; Fax: 54 972 91319.

Sweden

Swedish Tourist Office, PO Box 4649, Grand Central Station, New York, NY 10163-4649, USA. Ph: 212 885 9700 and at 11 Montagu Place, London W1H 2AL, UK. Ph: 171 724 5868

Top Ten Fishing Sweden, S-566 93 Brandstorp, Sweden. Ph: 50 25 02 00

Laholm Turistbryä, Box 78, S-312 22, Laholm, Sweden. Ph: 43 01 54 50

Simrishamns Turistbryå, Tullhausgatan 2, S-272 31, Simrishamn, Sweden. Ph: 43 12 22 30

Sportfiskecenterum 1 Belkinge, Saltsjöbadsvägen 53, S-374 30, Karlshamn, Sweden. Ph: 45 41 99 50

Ostersunds Tourist Board, Radhusgatan 44, 83182 Ostersunds, Sweden. Ph: 63 14 40 01

Sollefteå Tourist Office, Storgatan 49, Box 121, 88123 Solleftea, Sweden. Ph: 62 68 29 00

Sportfiskarna, Box 2, S-163 21, Spång, Sweden. Ph: 87 95 33 50

TuristRådet, Box 3030, Kungsgatan 36, S-10361, Stockholm, Sweden. Ph: 87 25 55 00

United States of America *Alaska*

Alaska Department of Fish and Game, Division of Sport Fishing, PO Box 25526, Juneau, AK 99802-5526, USA. Ph: 907 465 6186; http://www.state. ak.us/local/akpages/FISH.GAME/adfghome.htm

Accommodation

Boardwalk Wilderness Lodge, PO Box 19121, Throne Bay, AK 99919. Ph: 907 828 3918

Misty Fjords Lodge, 125 South Main St, Ketchikan, AK 99901. Ph: 888 295 5464

Afognak Wilderness Lodge, Seal Bay, AK 99697. Ph: 907 486 6442

Enchanted Lake Lodge, 2222 W. Lake Sammamish Way, SE, Bellevue, AK 98008. Ph: 907 246 6878

Mike Cusack's King Salmon Lodge, 3340 Providence Dr, Suite 555, Anchorage, AK 99508. Ph: 907 277 3033

Saltery Lake Lodge, 1516 Larch St, Kodiak, AK 99615. Ph: 907 486 7083

Talaheim Lodge, PO Box 190043, Anchorage, AK 99159-0043. Ph: 907 248 6205

Talstar Lodge, PO Box 870978, Wasilla, AK 99687. Ph: 907 688 1116

Osprey Alaska, PO Box 504, Cooper Landing, AK 99572. Ph: 800 533 5364

United States of America *east*

Maine Department of Inland Fisheries and Wildlife, 284 State Street #41, Augusta, ME 04333, USA. Ph: 207 287 8000. http://www.state.me.us/ifw. homepage.htm

New Hampshire Fish and Game Department, Div. Public Affairs, 2 Hazen Dr., Concord, NH 03301, USA. Ph: 603 271 3211. http://www.wildlife.state. nh.us/

New York Division of Fish, Wildlife and Marine Resources; 50 Wolf Road, Albany, NY 12233, USA. Ph: 518 457 5420. http://www.iloveny.state. ny.us/outdoor/fishing.html

Pennsylvania Fish and Boat Commission, Bureau of Boating and Education, Box 1673; Harrisburg, PA 17106-7000, USA. Ph: 717 657 4518. http://www.dcnr.state.pa.us/

Vermont Fish and Wildlife Department, 103 South Main St, Waterbury, VT 05676, USA. Ph: 802 241 3700. http://www.state.vt.us/anr

Wulff School of Fly Fishing, PO Box 948, Livingston Manor, NY 12758, USA. Ph: 914 439 5020

Accommodation

Libby Sporting Camps, PO Drawer V, Ashland, ME 04732. Ph: 207 435 8274

Red River Camps, PO Box 320, Portage, ME 04768. Ph: 207 435 6000

Wheaton's Lodge and Camps, HC81, Box 120, Forest City, ME 04413. Ph: 207 448 7723

Tall Timber Lodge, 231 Beach Road, Pittsburg, NH 03592. Ph: 800 835 6343

Equinox Hotel, PO Box 46, Manchester Village, VT 05254. Ph: 800 362 4747

Beaverkill Valley Inn, 136 Beaverkill Road, Lew Beach, NY 12753. Ph: 914 439 4844.

Starlight Lodge, PO Box 86, Starlight, PA 18461. Ph: 717 798 2350

Allenberry Resort Inn and Playhouse, PO Box 7, Rt. 174, Boiling Springs, PA 17007. Ph: 717 258 3211

United States of America *south*

Florida Game and Fresh Water Fish Commission, Office of Information Services, 620 S. Meridian, Tallahassee, FL 32399-1600, USA. Ph: 904 488 4676

Georgia State Game and Fish Division, 2070 US Highway 278 SE, Social Circle, GA 30279, USA. Ph: 770 918 6418. http://www.dnr.state.ga.us/

North Carolina Wildlife Resources Commission, Inland Fisheries Division, 512 N. Salisbury St, Raleigh, NC 27604-1188, USA.
Ph: 919 733 3633;
http://www.ehnr.nc.us/EHRC/files/division.htm

Tennessee Wildlife Resources Agency, Box 40747, Nashville, TN 37204, USA. Ph: 615 781 6500;
http://www.state.tn/environment

Great Smoky Mountains National Park, 107 Park Headquarters Road, Gatlinburg, TN 37738, USA. Ph: 423 453 1200

Accommodation

Fontana Village Resort, Highway 28, Box 68, Fontana Dam, NC 28733. Ph: 800 849 2258
Gillionville Plantation, 326 New Thompson Road, Albany, GA 31707. Ph: 912 439 2837

Roland Martin's Lakeside Resort, 920 E. Del Monte Ave., Clewiston, FL 33440. Ph: 941 983 3151

Cheeca Lodge, PO Box 527, Islamorada, FL 33036. Ph: 305 664 4651

United States of America *west*

Colorado Division of Wildlife, 6060 Broadway, Denver, CO 80216, USA. Ph: 303 291 7533.
http://www.dnr.state.co.us

Idaho Fish and Game Department, PO Box 25, 600 S. Walnut St, Boise, ID 83707, USA.
Ph: 800 377 7820; http://www.state.id.us/fishgame/fishgame.html

Montana Department of Fish, Wildlife and Parks, 1420 E. 6th Ave., Helena, MT 59620, USA.
Ph: 406 444 2535; http://travel.mt.gov/recadv/fishing/fishing.html#INDEX

Utah Division of Wildlife Resources, 1594 W. North Temple, Salt Lake City, UT 84116, USA. Ph: 801 538 7200; http://www.nr.state.ut.us/dwr

Wyoming Game and Fish Commission, 5400 Bishop Blvd, Cheyenne, WY 82006, USA.
Ph: 307 777 4600; http://gf.state.wy.us

Arizona Game and Fish Department, 2221 W. Greenway Rd, Phoenix, AZ 85023, USA.
Ph: 602 942-3000; http:/www.state.az.us/gf/welcome.html

California Department of Fish & Game, Inland Fisheries Div., 1416 9th St, PO Box 944209, Sacramento, CA 95814, USA. Ph: 916 653 7664;
http://www.dfg.ca.gov/

New Mexico Department of Game and Fish, PO Box 25112, Santa Fe, NM 87504, USA.
Ph: 505 827 7901; http://www.gmfsh.state.nm.us

Nevada Department of Conservation and Natural Resources, PO Box 10678, Reno, NV 89520, USA.
Ph: 702 688 1500; http://www.state.nv.us

Oregon Department of Fish and Wildlife, Fish Division, Box 59, Portland, OR 97207, USA.
Ph: 503 872 5252; http://www.dfw.state.or.us/

Trout Unlimited, 1500 Wilson Blvd, Arlington, VA 22209-2404, USA. http://www.tu.org

Washington Department of Fish and Wildlife, 600 Capitol Way North, Olympia, WA 9850-1091, USA.
Ph: 360 902 2200; http://www.wa.gov/wdfw/

Accommodation

Lee's Ferry Lodge, Vermilion Cliffs, HC67, Box 1, Marble Canyon, AZ 86036. Ph: 520 355 2231

Rizuto's San Juan River Lodge, PO Box 6309, 1796 Hwy 173, Navajo Dam, NM 87419. Ph: 505 632 3893

Seven Lakes Lodge, Meeker, CO 81641.
Ph: 970 878 4772

Flaming Gorge Lodge, 155 Greendale, Dutch John, UT 84023. Ph: 801 889 3773

Yellowstone Park Hotels, AmFac Parks and Resorts, PO Box 165, Yellowstone National Park, WY 82190. Ph: 307 334 7901

Henry's Fork Lodge, HC66, Box 600, Island Park, ID 83429. Ph: 208 558 7953

The Old Kirby Place, West Fork Bridge, Cameron, MT 59720. Ph: 406 682 4194

Hat Creek House, 18101 Doty Road, Hat Creek, CA 96040. Ph: 916 335 5270

Steamboat Inn, 42705 N. Umpqua Hwy, Steamboat, OR 97447-9703. Ph: 800 840 8825

Brightwater House, 440 Brightwater Dr., PO Box 1222, Forks, WA 98331. Ph: 360 374 5453

Wales

Welsh National Rivers Authority, St Mellons Business Park, Cardiff CF3 0LT, UK.
Ph: 1222 770088

The National Trust PO Box 536, Melsham, Wiltshire, SN12X 8SX, UK. Ph: 1225 791199

Foxon's Tackle, Lower Denbigh Rd, St Asaph, Denbyshire LL27 0ED, UK. Ph: 1745 583583

West Wales School of Fly Fishing, Ffoshelyg, Llancych, Boncath, SA37 0LJ, UK.
Ph: 1239 698678

Accommodation

Seiont Manor Hotel, Llanrug, Caernarfon, Gwynedd LL55 2 AQ. Ph: 1286 673366

Hand Hotel, Bridge Street, Langollen, LL20 8PL. Ph: 1978 860303

Pale Hall Country House, Llandderfel, Nr. Bala, LL23 7PS. Ph: 1678 530285

Lake Country House Hotel, Llangammarch, Powys LD4 4BS. Ph: 1591 620202

Gliffaes Country House Hotel, Crickhowell, Powys NP8 IRH. Ph: 1874 730371

The Black Lion Inn, Llansawel, nr Cenarth.
Ph: 1558 685263

The Cothi Bridge Hotel, Nantgaredig, Carmarthen, SA32 7NG. Ph: 1267 290251

Tynycornel Hotel, Talyllyn, Tywyn, LL36 9AJ.
Ph: 1654 782282

George III Hotel, Penmaenpool, Dolgellau, Gwynedd LL40 1YD. Ph: 1341 422525

Further reading

The Angler's Guide to Alaska, Evan and Margaret Swenson; *The Angler's Guide to Montana*, Michael S. Sample, Falcon Publishing.

Angling in Norway, Nortra Production, Norway.

Atlantic Salmon Fishing, Bill Cummings, International Marine/McGraw-Hill, USA.

BC Fishing: Freshwater Directory and Atlas; BC Fishing: Saltwater Directory and Atlas, Karl Bruin, Editor; OP Publishing Ltd, Canada.

Bonefish, Tarpon, Permit Fly Fishing Guide, Al Raychard, Frank Amato Publications, USA.

Bugging the Atlantic Salmon, Michael Brislan, Goose Lane Editions, Canada.

California Blue Ribbon Trout Streams, Bill Sunderland and Dale Lackey, Frank Amato Publications, USA.

Colorado Angling Guide, Chuck Fothergill and Bob Sterling, Stream Stalker Publishing Co., USA.

Directory of Scottish Salmon Waters, Durham Ranger Publishing, UK.

Due North of Montana, Chris Damson, Johnson Books, USA.

The Essential G.E.M. Skues, Kenneth Robson (Editor), The Lyons Press.

Fish the Southern Seas, by Charles Norman, South Africa. Out of print.

Fishing the Miramichi, Wayne Curtis, Goose Lane Editions, Canada.

Fishing in New Mexico, Ti Piper. Out of print.

Fishing in Oregon – Madelynne Diness Sheehan and Dan Casali, Flying Pencil Publications, USA.

Fishing in Florida, Kris Thoemke, Falcon Press, USA.

Fishing Vermont's Streams and Lakes, Peter E. Cammann. Out of print.

Fodor's Europe, Fodor's Travel Publication's Inc., New York, NY, USA.

Fly Fishing Across Russia, East Europe and Finland, Chris Hole, USA.

Fly Fishing for Salmon and Sea Trout, Arthur Oglesby, Crowood Press, UK.

Fly Fishing for Trout, Charles Jardine, Dorling Kindersley, UK.

Fly Fishing in Southern Africa: An Okavango Season. Out of print.

Fly Fishing in Northern New Mexico, Craig Martin, University of New Mexico Press, USA.

Good Fishing in the Catskills, Jim Capossela. Out of print.

Great Lakes Steelhead, a Guided Tour for Fly-Anglers, Bob Linsenman and Steve Nevala, Backcountry Publications, USA.

Iceland Fishing Guide, Iceland Farm Holidays, Iceland.

The Montana Angling Guide, Chuck Fothergill and Bob Sterling, Stream Stalker Publishing Co., USA.

New Zealand Fisherman, Review Publishing Co. Ltd., New Zealand.

New Zealand Handbook, Jane King, Moon Travel Handbooks, USA.

Northeast Guide to Saltwater Fishing & Boating, Vin T. Sparano (Editor), International Marine/ McGraw-Hill, USA.

North Umpqua Angler's Guide, Doc Crawford Frank Amato Publications, USA.

Pennsylvania Troutstreams and Their Hatches, Charles Meck, Backcountry Publications, USA.

River Journal: Yellowstone National Park, Bruce Staples, Frank Amato Publications, USA.

A River Runs Through It and Other Stories, Norman Maclean, University of Chicago Press, 1976.

Roadside Guide to Fly Fishing Alaska, Flies for Alaska, and *Flyfishing Alaska*, Anthony J. Route, Johnson Books, USA.

Salmon Fishing, a Practical Guide, Hugh Falkus, Witherby, UK.

Smoky Mountains Trout Fishing Guide

Smoky Mountain Fly Fishing, Don Kirk, Menasha Ridge Press, USA.

Trout and Salmon Rivers and Lochs of Scotland, Bruce Sandison, Merlin Unwin Books, UK.

Trout and Salmon Rivers of Ireland

Trout and Salmon Flies of Ireland, Peter O'Reilly, Merlin Unwin Books, UK.

The Trout and the Kingfisher

Trout Through the Looking-Glass, Malcolm Meintjes, South Africa. Out of print.

Trout Streams of Alberta, Jim McLennan, Johnson German Publishers, Canada.

21 Great New Zealand Trout Waters, Tony Orman, David Bateman Ltd, New Zealand; and Stackpole Books, USA.

Where to Fish, D.A. Horton, Harmsworth Publishing, UK.

The Wyoming Angling Guide, Chuck Fothergill and Bob Sterling, Stream Stalker Publishing Co., USA.

Index

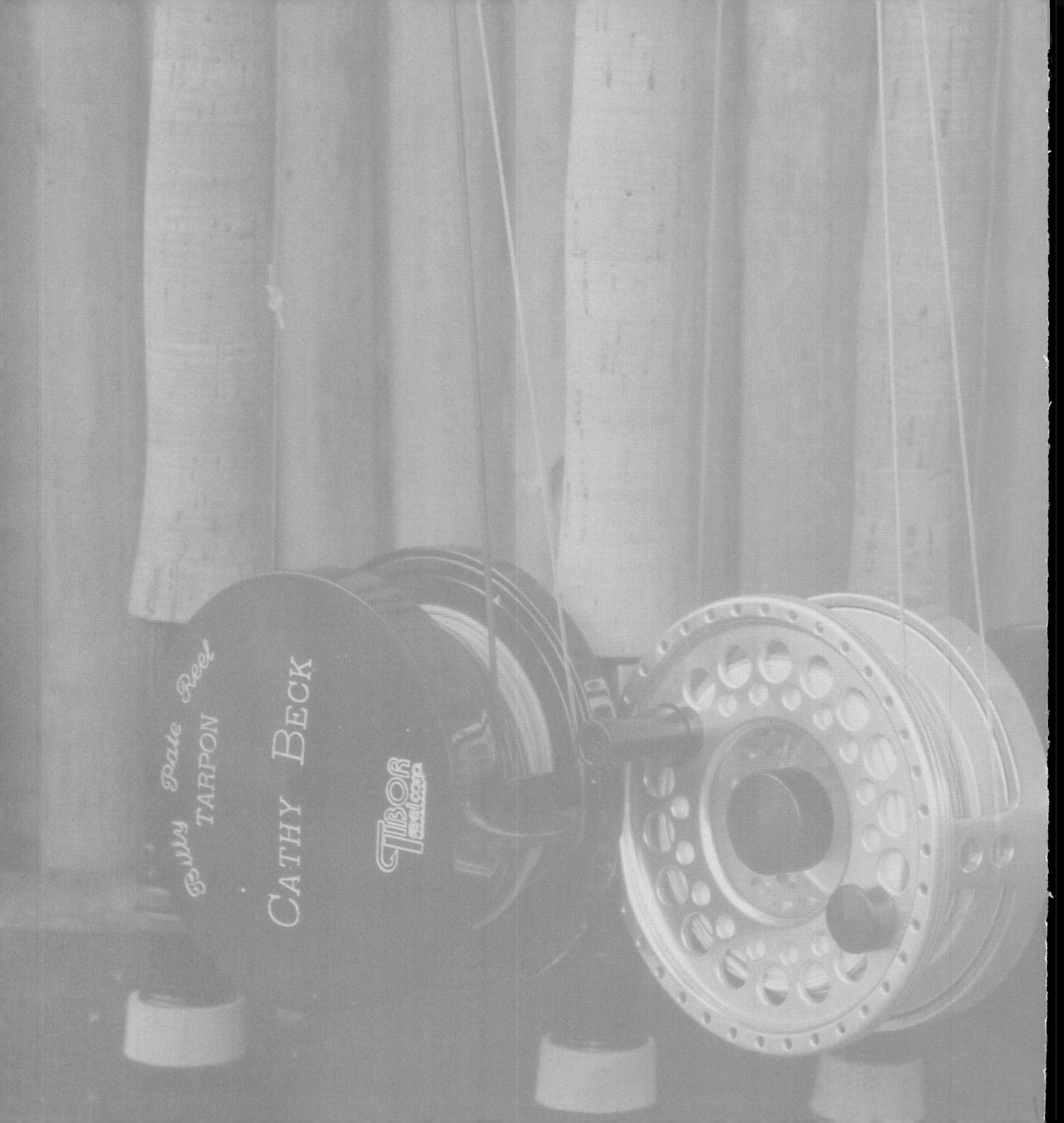
Billy Pate Reel
TARPON
CATHY BECK
TIBOR